Also by Max Cleland
Going for the Max!
Strong at the Broken Places

HEART
OF A
PATRIOT

How I Found the Courage
to Survive Vietnam,
Walter Reed and Karl Rove

MAX CLELAND
WITH BEN RAINES

SIMON & SCHUSTER   New York • London • Toronto • Sydney

SIMON & SCHUSTER
1230 Avenue of the Americas
New York, NY 10020

First Simon & Schuster hardcover edition October 2009

SIMON & SCHUSTER and colophon are registered
trademarks of Simon & Schuster, Inc.

For information about special discounts for bulk purchases,
please contact Simon & Schuster Special Sales at
1-866-506-1949 or business@simonandschuster.com.

The Simon & Schuster Speakers Bureau can bring authors
to your live event. For more information or to book an event,
contact the Simon & Schuster Speakers Bureau at
1-866-248-3049 or visit our website at www.simonspeakers.com.

Designed by Dana Sloan

Manufactured in the United States of America

10 9 8 7 6 5 4 3 2 1

Library of Congress Cataloging-in-Publication Data
Cleland, Max.
   Heart of a patriot: how I found the courage to survive Vietnam, Walter Reed
and Karl Rove / Max Cleland, with Ben Raines.
      p. cm.
1. Cleland, Max. 2. Legislators—United States—Biography. 3. United States.
Congress. Senate—Biography. 4. United States. Veterans Administration—
Officials and employees—Biography. 5. Disabled veterans—United States—
Biography. 6. Vietnam War, 1961–1975—Veterans. 7. Veterans—Civil rights—
United States. 8. Legislators—Georgia—Biography. I. Raines, Ben. II. Title.
   E840.8.C545A3   2009
   362.4'3092—dc22   2009011620
ISBN: 978-1-4391-2605-9

Photo of Max Cleland with President Obama: © LARRY DOWNING/Reuters/Corbis
All other photos courtesy of The Max Cleland Collection, duPont-Ball Library,
Stetson University

My parents, Hugh and Juanita Cleland, have been the
most powerful positive influence in my life . . .
and took care of me when it was most difficult to do so.
This book is dedicated to you.

★ CONTENTS ★

"[I]t is required of a man that he should share the passion and action of his time, at peril of being judged not to have lived."

—OLIVER WENDELL HOLMES, JR.
MEMORIAL DAY, MAY 30, 1884

✷ FOREWORD ✷

An Open Letter to America's Veterans

AMERICA SENDS THE flower of its youth abroad to fight its wars. Because of that, America's military is always staffed with the stoutest, finest, most courageous people in the country. If as soldiers we are not that way when we enter the military, the military makes us that way by the time we get out. In the end, the military is still made up of everyday people like you and me. As such, most of us have no special skills to cope with the challenges wartime military service presents. Regular life simply cannot prepare a person for the brutish sensory overload of combat.

Coming back from military service in a time of war, we may be wounded in ways that don't show to the world at large. Some of the deepest wounds we suffer may be inflicted without leaving so much as a scratch. No matter what you are feeling when you come home, no matter how crazy you feel inside, know that you are not mentally ill. As combat veterans, we have been through some of the most traumatic life experiences possible. War is as close to hell on earth as anything ever could be. That does make us different from

1

our loved ones back home. War marks us all, some more deeply than others.

As veterans, we have paid a price to serve our country. We have suffered. And we may suffer for a lifetime. The soldier never gets to choose his or her war. The wars choose us, and not all are just. I believe the emotional casualties of the misguided wars may be the hardest of all to bear.

The soldier's lot is to be exposed to traumatic, life-threatening events—happenings that take us to places no bodies, minds, or souls should ever visit. It is a journey to the dark places of life—terror, fear, pain, death, wounding, loss, grief, despair, and hopelessness. We have been traumatized physically, mentally, emotionally, and spiritually. Some of us cope with exposure to hell better than others. Some are able to think of their combat experiences as but unpleasant vignettes in a long and wonderful life. It is not to those veterans I am speaking. I love them, but I am not afraid for them.

I am speaking to the rest of my brothers and sisters, those who find themselves trapped in the misery of memories as I was for so long.

For them, I am afraid.

To those veterans I say, you are not alone.

Many of us have been overwhelmed by war. Many of us have been unable to cope on our own with what has happened to us or with what we have done. Many of us have been left hopeless, lost, and confused about ourselves and our lives in ways we never thought possible.

That does not make us victims.

It makes us veterans.

As veterans of war, we are vulnerable to the memories of those experiences for the rest of our lives. Movies, the nightly news, the death of a loved one, even simple stress can serve as a trigger that reminds us of the hell we were once in. Just that remembrance can sometimes be enough to undo all the buckles we used to put ourselves back together when we got home.

Our bodies, minds, and spirits react automatically to these memory triggers. They feel the hurts and fear and horror anew each time. The curse of the soldier is that he never forgets.

Having once felt mortal danger and pure terror, our bodies prepare for it again. That helped us survive on the battlefield. However, what saved us on the battlefield doesn't work very well back here at home. It is impossible to forget our experiences in the military. But it is possible to deal with them positively. It is possible to take control of them.

That's what I've had to do.

I've found in my own life that I had to exude positive energy into the world in order not to be overwhelmed with sadness and grief over what I have lost. My body, my soul, my spirit, and my belief in life itself were stolen from me by the disaster of the Vietnam War. I found solace in attempting to "turn my pain into somebody else's gain" by immersing myself in politics and public service. In particular, I devoted myself to helping my fellow veterans and disabled friends heal. This was a great help to me in my life. But when I lost my reelection bid for the U.S. Senate in 2002, my life fell apart. The staff that had helped me politically and physically so I could keep on running with no legs was gone. The pleasure of having a job worth doing and the money to keep me afloat were gone.

My relationships began to crumble, especially the one with my fiancée.

I went down in my life in every way it is possible to go down. Massive depression took over. I went down with a grief over my losses that I had never known before. I went down thinking that God was not for me anymore. I no longer wanted to live. With the start of the Iraq War, my own post-traumatic stress disorder came roaring back nearly 40 years after I was in combat. I never saw it coming. Thoughts of war and death simply consumed me. I thought I was past that.

It taught me that none of us are ever past it. But all of us can get past it enough to be happy.

When I went down, my sense of safety, organization, structure, and stability collapsed. My anxiety went sky-high. My brain chemicals, which had helped me stay hopeful and optimistic, dropped through the floor. My brain stopped working. My mind, which I had counted on all my life to pull me through and help clarify challenges, fell into despair. My spirit dropped like a rock as all hope I had for a good life went away. I was totally wounded and wiped out—hopeless and overwhelmed. Just like I had been on that April day in 1968 when the grenade ripped off my legs and my right arm. Emotionally, spiritually, physically, and mentally, I was bleeding and dying. I wound up at Walter Reed Army Medical Center almost 40 years after I had been treated there the first time. This time around, I was in search of being put back together again in my mind, heart, and soul. When I was there the first time, the doctors didn't really treat our hearts and minds, just our broken bodies. Post-traumatic stress disorder didn't officially exist. Neither did counseling for it. What a world of difference several decades make!

Recovery is possible. There are people who can help.

Through weekly counseling, medication for anxiety and depression, and weekly attendance at a spiritual Twelve Step recovery group, I began to heal. My personal recovery and renewal have taken years. I still talk to my PTSD counselor at Walter Reed occasionally when I need to do so. I still take a low dose of antianxiety and antidepression medication. I still stay in touch with my brothers in my Tuesday night Twelve Step group at the "last house on the block." As a brother in that group, I lean on my fellow attendees, especially my fellow veterans, and feed off their experience, strength, and hope.

Which is why I am writing this open letter especially to those who have suffered what Shakespeare referred to as "the slings and arrows of outrageous fortune" by getting blown up, shot up, or otherwise wounded in the service of our country. For me, the physical wounds were the first to heal and the easiest to deal with. It is not easy to run for political office or try to run forward in life with no legs. But I've been able to do it. The mental and emotional wounds—and a whole suite of spiritual wounds—have been far more difficult to overcome. They are the most subtle of all, and the hardest to heal. From time to time, I am overwhelmed by the sense of meaninglessness I feel regarding the Vietnam War, in which I was a young participant, and the Iraq War Resolution, which I voted for as a U.S. senator. To keep my sanity, I must not dwell on my part in those disastrous episodes in American history. I try not to blame myself too much. I work on my own recovery and renewal knowing that I can't help anyone else unless I get, as Hemingway put it after his war, "strong at the broken places."

I try to get enough sleep so my mind can regenerate. I exercise. I still walk with no legs, putting my stumps on pillows and sliding across the floor to get my aerobic workouts. Occasionally I do sit-ups and push-ups and curls with weights. I stay in touch with the members of my group and read literature like the Bible, which guides my prayer and meditation and helps me remember that God is with me, not against me. I work on my physical, spiritual, and mental recovery and renewal every day.

Recovery is possible from even the most grievous wounds of war, politics, and life. But we veterans remain painfully aware of our experiences. As my trauma counselor tells me, it is fine to look in the rearview mirror from time to time to see where you've been, but it is much more important to look through the windshield to see where you want to go. We can't let where we've been dominate and control where we are headed. Otherwise, we live an upside-down life.

In addition to trying to muster the courage and the faith to move forward each day, I try to remember that I am blessed to have the grace of God and the help of friends to point the way and help me along my path.

I wish you the same.

Max Cleland
Atlanta, Georgia
2009

The Charge of the Light Brigade

AT THE MOMENT Lyndon Johnson appeared on television to announce that he was dropping out of the presidential race and wanted to end the war he had started, I was preparing to board a chopper headed into battle.

I was scared out of my mind.

While Johnson's speech was heard at dinnertime on the last day of March back in the States, over in Vietnam we heard him live on the radio the morning of April Fools' Day. For soldiers about to risk everything in battle, the timing couldn't have been more dismal. We felt as if we were being abandoned on the battlefield. Everyone was left wondering if we were to be the last soldiers to die in a war our commander in chief had just bowed out of.

I was flabbergasted. President Johnson was my guy. He had received my first-ever vote for president in 1964. I volunteered for Vietnam because I believed in what he was doing there. Now, all of a sudden, the president I heard on the radio no longer sounded like he had faith in the mission. I didn't know what to make of it.

Everybody on the ground in Vietnam knew things were not going well for the United States in the early part of 1968. In a stunning strategic blunder, the U.S. commanders had been caught off-guard by the Tet offensive—a massive surprise attack by the North Vietnamese army involving more than 100,000 troops. Vietcong forces sacrificed themselves by the thousands in February and killed more than 500 Americans in a single week, the highest total of the war. Tet revealed the North Vietnamese to be resurgent despite all statements to the contrary by President Johnson and his cabinet. Still, I don't think anyone fighting in Vietnam expected him to call for an end to the war.

With the president's words of defeat ringing in my ears, I was one of more than 15,000 soldiers about to lift off as part of Operation Pegasus, a rescue mission named after the winged horse of mythical legend. My unit, the First Air Cavalry Division, was the U.S. Army's flying horse—the only all-helicopter unit in Vietnam. Everything we did, we did out of choppers. Our job was to rescue 5,000 marines who had been pinned down for several months by 20,000 North Vietnamese army soldiers at a place called Khe Sanh. It was to be the biggest battle of the war.

No one was sure if we would be able to rescue the marines. The North Vietnamese were digging tunnels all over the place and popping up within 100 yards of the base to snipe our guys. Mortars and rockets had been falling on the Khe Sanh base day and night since January, and the place was in danger of being overrun at any moment. Supply planes trying to land took so much fire that many of them were forced to pull up without ever touching down on the runway. The plight of the troops pinned down in that faraway jungle was front-page news back in the States, and it was a major embarrassment to Johnson and his war team.

One of the North Vietnamese divisions hemming in the marines was the famed 325th C Division, which had helped defeat the French at Dien Bien Phu in 1954. That bloody battle essentially ended the French Indochina War. The French defeat there was so profound and unexpected that it broke the will of the French people and turned the nation against the war and the long colonial occupation of Vietnam. With American media reporting on the soldiers trapped at Khe Sanh and already drawing parallels to the French experience, the Johnson administration was worried that a similar defeat would turn public opinion against its war. Under his orders, the American military put all its chips on the table in order to break the siege, with Johnson reportedly telling the Joint Chiefs of Staff, "I don't want no damn Dien Bien Phu."

I could see Khe Sanh was shaping up to be one of the largest and most important battles of the war. It was also my last chance to see major combat. I had just received my discharge orders and would be going home in a matter of weeks. Up to that point, my tour in Vietnam had been relatively uneventful. I had been through mortar attacks and light shelling, but nothing like what the marines were facing at Khe Sanh. That was part of why I volunteered for the mission. As a captain in charge of setting up radio relay stations and handling the logistical communication traffic for the 1st Cav, I didn't want to ship home from the war of my generation without having faced down the enemy and my own fears. I wanted to be tested. Men my age were getting killed every day. I had seen the stacks of shiny aluminum caskets at our air bases. I couldn't escape the feeling that I had to do my part, that it was my duty to volunteer. I wanted to lead men, but didn't see how I could send soldiers into combat unless I was brave enough to fight when it was my turn.

A few weeks before the massive rescue mission was set to launch, I asked to speak to my battalion commander. When I told him I wanted to go in as the signal officer for an infantry battalion being air-assaulted into Khe Sanh, he looked at me like I was nuts. Then he asked me if I was trying to get a Purple Heart. "You know they kill people out there," he said.

I wasn't fazed. Not right then anyway. I was a six-foot-two army paratrooper—tall, tan, and tantalizing. I'd jumped out of airplanes. I was trained to fight. I wanted to be tested under fire to see what I was made of.

But as the days before the battle slipped by, my courage failed. My bravado vanished. I began to dwell on what might happen, namely my own death. I started breaking out in cold sweats. I was flat-out scared.

I began to wonder why the hell I had volunteered for such a crazy mission. It was only after I insisted on going that I learned what a bare-bones force we were taking in. Soldiers from the First Air Cav were to be dropped on strategic hilltops and other spots to support a larger ground force moving in toward the base on land. The problem was that all our landing areas were well within reach of enemy weapons. That meant we were going in against entrenched guns, literally the same thing faced by the doomed soldiers in Tennyson's "Charge of the Light Brigade," with "Cannon to right of them / Cannon to left of them / Cannon in front of them." A soldier facing heavy artillery fire has no one to shoot at, because the big guns are so far away. There is but one thing to do: hunker down and hope nothing lands on you. That is what I would be doing with my men after our helicopter dropped us off, hunkering down and hoping for the best.

Before the war, I had read *Street Without Joy* and *Hell in a Very Small Place,* both by Bernard Fall, the great historian of the French Indochina War, and both about the battle of Dien Bien Phu. The books described in painstaking detail the mistakes of the French military in that war, including underestimating their Vietnamese enemy. I knew all of that history, and I knew I had just signed up for a battle that would be very much like the one Tennyson's poem described from the Crimean War. In this case, I would play one of the British soldiers sent to do or die, sent "Into the jaws of Death / Into the mouth of Hell."

With those thoughts swirling in my mind, the mission itself began to seem close to suicide. Before I volunteered, I was on the verge of going home in one piece. I had my orders. I had done my time. Why had I volunteered for a battle I didn't need to fight? I started feeling like I wanted out. With my tail between my legs, I went to the battalion commander and tried to back out by telling him I'd had a change of heart. He wouldn't let me off the hook. My orders stood. When I expressed my fears to an army major friend of mine, he said, "Congratulations on being normal. Just keep your mind on your job and you'll do fine." He told me that being afraid didn't mean I was a coward. Courage, he said, was doing what you had to do in the face of your fear.

That bucked me up some, and I pulled myself together. But then Johnson pulled the rug out from under every soldier he had put in harm's way.

We loaded up the day after his speech, hundreds of choppers strong, and lifted off toward Khe Sanh. We spent the night at a staging area called Landing Zone Stud, near a Vietnamese village named Ca Lu. The morning of April 3, 1968, we touched down in hills about a mile east of the Khe Sanh perimeter. The B-52s had done their job in prepping the landing zone. The hillsides were barren and burned, pockmarked with hundreds of massive craters. The devastation stretched all the way down the hill we were on to the bottom of the valley where the marine base was located. Instantly I understood why the jungle had been cleared—to take away as many hiding places as possible from the North Vietnamese. I wondered what had been there before we created this bleak moonscape. Villages? Trees? What would be there after we were gone?

I led my small signal unit into a deep bomb crater next to the landing site because there was nowhere else to hide. There were no trees, no bushes—nothing. It was 20 feet across and about 20 feet deep, and it still reeked of burned explosives. We set up our radio equipment and waited. Nothing happened all day and into the night. The night of April 4, as I was writing a letter to a friend by flashlight at the bottom of the bomb crater, I heard the distinctive whistle of what I later learned was a Russian-made rocket. Incoming! The battle was on. Rocket after rocket pounded down around us. The explosions sent thudding shivers through the ground. I could hear the cries of soldiers who had been hit around me. I clutched my M-16 tight as an old, battle-hardened sergeant screamed, "Take care of the wounded! Prepare for a ground attack!" My rifle trembled in my hands and I cursed myself for being stupid enough to ask for this mission. Then I heard a new round of shelling. I watched bright yellow flashes bloom like dandelions against black velvet as our shells pounded back at North Vietnamese positions miles across the valley. The two sides bombed the hell out of each other that night.

As gray shards of first light spread over the valley, I saw that four men in our battalion were dead. Their bodies had been laid in a row. My eyes fell upon one of the dead men. The splintered shafts of his shinbones protruded from the gore of his legs.

I found a telegram that had been dropped on the ground by a newsman. It read, "MLK story front page news. Khe Sanh relief not headline anymore." It was April 4. Martin Luther King Jr. had just been assassinated. Within the blink of an eye, pulling America's chestnuts out of the fire at Khe Sanh didn't seem to matter much anymore.

Four days later, with 200 men in my division dead and thousands of rounds of artillery spent, the siege was broken. It was April 8, 1968. A giant golden sun rose above the horizon and tinted the puffy clouds pink. We had done what we came to do. The 5,000 marines were rescued. And I had faced down the demons of my fear. I had found new courage. In another month, I'd be stateside, my tour of duty over, my heart battle-tested forever.

Blinking into the brightening sun, I heard someone call my name. It was Major Maury Cralle. He was on the battalion staff and asked me to send a radio unit back to the division base camp at Ca Lu to upgrade our communications capabilities and set up a radio-relay site for the battalion in preparation for its move into the Khe Sanh perimeter. My team and I loaded up a couple of generators, some radios, antennas, and the rest of our gear and took off for Landing Zone Stud. There was a new soldier on the chopper. I had never met him before. It was a short, uneventful hop to the base. I was the last man off the chopper, and ran in a low crouch until I was clear of the whirling blades. As the chopper lifted off, I saw the grenade. It was on the ground where I had landed. I thought it had fallen off my web gear. Slinging my M-16 behind my back with my left hand, I reached over to pick it up.

Just as I was about to touch it, there was a white flash and a massive explosion. I was hurtling through the air. The blast rattled every part of me, and then I slammed back into the earth. I could feel my eyes pressing deeper into their sockets in my skull. For a moment I couldn't see. The boom of the explosion echoed in my ears and drowned out all other sounds.

My eyes came back first. I was on my back and looked up and saw the sky. Then I looked toward my right hand. There was nothing there. It was gone. My shirtsleeve was shredded, the tattered end sopped in blood. A splinter of bone jutted from where my arm had been. Using my left hand, I felt my head. My steel pot helmet had been blown off, but my face and head seemed intact. I reached between my legs and felt for my sex life. Everything was still there. My flak jacket had protected my torso and groin. Using my left hand to push myself up, I tried to stand, but I couldn't. Something was badly wrong with my legs. Looking down, I saw that I had no right leg below my thigh. The left leg was there, but my combat boot was askew, sitting almost next to my knee at an impossible angle. My green fatigue pants were smoking and soaked in blood.

Then I felt nothing but pain all over my body. There was the smell of burned meat, like a steak scorched black. It was my flesh. I started fading, like I was falling backward, dropping down a shaft into the earth beneath me. My ears were still ringing. My body was on fire. I tried to call out to the guys who had been on the chopper with me for help, but my voice was just a hiss, lost in my throat. I couldn't yell. My windpipe had been ripped open.

Somebody came toward me and told me to hold on. My crew had apparently jumped for cover when the grenade went off, thinking it was a rocket attack. Someone I didn't recognize was making a tourniquet out of a belt and tying off my leg. My pants were being cut off me. I heard people calling for medics. Soldiers surrounded me now, their faces pale and scared, their eyes shifting away from mine. I knew the look. It had been on my face at Khe Sanh when I looked at the dead. It was a look that said, Thank God, that's not me. Someone was wrapping a T-shirt around my arm stump. Waves of pain coursed through me. A navy medic showed up. I kept thinking, Oh, God! Why me?

A medevac chopper came and lifted me to the division aid station. I was put on a table and medics began to work on me quickly. A medic gave me a shot of morphine. I looked up at him and hissed, "Am I going to make it?"

"You just might," he said in almost a casual way, as if a coin would be flipped and one side said "live" and the other side said "die." I fought to stay conscious.

I shouted out through my hissing, "Look me up in twenty years . . . ," my voice trailing off to nothingness.

I was bleeding to death.

My heart raced and I felt the life ebb out of me with each beat. My skin was on fire and waves of pain throbbed through my body. It had been less than an hour since the grenade went off. I was close to passing out. I fought against it. I fought with everything I had to stay awake. I knew if I collapsed into unconsciousness, I would never make it back. I don't want to die here, I thought over and over. I faded in and out of consciousness as they carried me into the operating room and could barely breathe through my slashed windpipe. Five doctors rushed toward me and began working as soon as I was set down on the surgical table. Someone was putting the gas breather over my mouth and nose. Other hands were holding the gash in my throat open.

I could feel the anesthesia coming on.

"Please save my left leg if you can," I whispered.

"We'll do all we can," was the last thing I heard as I drifted into the ether. I couldn't help wondering how many legs and arms I had given away in such a short period of time.

★ 2 ★

Beginnings

I WAS BORN on the night of the first total blackout in the city of Atlanta's history, August 24, 1942. In the wake of Pearl Harbor, the city fathers had come to believe an air assault on Atlanta was imminent and they wanted to be ready for it. The blackout was a dry run, complete with air-raid sirens and small planes dropping sacks of flour on top of airstrips and hospitals as make-believe bombs. So it was that little Max Cleland came into the world, a war baby born into a city pretending not to exist.

With the nation at war, my father, two of his brothers, and both my mother's brothers joined the military to fight Hitler and the Japanese. My daddy joined the navy. That meant my mother went to work and I was left in the care of my grandmother. Like a generation of war babies, I wasn't even talking when my father left home. Stories from my mother and grandmother brought him to life for me while he was gone, but in reality, I was too young when he left to even remember him.

He came home December 8, 1945. I was three and a half. I can still remember the magic of the night I saw my father, and how happy my mother was when she woke me up out of bed shouting,

"Daddy's home! Daddy's home!" I ran on my little legs and jumped into my father's arms for what seemed to me to be the first time ever. He pulled me up to his chest and hugged me and kissed me and stared at me for a long while. In the way of gifts, he brought me a pack of crackers and a little red wagon that I pulled around for years. He was still in his navy uniform, and I remember the long strips of battle ribbons on his chest. They were striped and colored and I kept picking at them while he held me because I thought they were Dentyne chewing gum.

After the war, Daddy moved us out to Lithonia, Georgia, a little village about 30 miles from Atlanta near the farm where he had grown up. The village was founded in 1856 by early settlers who had worked in granite quarries before launching out for the West. The hills outside Atlanta contain massive granite deposits, and the famously sturdy, hardworking Scotch-Irish set up shop right away. Several quarries were opened around my hometown. My father's first paying job was carrying tools for a team of masons at one of the quarries, earning 50 cents a day. He worked hard all his life, but never again in the quarries after that first job. I think early exposure to the rough work of cleaving great stones from the hard earth was one of the primary reasons he spent the rest of his life as a salesman.

We lived on Main Street, just a few blocks from Lithonia's tiny downtown, in a house purchased with a GI Bill home loan. It took Daddy eight years to pay off the mortgage. I couldn't have had better parents, or a more perfect *Leave It to Beaver* upbringing. My mother, Juanita, was a lovely, slender brunette. She came from a family where everyone, the men and the women, were tall and a pleasure to look at, with beautiful arms and legs. She was a natural athlete, playing on her high school basketball team even in the midst of the Great Depression. Shortly after I was born, right after Daddy shipped out to Pearl Harbor for his World War II navy service, she went to work as a secretary for the Standard Oil Company. I still don't think I've ever known anyone who answered the phone more exquisitely. Her family was a little more sophisticated than my father's, and she was raised to have great articulation and diction, to "speak like a lady," as they used to say.

During my elementary school years, my father's mother stayed at home with me while both my parents worked. When I turned 13, my mother announced she was giving up her job. She told her boss she was "going home to raise my son."

Both my parents were reared on farms during the Great Depression, and that experience colored how they lived their lives, saved their money, and saw the world.

My father was, by his own description, the "number one plowboy" in his family, one of those desperately poor Depression-era families with seven brothers and sisters. He went to a one-room schoolhouse until fifth grade, the only schooling he ever had. Daddy was part of a generation whose education was cut short by the poverty of the Depression and a life of full-time work that began before adolescence. He never got to play ball as a child, and even as an adult didn't understand the rules of games like baseball or basketball. The rules he learned as a kid had more to do with bare survival: Work hard, take care of your family, and save your money.

By the time he was eight, my father was up feeding the family mule at 4:00 a.m. every day. Even at that tender age, he was tasked with plowing the family's sugarcane field with the mule, or hitching it to the big grinder mill that my grandfather used to crush the cane into sorghum syrup. That was the family's only cash crop, sorghum syrup, plus one bale of cotton a year. When the cotton came in, my grandfather would take Daddy to town with him to sell it. Each year, my father would get "a wienie, a pack of crackers, and some new shoes."

That wasn't my life. My father made sure we never wanted for anything. When I was a toddler, he worked 12-hour days driving as a route man for the Atlanta Linen Service. After the war, he traveled the state selling automobile polish out of the trunk of his car. He was one of the last of the great traveling salesmen of the postwar era and didn't retire until he turned 80. As a child, all that was asked of me was that I do well in school, take piano lessons, and go to church.

There was a lot of going to church. My mother was a Methodist, and Daddy was a Baptist. For me, that meant that most Sundays I got the best—or worst—of both worlds. First would come a few hours of Sunday school at the Lithonia Methodist Church, where Mother and I were members. Then the whole family would pack up and drive to the Turner Hill Road Baptist Church in the country, where Daddy was a member. I got a double dose of the Good Word every weekend.

The two churches and their competing visions of the Lord could not have been more different.

The Methodist church was in downtown Lithonia, a magnificent edifice made of hand-laid granite stone with a huge bell on top. Beautiful stained-glass windows glowed against the granite walls and made the building look almost like a Gothic cathedral. The service was predictable, structured, and focused, with printed bulletins outlining the theme of the service each Sunday, a giant organ that sounded like heaven itself, and a big choir in matching robes. The minister hardly ever raised his voice and always spoke reverently of God's love.

Turner Hill Baptist had a thundering country preacher delivering promises of hellfire and damnation for all. Adding to the sense of hell, the old clapboard church had no air-conditioning. If you were thirsty and wanted a drink of water, you had to drink from the "common cup," a big aluminum dipper that served everybody—rich and poor alike—from the church well. The church sat on a red clay dirt road in the midst of farmland where my daddy had grown up, and was the classic little brown church in the vale—except it was white. When summer came, it was revival time. That meant "dinner on the grounds." The women of the church would lay out a spread of collards, ham, fried chicken, black-eyed peas, cornbread, creamed corn, pies, cakes, and all the other high points of fine country cooking. The food we took home from the revivals lasted for days.

I didn't mind church so much back then, because it was one of the only things going on in our little town that qualified as live entertainment in the late '40s and early '50s.

Then came television. That changed everything for me.

In 1950, my father paid $50 for our first television. It was a 12-inch Sylvania black-and-white TV with a rabbit-ear antenna that sat on top of the console. This was just a few months after I saw television for the first time while visiting family friends. I remember when they turned the TV on, I could hear the vacuum tubes crackling inside as they warmed up. They told me the cobwebs and bugs that had collected inside the cabinet were burning up. I sat right in front of the TV and watched a glowing pinprick in the center of the screen get bigger and bigger. Then suddenly the dot swelled and blossomed into a moving picture. It was the Lone Ranger! That was the very first thing I ever saw on TV, and from that moment on, the Lone Ranger became my personal hero.

Television was a true wonder and made anything seem possible—rockets, spacemen, the future! It was literally my window to the world, connecting me to life outside Lithonia. I was hooked on it instantly. I became part of the first TV generation, a true baby boomer. Milton Berle, *I Love Lucy, Woody Woodpecker, Bugs Bunny,* Sid Caesar, Jackie Gleason, Roy Rogers, *Gunsmoke, Hopalong Cassidy*—I watched them all. But I still loved the Lone Ranger best.

For some reason the image, the character, the persona of the Lone Ranger stuck with me. I was an only child. The Lone Ranger was alone too, except for Tonto, his Kemo Sabe, his "trusty scout." I was fascinated by his mask and the silver bullets he shot, "never to kill, but to wound." As a young boy, I would put myself to sleep "returning to the days of yesteryear" and pretending that I *was* the Lone Ranger. I named my first dog Ranger. I had Lone Ranger saddlebags on my bike and wore my cap guns everywhere. The Lone Ranger's ethic of hard work and fighting for peace and justice became my ethic. That was how I thought you measured up as a man.

Years later, as an adult, I got a chance to meet Clayton Moore, the man behind the Lone Ranger's mask. It was a magical moment for me, more powerful in a way than meeting the presidents I've known. Like the Willie Nelson song says, "My heroes have always been cowboys," and Clayton was the best of them all. We spent several hours together shortly before he died, and I loved it. The silver bullet he gave me is one of my prized possessions.

That show shaped my entire life.

But it wasn't long before the boob tube gave me a gift of more lasting import than even my Lone Ranger–inspired morals.

Summers in Georgia are brutal. We had no air-conditioning. Playing outside under the big pecan tree in my backyard became my favorite way of cooling off. One day, I came into the house to rest from playing and turned on the TV. I saw the most amazing thing. A group of people were parading, shouting, wearing funny hats, and waving placards with names on them. It looked like a big party, and it was. It was the Democratic Party at the 1952 Democratic National Convention. I had never seen anything like it. The name "Russell" was written on a lot of the placards. I knew he was from Georgia and that people called him "Senator." Watching television, I figured out he was running for president. Wow! There was a Georgia connection to all the stuff I was seeing on the magic TV!

How cool!

Dick Russell's boomlet for the presidency did not last long, but it connected with me that somehow folks in Georgia were tied into something big. I watched the rest of the convention as Adlai Stevenson became the Democrats' nominee for president in 1952.

The parading and hollering in the convention hall got really fierce, and I could see people pumping signs with his name on them in an increasingly vigorous way as they tooted horns and danced in the aisles. That was where I wanted to be. It seemed like a grand old time.

In my family, we were die-hard Democrats. The gospel according to my parents held that FDR saved the nation from a Depression caused by Republicans. My father did two stints in FDR's Civilian Conservation Corps during the Depression, one of thousands of people whose lives were resurrected with such projects. FDR's picture still hangs in our family home, the only president my parents ever saw fit to honor on our walls.

The Democrats on TV were campaigning and celebrating, so I decided I should campaign and celebrate too. With nothing but time on my hands that hot summer, I convinced the girl next door, Julie Davidson, to campaign with me. We took pecan sticks from the yard as our sign poles, made posters with the cardboard out of my daddy's shirts that came home from the cleaners, and wrote "Adlai Stevenson for president" on them with my mother's lipstick. Though I lived on Main Street in Lithonia, the busiest street in town, I seldom saw a car in those days. Ten or fifteen minutes might go by with no traffic. When the occasional car did come down the street, Julie and I would run alongside, whooping it up and hollering, "Stevenson for president!" We jumped around and danced on the sidewalk, waving our little pecan-stick placards and pumping them up and down just like the people on TV. Cars honked and people smiled and waved. It was great fun. I realized for the first time that I liked campaigning.

That was the summer before fifth grade. By then, I could play piano pretty well, but I hated it. I begged my mother to let me switch instruments. I had been seduced by the gorgeous sound of the trumpet. After much prodding, she agreed, and since I could already read music, I was playing pretty well in a matter of weeks. Word got to the director of the Lithonia High School band, and he recruited me right out of fifth grade.

I was a 10-year-old thrown in with all these high school juniors and seniors. I remember my first practice with all those giant kids. I was the last-chair trumpet in this long line of trumpet players. The band director asked the first-trumpet how to finger a certain note, but he didn't know. The director went on down the line. None of the other trumpet players ahead of me knew how to finger it either. While they were being questioned, I peeked in my "Beginning Trumpet" book, which I still had because, unlike all the high school players, I had only started playing a few months before. Nobody saw me sneak a peek into the book and find the note. I ended up the only trumpet player, a mere 10 years old, who could tell the band director how to make the note. I was one of his favorites from then on and he made me a permanent part of the high school band right then, at my first practice.

The next year, when I was in sixth grade, the band went to the state competition and came in third, not bad for a small-town band playing against everybody else in Georgia. But that was not how the bandleader felt. He was new to the high school and was so displeased with third place that he actually went to the principal and tried to resign. The principal talked him into staying, but the director swore that if the band didn't come in first place the next year, he would quit. He even delivered his ultimatum to the band. He worked our butts off for all of my seventh-grade year trying to win that first-place award, drilling us over and over. It was the first real hard coaching I ever had and I still remember it, even more than all the yelling from my sports coaches. He was so insistent on perfection that I found it rubbing off on me. He kept telling us we could be first, so we should be first. Nothing else would do.

The state finals came around again at the end of my seventh-grade year. By this time, we had a great band. We went to the competition and blew the doors off the auditorium. We won a "Superior" rating against schools from all over the state. I remember going home with the little blue medal they gave each of us still in its paperboard box. I put it on the mantel and stood back and looked at it. First place. Number one. Superior. It meant we were the best there was. I was the best I could be. I liked that feeling, the feeling of winning. Oh yeah, I thought. There are going to be a lot more of those up there on the mantel before long. I'm going to be the best at whatever I do.

As seventh grade drew to a close, it was time for that great American institution, the school trip to Washington, D.C. Tired kids in T-shirts, confused parents, and lonely bus drivers trying to pick through the iconic monuments in the nation's capital—those scenes are repeated every spring and summer in Washington to this day. That school trip was the first time I ever set foot in the capital city. My seventh-grade teacher, Mrs. Craven, had rigorously prepared us for the adventure. In our schoolroom, we had little figurines of all the presidents that we studied, and we had memorized their names—even if we had had no instruction as to what they actually stood for.

For me and most of my class, this would be the first time we had ever been "North." We had one boy in our class who was born in Pennsylvania. We nicknamed him "Yankee." That's how we felt about Northerners. This was in the 1950s, and going "up North" was like going to a foreign country. It was exciting. Even the lectures Mrs. Craven gave us before the trip were spellbinding. She told our class that we might even see black men dating white women—an unimaginable breach of ethics in the South at that time. And she told us that one of the trains we would be riding on would go 80 miles an hour—faster than anyone in the class had ever traveled before!

My mother came along on the trip, and one particular moment in Washington with her still stands out for me. At the base of the Lincoln Memorial, you can stand and look east at the long expanse across the Reflecting Pool to the Washington Monument. In the distance, beyond the Washington Monument, you can see the U.S. Capitol sitting on the highest point in the city. For some reason, my mother and I were both captivated by that view. I loved it. I was mesmerized by it, as apparently was she. We were so seduced that we failed to notice that Mrs. Craven, my classmates, and our tour bus had disappeared without us. They were headed to Arlington Cemetery, our next destination. No one noticed we were missing until much later that afternoon. Eventually, hours later, someone figured it out and the bus came back for us. We were teased endlessly, but it was worth it. I have always treasured the memory of that afternoon spent lost and alone looking at the Capitol with my mother.

As eighth grade kicked off, I got obsessed with ball—any kind of ball. Baseball, football, tennis, any sport with a ball. I played all the time. My best friend, Edgar Abbott, lived right behind our house. He was a year older than I was and a year better at everything, particularly sports. He became my big brother and I idolized him. He could whip me at anything and everything. And he did. But he would also teach me. He had an instinct for teaching, and actually went on to become a teacher in his adult life. But back then, Edgar and I played ball almost every day, from the moment school got out until the sun went down. He'd show me how to hold the ball, or how to dribble or shoot a hook shot or grip a tennis racket—anything! The one constant was that he could always beat me. That was part of what fired my competitive drive, which had become fierce after winning the band medal. Ever after that, I wanted to be a winner. For me, the ultimate had become to demonstrate physical prowess in sports. I didn't get into fistfights. That wasn't my bag. I wanted to beat people in sports. It was an obsession.

If Edgar couldn't play ball with me, I'd play by myself, throwing the ball against a wall and fielding grounders or bouncing it off the roof to practice snagging fly balls. I'd shoot hoops alone, practice my tennis serve, whatever I could do. As school went on, competition became the way I defined myself. I was an athlete, purely physical. And I was damn good.

I made the varsity baseball team as a starter in the ninth grade, the first kid in my class to earn a letter. I played third base for four years. The coach made me leadoff hitter, and I was written up in the Atlanta paper as the "spark plug of the team." I remember carrying my glove to class on the day of the first tryout. I kept hitting my glove with my hand all day, saying, "I can do it. I can do it."

Sophomore year, I made the varsity basketball team, but didn't really break out until a game against our archrivals from Conyers, a little town about six miles away. The star forward on our team was sick and couldn't play, so the coach moved me over from guard. It was the best game I ever played. Something happened that night and I just couldn't miss the basket. We beat them by two points in over-time and I was the star of the game. What a feeling! My high game over two years had been four points, but that night I scored 15. From then on, I was the starting forward on the team. As it happened, that was the only game we won all year. We had a record of one win and 19 losses. My junior year, we had a winning season, and senior year I led the team in free-throw percentage and in total offense, scoring over 200 points.

We played in a little cracker-box gym just like in the movie *Hoosiers,* with steep, old wooden bleachers crammed so close up against the court you felt like you were a part of the game even if you sat in the top row. The cheerleaders wore their little brown and white oxfords and stood about two inches outside the baseline on the most fabulously shellacked floor I've ever seen. We didn't mess with that floor. It was sacred, and it was the best basketball floor I ever played on. We had plywood backboards, but I never used them. I always aimed for the basket because I wanted to see the swish of the net. My best shot was a fadeaway jump shot from the corner about 20 feet out, fading into the popcorn stand and on top of the cheerleaders. For me, that was the ultimate athletic move, crashing into a wall of pretty, giggling girls.

Edgar taught me tennis beginning in seventh grade. I loved the one-on-one aspect of it. There was no one else to blame if you lost. It was just you and the guy across the net. Once again, Edgar was my main competition. For four years in a row in high school, he was the runner-up for the state singles championship. But by my senior year in 1960, Edgar had graduated and I was the one playing for the state championship. I got beaten, but I became runner-up for best high school tennis player in Georgia in my class. After that came the city championships, open to anyone in Lithonia, young or old. Edgar and I teamed up to win the doubles title. Then it was time for singles. Edgar and I both played through the field and ended up going one-on-one against each other in the championship match. Finally, for the first time ever, I beat him. I was officially the best tennis player in all of Lithonia. It was the greatest athletic victory I ever had.

Senior year, I was president of several clubs and editor of the school yearbook. The teachers at my school voted me "Outstanding Senior." As part of the honor, I got a loving cup with my name engraved on it from the *Atlanta Journal* newspaper. Today that cup sits in a place of honor in my home, surrounded by the rest of my medals from high school. It remains my favorite trophy.

Unfortunately, I wasn't clever enough to take full advantage of the benefits of athletic stardom in high school, meaning girls. I did finally get a girlfriend toward the end of my junior year. We'd go eat at the drive-in and she'd wear my school letter jacket, but I didn't even know what a move was, let alone how to try to make one. I finally kissed her on Christmas night in our senior year. After such a long buildup, I got excited real fast and it scared the hell out of me. I had no idea how that sort of stuff worked. My understanding of the sexual world was nonexistent, even by 1950s standards. All through high school, while everybody else was off kissing and drinking beer, I was doing homework or bouncing balls off the roof of the house.

That fall, I was accepted to Stetson University in Deland, Florida. I left home for the first time to begin my college experience just a few months after that first overwhelming kiss. I had no idea how big my world was about to become.

✯ 3 ✯

Discovery

BY THE TIME I graduated from high school and headed off to Stetson, my ardor for politics had dimmed. In fact, I had lost all interest in politics within days of my impromptu Main Street campaigning for Adlai Stevenson.

My mind was instead focused on the stars. It was the dawn of the jet age and I had been inspired by the American space program and the rockets taking off from Cape Canaveral. Stetson was only 100 miles from the Cape, which was a big attraction for me. The campus was close enough that you could see rockets in the sky after blastoff. Before I reported in for freshman orientation, I had decided I would become a high school science teacher.

I set out to major in physics. That lasted three short and sometimes humiliating days. It was quickly revealed that I didn't have enough math for college physics. Told I had to pick a new major—one that didn't involve arithmetic or any of its more complex relatives—I chose English. Unfortunately, I failed the writing sample and the grammar test, and was put in a remedial English class. I discovered that when it came to my native tongue, I was actually bilingual. I spoke Southern and a little English.

That first semester I suffered a rather rude introduction to the "big fish, small pond" phenomenon. Stetson was a bigger pond than Lithonia High School, and I wasn't measuring up. In fact, I was a veritable minnow. I spent my first months in college fighting for sheer academic survival. So much for my days as "Outstanding Senior" back home. I desperately wanted to go out for intramural sports that first semester, but my father was spending too much of his hard-earned money on my education and I was doing too poorly to waste any time playing ball.

On the upside, I became captivated by the nation's electoral drama, which was unfolding anew in the fall of 1960. Politics was in the air and once again I couldn't get enough. Over the summer I had watched John Kennedy accept the Democratic nomination at the convention, and I was ready to parade on Main Street all over again. My dorm room had no TV, so every night I hiked about a block in the dark to a central TV room to watch the nightly news. I sat rapt in front of the television, watching the Kennedy-Nixon debates. I had become fascinated by Senator John Kennedy. He was young and good-looking, and so was his whole family. He had hopeful ambitions for the country and talked a lot about the future and my generation's role in it. In particular, he talked about young people involving themselves in politics. For the first time in my life, I wanted to vote for somebody. I wanted to vote for John Kennedy and volunteer for his campaign.

I ventured off-campus into downtown Deland and dropped by the local Democratic Party office, where I was greeted by a lady volunteer. It was the first campaign office I had ever been in. I proudly told her that I wanted to vote for Kennedy. When she learned that I was just 18, she told me that I couldn't vote in Florida. "Sorry. I'd like to help you, but you have to be twenty-one years old to be registered to vote." I was crestfallen. In Georgia in those days, you could register to vote at 18 thanks to Ellis Arnall, a progressive governor in the

1940s. It would be 1970 before the U.S. Constitution was amended to reduce the voting age from 21 to 18 nationwide. In large measure, the law was changed due to Vietnam War protesters, who argued, "Old enough to fight, old enough to vote." I was left to agonize over the extremely close Kennedy-Nixon presidential balloting, wishing I could have pulled the lever for my guy myself. In the end, he won, but no thanks to me.

I got my feet under me over the course of the next year, and was able to join a fraternity and keep up with both my studies and my duties as a U.S. Army ROTC cadet. My plan at the time was to graduate from college and be sworn in as a second lieutenant in the U.S. Army on the same day. I owed the army two years of active duty immediately after graduation and I couldn't wait. I loved the idea of being a soldier.

I walked into the fraternity house one Monday evening in October 1962 and saw the president on television. I know it was a Monday because I was still in my ROTC uniform from drill practice. Every seat was taken, so I leaned up against a window as John Kennedy looked into the TV camera and told the nation that the Soviet Union was installing offensive nuclear missiles in Cuba. In response, he was ordering a U.S. naval blockade around the island. I felt cold chills run down my spine. I was in the pipeline for military duty and had two years of training under my belt by that point. It occurred to me that I might get called up early if we entered into a full-blown war with the Soviets.

Stetson's campus was only a few hundred miles north of Cuba. During the 13 days of the crisis, U.S. military movement to south Florida was powerfully evident to me. U.S. Highway 17 runs north and south along the eastern coast of the United States and bisects the Stetson University campus in Deland. Every day as I changed classes, I watched elements of the 82nd Airborne Division and the 101st Airborne Division roll their massive artillery pieces, trucks, and machinery through campus toward Miami and Key West. Obviously, they were preparing for the invasion of Cuba!

For the first time, I was connected to military service and what it took to defend the nation in a palpable way. I was not officially ready for prime time in the army, because I was just in my junior year of studies, but I was beginning to understand what it might be like to go to war. Watching the soldiers drive by, young guys just like me, I realized that I had put myself on a path that might get me killed.

The missiles were discovered in the fall of my junior year, by which time I had changed my major field of study from English to history. I was captivated by the lessons of those who had gone before us. As I progressed through my ROTC training, the study of American history began to seem more relevant than courses in seventeenth-century literary criticism. I was taking a course in the history of Russia when the crisis erupted. My professor was Russian and confided privately to the class that he didn't see how the crisis could be resolved peacefully. He said he couldn't see either side backing down.

Neither could I.

Thank God, President Kennedy did not take the advice of General Curtis LeMay and order air strikes on the missile sites in Cuba. Thank God, Kennedy did not take the advice of Georgia senator Dick Russell and invade Cuba. We now know there was a missile under the command of the Cubans that even the Soviets did not know about. It was pointed at Miami. How different and tragic our history would have been if we had attacked or invaded Cuba and started a nuclear holocaust.

During the discussion about a preemptive war against Cuba, Bobby Kennedy, the president's brother and then attorney general, is reported to have handed the president a note. The note said, "I now know how Tojo felt when he was planning Pearl Harbor."

Historical accounts have revealed that almost all of Kennedy's advisers—save for Bobby—were in favor of an aggressive course of action that would have likely led the United States and the Soviet Union to engage in nuclear war. Bobby famously said, "Jack, I'm as conniving as they come, but a sneak attack is just wrong." President Kennedy, who had seen war firsthand, chose to try to preserve the tense peace we had with the Soviet Union rather than risk starting a conflict that could destroy both nations.

Avoiding that war instead of starting it changed the course of world history.

And it proved that it *does* matter who is president. History, in the wake of the wars in Vietnam and Iraq, has proved that fact again. And history bears out the wisdom of presidential restraint. We can see the folly of presidents like Lyndon Johnson and George W. Bush. Both went off half-cocked and got a bunch of Americans killed in wars waged for highly questionable reasons. It is a shame neither man learned from Kennedy's forbearance.

In 13 days, the crisis was over. The Russians backed down. The missiles in Cuba were removed. "We were eyeball to eyeball and I think the other fella just blinked," Secretary of State Dean Rusk quipped. What followed was monumental. It was rapprochement with the Soviet Union, the hallmark of Kennedy's foreign policy. An emergency hotline was installed between Washington and Moscow to avoid any misunderstanding between the two countries. To articulate the new approach, President Kennedy gave a historic address during the commencement ceremony at American University in the early summer of 1963.

I discovered the president's speech accidentally while trying to tune my transistor radio to some rock-and-roll music. I was lying on the sand in South Beach, across the bay from Miami, wearing a bathing suit and army combat boots. I was staying with my aunt who lived in Miami and had been running wind sprints up and down the beach in my boots to strengthen my legs and my endurance before I left for ROTC Summer Camp at Fort Benning, Georgia.

My ears pricked up when I heard the announcer say the president was speaking at American University in Washington. I was headed there in the fall for the Washington Semester Program. I had been selected to spend a semester in the capital to see "government in action." As a 21-year-old single man, I was definitely more interested in the "action" of that equation than the "government" part.

Mostly, I was interested in getting out of Deland, which I had come to call "Deadland." I was tired of school and tired of going nowhere. I had changed my major three times in three years. I wanted some excitement. One day, as I was flipping through the pages of the student newspaper, I came across a photo of Bobby Kennedy shaking hands with some students from Stetson. I wondered how they pulled that off. Meeting a Kennedy face-to-face beat the hell out of hanging around Stetson for another year. The caption said something about "Students in the Washington Semester Program." I asked a professor and learned there were four slots available for the fall. I didn't expect to get picked, but as one of just four students who applied, I was automatically "selected." It was my first lesson in American politics: You can't win if you don't play.

Despite my resurgent fascination with politics, I had never taken a course in government or political science. The last class I had that even touched on the subjects was a ninth-grade civics lesson entitled "How a Bill Becomes a Law." That had proved as boring as dirt. But with Kennedy in the White House, things seemed different. Government seemed sexy. Sprawled on my back in the sand at South Beach listening as the president proposed the first Nuclear Test-Ban Treaty, the idea of going to D.C. began to make me tingle.

American politics, here I come.

★ 4 ★

Splendor in the Grass

ON SEPTEMBER 10, 1963, I landed at National Airport to begin the Washington Semester Program at American University.

It was a turning point in my life.

Within that first week, I caught one of the deadliest fevers known to man—Potomac fever. I didn't know it at the time, but I was permanently afflicted. "The only cure for politics," Hubert Humphrey once observed, "is embalming fluid."

At 21 years of age, and released for a semester from my army ROTC obligations, I had the time of my life in Washington. I ate, drank, and breathed American politics by day and learned about grown-up girls at night. My classes at AU were all in government and politics-related subjects.

Since I had never taken Government 101, I had to take the basic course on how the U.S. Congress worked. Additionally, I had a senior seminar in American government that required a term paper, and took a graduate course in American "pressure groups." Those groups are now called "special interests" or political action committees. Whatever you call them, they are the groups in Washington that put pressure on the political system to have things turn out their way.

Later in my life, when I was in the U.S. Senate, I heard President Clinton declare that there were 88,000 lobbyists and lawyers in Washington. He said he could go for weeks without meeting "a real citizen."

With my studies, I was introduced to a new group of friends. My fellow students came from all over the country. They were talented, interested, and motivated young men and women who, like me, had come to Washington for "the action," and to see government, up close and personal. I had a splendid time. For the first time in my young adult life, I was able to drink beer and whiskey in off-campus bars. I began to develop a real social life. At the time, Stetson was affiliated with the Florida Baptist Convention. Drinking on or off campus could get you expelled. Drinking and dancing were permitted only in the fraternity houses, which were privately leased. I didn't drink at Stetson, but I loved to dance, to rock and roll. I grew up in the golden era of rock, 1956 to 1967, and the music thrilled me.

I really began to swing with some of the girls in the WS program, mostly college juniors and seniors. They were attractive, smart, and available. I was coming of age and beginning to feel my oats. I wore a flattop buzz cut and a sport coat. That fall of 1963, on the loose in the big city for the first time, I had my first taste of liquor, politics, and sex. It was all wrapped up together as far as I was concerned. It was a time of pure sunshine.

Wordsworth wrote in one of his poems, "Bliss was it in that dawn to be alive / But to be young was very heaven!" It was. It was a time "of splendor in the grass, of glory in the flower." Life was coming together for a little kid from Lithonia, Georgia, at last. I was growing up, the lights were all coming on, and I loved every minute. I was doing my thing—American politics.

In my first week in D.C., I went to see my congressman, Charlie Weltner, from Atlanta. Weltner sat on the now defunct House Un-American Activities Committee, which was a holdover from the "Red scare" days of the early '50s. A hearing the committee was holding on some students who had broken a U.S. government–imposed travel ban to Cuba was big news at the time. I got approval from Weltner's office to attend so I could see what a congressional hearing looked like.

It was held in the venerable old Cannon House Office Building. Named for House Speaker Joseph Gurney Cannon, who presided over the U.S. House of Representatives in the early part of the twentieth century, it was the oldest office building on the House side. The day I chose to attend the hearings, the building was jam-packed. Fighting my way to the front of the line, I said the magic words to the guard at the door: "I am a student in the Washington Semester Program, and Congressman Weltner said I could attend the hearing."

The guard let me in.

I had on a coat and tie and was seated about three-quarters of the way back from the dais upon which the committee sat. I was near the door. The students who had gone to Cuba illegally were seated together near the front. The hearing hadn't even started when the students suddenly stood up as one and started shouting. The committee members looked stunned. I saw one student take off his glasses and put them in his pocket like he was getting ready to fight. Chairman Edwin Willis from Louisiana motioned to the security guards lining the room to move in on the students. A real honest-to-goodness fistfight broke out right there in the committee room. People were running and screaming all over the place. The klieg lights on the TV cameras came on, and the melee was captured for the evening news. The guards started hauling the students out the door right next to me. They were grabbing any casually clad people of college age and ushering them out, even if they weren't part of the accused group. Since I was by the door, I thought I would be next. They passed me by. I guess my coat and tie saved me from being thrown out right then and there. All I could think of while the cameras were rolling and the students were being dragged away was, What will my mother think of me if I get thrown out of my first Washington, D.C., committee meeting? What will she think if she sees me on the evening news?

As time went by in the WS program, our professors took us to seminars to see and hear real, live congressmen, senators, Supreme Court justices, and federal bureaucrats. The most intriguing visit I had was with a senator from Georgia, Herman Talmadge. The former mayor of Lithonia, Charlie Davidson Sr., had set up the visit. Back home, his family owned the local granite quarry and he was known to everyone as Mr. Charlie. He and his family were hard-core Republicans, but they supported their friend Herman Talmadge, a conservative Democrat, in a big way. In the late '50s, Mr. Charlie actually got "Hummon" to come to Lithonia so he could show off the city's new tennis court, park, and swimming pool. When Mr. Charlie found out I was going to Washington, he said, "Go by and see Herman Talmadge and tell him I sent you."

As I approached Senator Talmadge's office in the old Senate office building (later named the Russell Senate Office Building after Senator Dick Russell), I felt nervous about bothering such an important man. When I got to the door with the Georgia seal on it, I twisted the knob and went in. It was the first Senate office I had ever seen. The receptionist gave me a warm Southern "How y'all doin'? May I he'p you?" She was an attractive lady, midthirties, with the biggest beehive hairdo I had ever seen. It was 1963, after all. I told her that Mr. Charlie Davidson, the mayor of Lithonia, had sent me by to meet Senator Talmadge. I also told her I was a student in the Washington Semester Program, studying government.

She wrote the information down on a piece of paper and told me to wait, disappearing behind a large mahogany door. About a minute later, she came out. "Senator Talmadge will be out to see you in a moment." I just stood there in front of her desk, not knowing what to do. She offered me a Coca-Cola. I passed on the opportunity. Later, after I became a senator myself, I would discover that all of the congressional offices from Georgia got their Cokes for free because Coke's headquarters were in Atlanta.

The heavy door opened again and out stepped a stout, middle-aged man. He stuck out his hand briskly and said, "Hi, I'm Herman Talmadge." I thought it very strange that he would introduce himself to me that way, using his full name.

"Hi, I'm Max Cleland from Lithonia, Georgia, and Mr. Charlie Davidson said I should come by to see you," I mumbled, completely taken aback that I was talking to a real U.S. senator. Later, after years of campaigning myself, I came to understand why Senator Talmadge used his full name when introducing himself to me. It's your full name that's on the ballot. You want your constituents to remember it.

Talmadge showed me in to his office and invited me to sit on a couch directly in front of his desk. The back of his chair faced a window overlooking the Senate courtyard. The senator leaned back, and we started to chat. Without any warning, he bolted upright in his chair and launched a spit of tobacco juice across his desk into a spittoon by the wall. He hit it expertly, the spittle plonking into the brass urn. I couldn't believe it. I didn't know whether he was doing it for show, trying to impress me with how Southern he was, or whether it was a natural thing for him to do. Apparently, it was natural. Talmadge chewed tobacco most of his adult life. He later died of throat cancer.

After chatting about my studies at AU, how long I had known Mr. Charlie, and how long I was going to stay in D.C., Talmadge sat upright in his chair and boomed out in a loud voice, "Is there anything else I can do for you?" I had never been in a senator's office before, but I understood our time together was up. He escorted me out of his suite and then asked where I was headed next. I told him I wanted to go see the Senate and sit in the gallery. He said he was headed to the Senate himself and invited me to ride with him in his car. I said I would love to.

We exited his office and went down the hall. Facing the elevator, he hit the button marked "Senators Only." In a split second an
elevator appeared, with an operator who addressed Talmadge with a
deferential "Good afternoon, Senator." The elevator took us down to
the main floor, where Talmadge parked his car. As we drove over to
the Capitol Plaza, I engaged him about a Walter Lippmann column I
had read in the *Washington Post*. He responded gruffly, making clear
he was no fan of Lippmann or the *Post*. As we got out of the car and
faced the steps of the Capitol, he paused for a moment before he went
inside. The sun was setting in the distance, and the scene for me was
golden. The air was clear and the summer heat in D.C. was beginning
to dissipate. I felt like I was standing on top of the world. I was scared
to speak, lest I break the spell, but I ventured to ask Senator Talmadge
if he liked being in the Senate. Expecting him to say he loved it, I
was shocked by his answer. In a thick and rolling Southern drawl, he
looked out into the distance wistfully and said, "When I was guv'ner,
I could make a decision and have it carried out. Here"—he pointed
toward the Senate—"I make a decision and we *talk* about it."

I was stunned. Herman Talmadge had a safe seat in the U.S. Senate.
A poster in his office lobby proudly announced that he had carried all
the counties in Georgia in his last election. The man was at the center
of power in American politics. How could he be dissatisfied? Later,
Zell Miller, another former Georgia governor, came to the United
States Senate. It was painfully obvious that he didn't like it either.

As time went on and my love of politics deepened, I learned that
governors are generally disappointed when they come to the U.S.
Senate. In their states, they control the offices and agencies of state
government. In the Senate, their individual power is gone. Power
there is all about building a coalition, building a consensus, and staying
there long enough to gain seniority. The former distinguished senator
from Illinois Everett Dirksen, after whom a Senate office building is
named, used to respond to questions about the Senate's seniority sys-

tem with the remark "The longer I stay here, the better I like it." From time to time, for as long as he was in the U.S. Senate, rumors would spread that Talmadge was going back to Georgia to run for governor again. He never did.

Through the years, Herman Talmadge and I became close friends, mutual admirers, and supporters. Before he got beaten in 1980 on ethics charges levied by the Senate, Talmadge was one of the most respected members of that body. His tenure as chairman of the Agriculture Committee was known for its effectiveness in rural and farm matters. In that regard, he struck up an unusual friendship with a fellow senator who was his political opposite—Hubert Humphrey. Though different as night and day in their politics, they were united in fighting for the American farmer. Neither one of them ever forgot his humble roots. Talmadge once quipped that Hubert Humphrey had the greatest coordination between mind and tongue of anybody he ever knew. I had the same impression as I watched Humphrey from the Senate gallery. He was a silver-tongued orator. Once I heard him speak to a group of government interns in the summer of 1965. By then, he was vice president. I sat in the front row and could see his eyes tear up and glisten when he talked about young people getting involved in politics, government, and American democracy. The joke about Humphrey was that he had more answers than there were questions. To me, though, he was one of the last of a dying breed of great statesmen and orators who could bring tears to your eyes no matter what he was talking about.

After I got beaten in 1974 in my race for lieutenant governor of Georgia, Herman Talmadge went out of his way to back me for a position as a staff member of the Senate Veterans' Affairs Committee. He picked up the phone and called the then chairman of the committee, Senator Vance Hartke, and asked him to hire me as a personal favor. Talmadge knew what he was doing. He knew that helping me might come back to haunt him if Hartke ever needed anything. But

Talmadge stuck by me anyway. I never forgot that. When Talmadge was dying of throat cancer in Atlanta, I went by to see him in the hospital. I wanted to thank him for helping out a young man at the dawn of his career.

Getting to chat with a real senator wasn't the only thing I loved about my time in Washington. Just being in the capital with President Kennedy in the White House was to me an incredible, mystifying, and exhilarating experience. There was an air of enthusiasm, new purpose, and a new destiny for America. During his "thousand days," John F. Kennedy lit a fire in my generation, and made government and politics sexy. He made politics de rigueur—what one ought to do. It's still hard for me to imagine that at one time, John F. Kennedy was president, Bobby Kennedy was attorney general, and Ted Kennedy was in the Senate. I bought into the Kennedy mystique all the way. I loved the spirit of "vigor" and "new frontier" that John Kennedy brought to Washington. It seemed as if I was coming of age personally while my generation was coming of age politically. That fall in Washington, I felt like everything in my life and in the country was coming together all at the same time. "The energy, the faith, the devotion which we bring to this endeavor will light our country and all who serve it—and the glow from that fire can truly light the world." So said the president in his inaugural address in 1961. He said it. I believed it. "Ask not what your country can do for you—ask what you can do for your country." That phrase became my personal mantra. I was the Lone Ranger. I was shooting silver bullets.

Hi-ho, Silver, away!

★ 5 ★

The Oval Office

AFTER TWO MONTHS in D.C., I started to feel that the halls of power were old hat. I'd spent hours and hours in the House chambers, been in a car with a senator, had audiences with congressmen, Supreme Court justices, and other major players in the nation's capital. But the field trip planned for November 19, 1963, had me as giddy as a schoolgirl.

One of our professors had lined up a meeting with President Kennedy's National Security Affairs adviser, McGeorge Bundy. He had helped Kennedy navigate the cold war without starting a global nuclear one. He was as close to the center of power and my idol, President Kennedy, as one could be. "There's no substitute for brains," the president once said of him. Now, the afternoon of November 19, 1963, our small group of students had a seminar with Bundy at the White House.

Bundy discussed the affairs of the day, which included the rise of communism around the world and especially in Southeast Asia. In the discussion, he mentioned a settlement negotiated in 1962 with Laos. Apparently, Laos was to be a neutral country now. It adjoined both North Vietnam and South Vietnam. At the time, no one in our group questioned the agreement with Laos. It sounded like a peace deal, which I'm sure is the way Bundy and President Kennedy regarded it.

But looking back on the treaty as an educated grown-up, I know that Laos was a key staging ground for the assault on American troops in Vietnam. It became a key part of the Ho Chi Minh Trail supply route, down which hundreds of thousands of North Vietnamese soldiers and millions of tons of supplies were moved by our enemies. All those troops and all those supplies pouring into South Vietnam meant death over the next 10 years for tens of thousands of Americans.

After the Vietnam War, the North Vietnamese admitted that if American ground forces had invaded Laos and cut off supply routes to South Vietnam, there was no way they could have won the war. But Laos was off-limits to American forces (at least officially) because of the agreement the Kennedy administration had signed. Ultimately, that agreement helped seal the fate of the American military in South Vietnam before the war even started.

After dazzling us with his grasp of the minutiae of American foreign policy and the country's place in the world, Bundy adjourned the meeting. Rising from the conference table, he asked the magic question:

"Would you like to see the Oval Office?"

We all smiled with glee. Kennedy in 1963 was like a rock star, only he was more famous, more popular, and infinitely more powerful.

The president was away on a trip to Miami. There was a rope cord draped across the entrance to the Oval Office. Bundy removed the rope and we followed him in. I literally gasped as I saw the place where the most powerful man in the world worked. A turquoise rug displaying the Great Seal of the United States covered the floor. There was the famous ladder-back rocking chair the president sat in due to back injuries sustained when a Japanese destroyer cut his PT boat in half. There were photos and models of sailing ships on top of a bookcase across from the president's desk. We studied the pictures of Jackie and the kids.

The desk that Kennedy had chosen for the Oval Office was historic.

Queen Victoria had given it to President Hayes in the nineteenth century as a gesture of friendship and good relations. It was constructed of wood from the HMS *Resolute,* a British ship rescued by the Americans in the 1850s and restored to service in the Royal Navy. It had a special kneehole panel in the bottom front that became known to the nation because of a famous photo of John-John crawling through it while his father worked.

We said our good-byes to Mr. Bundy and were ushered back outside through the wrought-iron gates fronting Pennsylvania Avenue.

Three days later, I was in the dorm bathroom at AU getting ready for a trip to Capitol Hill. I had interviews scheduled for my term paper on how a Senate office is run. The paper was entitled "Administrative Assistant—Right-Hand Man of the Senator." My research came in handy many years later when I had to put together a Senate office myself. After brushing my teeth, I went back to my room and saw my roommate kneeling on the floor listening to the radio. He was trying to tune in the news. He looked up at me with wild eyes that I've never forgotten. His words froze my heart.

"The president has been shot."

"You're kidding! Are you sure?" I couldn't believe it.

We ran down the hall to the dorm TV room. Students had already gathered to listen to the news. Walter Cronkite was on the air in cold black and white reporting that the president of the United States had died shortly after 1:00 p.m. Central time. I walked out of the room stunned. For some strange reason, I felt compelled to go back down to the White House. I knew I couldn't get into the Oval Office this time, but I had to get as close as I could to the presence of President Kennedy. It dawned on me that I had just become one of the last people to see the Oval Office as it was under Kennedy. I dressed quickly, ran out of my dorm, and flagged down a cab. All along the route to downtown D.C., I saw Americans who had just heard the news darting across lawns, running down sidewalks, and crying in disbelief.

In a crisis, people do strange things. For some unknown reason, I asked the cab to stop at the British embassy on its way down Massachusetts Avenue, which is also known as Embassy Row. The British embassy is on the right going south down Massachusetts Avenue toward the White House, so it was on my way. I hopped out of the cab and ran into the first building I could find on the embassy grounds. I came across a receptionist. I asked her perhaps the stupidest question of all: "How do the British people feel about today?" How dumb!

"We are saddened, of course," the lady said in a quiet British accent.

I ran back to the cab and continued my journey to the White House, now armed with this trivial bit of information that I must have thought someone might need.

About five blocks from the White House, traffic came to a standstill. It seemed as if everybody in town had the same idea that I did. They all seemed to want to go to the White House and feel the presence of JFK. I ran the five blocks to Pennsylvania Avenue and took a left toward the White House grounds. The *Washington Star* newspaper (now defunct) already had an edition out with headlines screaming about the death of the president. I continued moving through the thickening crowd until I found a spot along the White House fence. As I peered through the wrought-iron bars, I saw that the White House staff had already draped black crepe around the doors and windows of the presidential mansion. When I was in that house but 72 hours earlier, it had held the promise and hope of the world. Now it was in mourning.

I stayed downtown well beyond nightfall. The crowds around the White House remained. I found a spot at the south end of the White House lawn to get a perspective on what was happening. Eerie lights were shining on the front and rear of the White House. The mansion had a ghostly feeling about it, with the stark contrast between the mourning cloth and the whitewashed walls. The crowd was silent.

Sometime after 9:00 p.m. that night, President Lyndon Johnson's helicopter landed on the South Lawn for the first time. Several other helicopters followed close behind. It seemed so strange to say "President Lyndon Johnson." People stepped out of the choppers and moved quickly inside to the ground floor of the White House. One of them was Johnson, but I couldn't tell which in the gloom. The Kennedy era was over.

The assassination took a toll on this nation that lasts to our present day. The tragedy of the Vietnam War may not have been played out in the same way by Kennedy as it was by Lyndon Johnson. Years later, I had breakfast with Walt Rostow at the University of Texas at Austin. Rostow, who served as a White House adviser to Kennedy and Johnson, thought that Kennedy would have acted differently than Johnson in regard to Vietnam. He believed Kennedy would have opted for more air and naval power instead of the massive buildup of ground forces that Johnson ordered. We will never know. Between the assassination and the interment of his body at Arlington National Cemetery, TV, radio, and other news outlets played Kennedy's speeches, press conferences, and news coverage over and over again. They played the inaugural address over and over again. "Ask not what your country can do for you—ask what you can do for your country." That phrase was played repeatedly in our national hour of grief. The country couldn't get enough of John Kennedy.

The assassination affected us all. Across the street from American University is a Methodist church. I went to that church shortly after the assassination. There I saw Representative Leslie Arends, the Republican leader in the House. He was crying silently in a pew. I recognized him because we had had a seminar with him in the Capitol. In a strange way, I felt very close to him.

While President Kennedy's body lay in state in the Capitol, I did not stand in line or seek to touch the casket. Rather, I stood in the Capitol Plaza with the throng that had gathered around the building. I stood on that cold November day and watched the honor guard bring the president's casket down the east Capitol steps as the Navy

Hymn was played. Somehow the Navy Hymn has always seemed to me more like a funeral dirge. It suited the mood that day. Suddenly a ripple of hushed voices went through the crowd. Lee Harvey Oswald had been shot in Dallas. Unbelievable! The man who allegedly shot JFK was dead. As someone said later about the year of 1968, with the assassinations of Martin Luther King Jr. and Bobby Kennedy, we in late November 1963 seemed to be going through "more history than we could consume."

When it was time for President Kennedy's body to be interred at Arlington, I was there. I stood atop a tombstone for five hours to get an up-close view. I was 30 feet from the most dramatic moment in my lifetime—the burial of the president of the United States. Standing there, I could see the cortege march slowly across Memorial Bridge before it wound its long tail up the back roads of Arlington Cemetery. Finally, the honor guard pulled up to a hastily arranged temporary burial site. Months later, the president's body was moved down the hill at Arlington to a more accessible site for his eternal flame. I watched aghast as I saw the leaders of the world parade before my eyes. One of the world leaders I recognized was the emperor of Ethiopia, Haile Selassie. I had watched him standing up in an open convertible, with JFK sitting in the rear, just weeks before the assassination. In addition to Haile Selassie, I saw Jackie, the children, Bobby and Teddy Kennedy, and their families. I watched the Irish Black Watch march in, with American Special Forces not far behind.

The death of the president had a powerful impact on my life. I can vividly remember strolling down a walkway covered with autumn leaves near the American University campus one evening after the assassination. I was kicking the leaves and thinking on the most powerful event in my life up to that point. The president's quotes, so freshly etched in my mind from their heavy rotation on TV and radio, came to have powerful meaning for me. The torch *had* been passed to a new generation of Americans. For the first time in my life, I truly believed

the torch had been passed to *me*. I shuffled through that night searching for answers. Somehow I knew that from now on, my life would be
different. I knew I had to find a place in American politics. The seed
had been planted. My duty was clear. But first, I had to learn what
this thing called politics was all about. Up to that point in my life, I
had anticipated graduating from Stetson and going to Vietnam as a
helicopter pilot. Instead, I decided to go to graduate school to study
my craft. Vietnam would have to wait.

★ 6 ★

Vietnam

WAR, THE GREAT German battle theoretician Carl von Clausewitz, once observed, is the continuation of politics by different means.

President Lyndon Johnson didn't know much about war, but he knew a hell of a lot about politics.

Johnson had been in the U.S. Senate when the Republicans accused President Truman and Secretary of State Dean Acheson of "losing" China to the communists after WWII. But the future of China was up to the Chinese. One of President Woodrow Wilson's Fourteen Points, ending WWI, was self-determination of nations. It was up to China to save itself or lose itself. Later, President Kennedy would articulate the need for America to keep the world not necessarily safe for "democracy," as Wilson had once said, but for "diversity."

When it came to Vietnam, Lyndon Johnson had other ideas. He said he wanted to go in to stop communism in a small, impoverished country all the way on the other side of the world just to protect the poor people who lived there. But he had political reasons as well.

Winston Churchill once warned about great nations getting involved in the affairs of smaller nations. Wellington, the great British general who defeated Napoléon at the battle of Waterloo, knew the danger of a great nation getting entangled in a war with a smaller nation. "A great country can have no such thing as a little war," he observed. The inference is obvious. When a great nation like the United States goes to war, it must be successful or its greatness is compromised. In Lyndon Johnson's reckoning, the Democratic Party could not be accused, again, of "losing" another country to the communists or the party's ability to lead the nation would be compromised. Johnson had seen close-up from his seat in the U.S. Senate how the "Red scare" and the McCarthy era propelled Republicans to power. The political charge used by Republicans in the late '40s and the entire decade of the '50s was that the Democrats were "soft on communism." Johnson resolved he would not be accused of being soft on anything.

To start a war, Johnson knew he had to bring in the Congress. On national TV, on the night of August 4, 1964, he addressed the nation. He told of two attacks by North Vietnamese naval forces on two U.S. Navy ships off the coast of Vietnam in the Gulf of Tonkin, on August 2 and August 4. Johnson argued that a military response was necessary. He ordered an air attack on oil and shipping facilities in North Vietnam in retaliation.

The report of the second attack on our ships was revealed to be a sham years after the fact, something cooked up by the National Security Agency. Johnson used the trumped-up account to ask Congress for a resolution to use "all necessary means" against North Vietnam. Thus the Gulf of Tonkin Resolution was born. It gave Lyndon Johnson a blank check to do whatever he wanted to do militarily in the name of fighting communism and defending the nation. The resolution had only two votes against it in the U.S. Senate. It resulted in a 10-year war that killed 58,000 Americans, wounded 350,000, and led to the death of the modern, idealistic, progressive Great Society Democratic Party for decades.

Forty years later, President George W. Bush would do exactly the same thing: start a war that didn't need to be fought, using trumped-up intelligence. Knowing that he wanted to attack Iraq, although Iraq had not attacked the United States, Bush sought a resolution from the Congress that essentially gave him a blank check to prosecute his war of choice. The Vietnam War destroyed Lyndon Johnson's presidency. The Iraq War destroyed the presidency of George W. Bush.

But in the summer of 1965, none of that had yet come to pass. I had completed all the course work for my master's degree except my thesis. I was flying high as an intern for Congressman James Mackay, from Georgia. I was in the prime of my life and was in Washington, D.C., my favorite city in the world. At the age of 23, I had been in the Oval Office, the U.S. Senate, and the U.S. House. I had begun to dream that one day I might be lucky enough to sit in the U.S. House. I never considered running for the Senate. That seemed unattainable.

In July 1965, Lyndon Johnson made the most fateful decision of his life. He decided to begin a massive buildup of U.S. ground forces in Vietnam. He hoped to stave off the growing threat that the North Vietnamese military would cut the south in two, taking South Vietnam's strategic Central Highlands in the process. Such an action might lead to a defeat for the South Vietnamese *and* the United States. Lyndon Johnson didn't want to "lose" South Vietnam.

I was sitting in a restaurant on Pennsylvania Avenue a few blocks east of the Capitol eating lunch on a sunny summer day. It was the third week of July 1965. The president came on TV. He announced that he was sending the First Air Cavalry Division, the U.S. Army's only all-helicopter outfit, to Vietnam.

In an instant, I knew where I was headed. I had seen the airmobile concept of an all-helicopter division tested at Fort Benning in the summer of 1963 when I was there at ROTC camp. Everything moved by helicopter in that division. It was the only one of its kind in the world. Even at Fort Benning back in 1963, I wanted to be in that out-fit. Now it was headed to war, and that meant I was headed there too. After my summer internship ended in Washington, I was headed for active duty in the army as a young officer. I was to report October 18, 1965. I already had my orders. My devotion to politics now became a devotion to military service.

That same week in July, just before President Johnson announced his historic decision, the interns who worked for Georgia congress-men were invited to spend some time with Georgia's senior sena-tor, Dick Russell. We met Russell in the Armed Services Committee room. Russell sat at the head of the table because he was chairman of the committee. We sat around the table in oversized leather armchairs like we were all committee members. Behind Russell, there were flags of all the different branches of the military with their combat stream-ers hanging down.

We were not supposed to take notes, and the senator's staff told us the meeting was off the record. I took notes anyway, especially when Russell talked about Vietnam, where I was headed in a matter of months. Later those notes were published in 1968 in the Atlanta paper after I was wounded. They reflected Russell's deep concern about a U.S.-led war in Vietnam.

Dick Russell was the premier expert on defense and war on Capitol Hill. He knew well the failure of the French in their Indochina ad-venture. He knew the story of the French defeat at Dien Bien Phu in 1954. With deep chagrin, he told our group of students, "The French had ten times better intelligence then than we do now." He touched upon the long history of how the Vietminh, precursor of the North Vietnamese army, had fought the Japanese successfully in World War II. After that, the French, he said, were looked upon as invaders and oc-cupiers. He feared the Americans would be looked upon as "the new French."

During the Vietnam War, Russell talked publicly about the need in Vietnam to "fish or cut bait." He said that he supported the troops and the flag. But privately, he was very disturbed by the American buildup in Vietnam and its possible outcome. One of his aides later related to me that Russell spent most of one night trying to talk Lyndon Johnson out of increasing the number of American troops there. Russell told us about the Indochina War and how the 1954 Geneva Accords called for elections in South Vietnam. Eisenhower's secretary of state, John Foster Dulles, had refused to sign those accords, and only "noted" them. Thus, those elections in the south were never held. Russell said that if they had been held, Ho Chi Minh would have won 80 percent of the vote and the United States would have had no need for military action there.

While I was in Vietnam in 1967 serving with the First Air Cavalry Division, Lyndon Johnson made a big deal of the elections in South Vietnam in the fall of that year. I was actually in Saigon watching them unfold. There was only one party on the ballot—the South Vietnamese government. The Vietcong were frozen out of the process. How, I wondered, could America, the greatest force for democracy on the planet, sanction a single-party election? A few months later, by February 1968, nobody worried about elections in South Vietnam anymore. Everyone there, including me, was fighting for their lives in the midst of the Tet offensive—the massive North Vietnamese attack on the south.

Tet led to Walter Cronkite's famous commentary on the *CBS Evening News* at the end of February 1968. The great newsman had been in Vietnam earlier that month during the opening of the Tet offensive. "It is increasingly clear to this reporter," Cronkite told the nation, "that the only rational way out then will be to negotiate, not as victors, but as an honorable people who lived up to their pledge to defend democracy, and did the best they could."

But, years before that was to happen, I reported for duty as a second lieutenant in October 1965. The first two years of my service were stateside, one year as an aide to the commanding general of the U.S. Army Signal Center and School at Fort Monmouth, New Jersey, Brigadier General Tom Rienzi. Those years were absolutely the happiest of my life. I was young and handsome and felt like I was the cat's meow. I dated pretty girls and made the most of my weekend passes. The general wanted me to stay on with him at Fort Monmouth, offering me the chance to finish out my hitch in the army without ever leaving the country or seeing combat. But that wasn't me. Instead, I told him that I felt I had to go to Vietnam, that it was my duty. He had promised me that if I spent a year working for him, he'd sign my orders for Vietnam. In the end, I actually had to extend my service for a third year in order to get there. I was glad to do it.

I arrived in June 1967. Approximately 10 months later, I was climbing aboard a chopper heading for the battle of Khe Sanh the day after Johnson's withdrawal from the presidential race.

I was wounded by the grenade on April 8, 1968, eight days after Johnson called for an end to the war. By June, the Khe Sanh base—which this country moved heaven and earth to defend and which I had risked my life to protect—was scuttled. The airstrip was plowed under and the territory ceded to the North Vietnamese army.

It all seemed not to matter anymore. As Bernard Fall wrote in *Hell in a Very Small Place,* battles were fought in the Indochina War after the French defeat at Dien Bien Phu, but one side had lost what it had hoped to gain by prosecuting the war.

In the same way, battles were fought in Vietnam after the Tet offensive and the siege of Khe Sanh, but they did not matter. America had nothing left to gain. Still, it took another five years for the country to finally admit the war was lost and to bring our troops home.

The decade of the '60s started out with such hope and promise. I had graduated from high school and gone to college. John F. Kennedy had been elected president. I had walked the halls of power in the nation's capital and been promoted to captain at the age of 25. Then, in a flash, my great, wonderful, promising life—everything I had worked for—was blown to bits.

★ 7 ★

Hanging in the Balance

FIVE HOURS AND 42 pints of blood after the grenade exploded, I woke up.

There was a girl there. She seemed impossibly young. When she saw that I was awake, she came over to the bed. My head was swimming, and it was hard to focus over the morphine.

"Have I got my leg?" I rasped.

"No." She spoke in the barest of whispers. A tear collected in her eyelashes.

My God! I've lost both legs! The thought just crashed around me, stealing my breath. My arm! I've lost everything. From the moment I woke up, I couldn't escape the idea that my life was over, that I was horribly crippled forever. All I had was one arm for the rest of my life! What on earth could I ever do but lie in a bed? For the next 24 hours, I drifted in and out of a morphine-induced haze, barely clinging to life and thinking I'd be lying on my back for the rest of my days. My body was racked by fever and infections that had set in when all the dirt and debris blasted into my wounds. I should have died. Truly. The ends of my thighs were still open and draining, and my remaining arm was pricked with IVs.

Years later, when I was the head of the Veterans Administration, one of the doctors who had operated on me wrote me a letter. He said that five surgeons had worked on me at once, all speeding to close gushing wounds. He revealed that it was an anesthesiologist who actually saved me. The anesthesiologist monitored my blood pressure, stopping the various operations when my pressure dropped too low. Then, when my pressure built back up again, he'd let the doctors work until I started fading again. He kept me teetering on the edge of living and dying, just hanging in the balance. The author of the letter said that he couldn't bear to face me after the operation because he was so traumatized by what he had been forced to do.

Two days after my surgery, it was time to begin the series of short plane rides and helicopter hops that would get me to a better hospital. First I was moved to a navy hospital on the coast in Da Nang for a night, then to a tiny army intensive care unit in another hut in Tuy Hoa. The air inside was suffocating. It was steaming hot and rank. There were about 12 patients inside. I was one of the few Americans there. The hospital treated both the Vietnamese fighting with the Americans and the Vietnamese trying to kill Americans. On the bed to my right was a Vietcong soldier whose eyes were empty and blank, like there was no longer anyone inside. To my left was a North Vietnamese prisoner of war who never said a word.

One afternoon after I arrived at that hellhole, I went through the worst pain I have ever experienced. A doctor decided to change the dressings on my wounds. The jagged shaft of bone still jutted from my stump of a right arm. The ends of my thighs were like exposed slabs of raw beef, only still alive and oozing blood. As the doctor pulled away the sodden gauze, my legs burned as if he were peeling off my skin. They shot me full of Demerol, but it didn't even cut the pain. The raw nerve endings in the exposed flesh continued to scream their alarm messages into my brain. My fever continued to soar out of control. The first night, nurses rubbed me with alcohol in a last-ditch effort to bring it down. My body quaked with chills, and I knew I was precariously close to death.

I could tell something was wrong at the hospital. I had sensed it as soon as I was carried in. The staff moved about like zombies, no one home behind their glazed eyes. Their war had been nothing but blood and guts and horror. These people had seen so much death they were just broken. Looking back, remembering the stench, the heat, the 24-hour-a-day exposure to total misery in conditions as bad as any on earth, I can see how horrific war must be for those trained to preserve life at any cost. What a paradox to find yourself treating both your fellow countrymen and the VC and the North Vietnamese who were blowing your countrymen up. I realized at that jungle outpost that doctors and nurses could be war casualties, and so could the guys carrying in the wounded, even if they'd never seen combat. Their nightmares would never be the same. Their fears and emotions would be with them until they died. Just like me.

For seven days in that hospital I drifted in and out of consciousness. Both the fever and the infections in my limbs rose and fell like tides in response to massive doses of IV antibiotics. I was on the verge of dying every moment. At one point, the male Vietnamese nurse checking my blood pressure reacted so suddenly and with such alarm that I knew my life was still hanging in the balance. I began to realize how desperate my future was, and how limited my potential had become. I didn't even have two arms to push myself around in a wheelchair.

I had not talked to my parents since the explosion, but I knew they would have gotten a telegram from the army saying I had been wounded. It would have no details, just that I was on the "seriously ill" list. My poor mother, like any mother, had to be wild with horror after receiving a note like that. But it would be almost impossible for her to imagine anything worse than what had actually happened to me. The hospital had a phone that was connected to a military radio system. When I called, a ham radio operator in California picked up the signal and patched me through to Lithonia. My mother answered. It was so good to hear her voice, even from 12,000 miles away. It made me feel like I might make it out of there after all. I told her I was fine and that I'd be coming home. That was all I told her. It was all I could bring myself to tell her. She would see what was left of me soon enough. I said we could build a swimming pool in the backyard.

We never did.

After a week, I was sent to the U.S. Army 106th General Hospital in Yokohama, Japan. I was back in civilization. The hospital was clean. The staff was lively, even pleasant. The first day I was there, they operated on me again, closing the wounds in my legs and neck and cleaning up the various shrapnel divots scattered over my body. I soon got to where I could move around in the bed and sit up unaided. I was alive, and things were looking up. I woke up one night and tried to swing my legs over the edge of the bed to walk to the bathroom. Reality hit me like a sandbag and left me crying in the dark.

Those first days were a roller coaster. One minute things would seem OK. I was out of immediate danger and I could still see and talk and think. While I didn't have any legs, it seemed like there was enough thigh left on both sides that maybe I could get artificial ones. Then, an instant later, just as I was finding reasons to be grateful, my new, mangled body would remind me of how much I had lost. I would never walk again on my own two feet. I would never be an able-bodied man again.

In my mind, I replayed the grenade explosion again and again. Ducking under the wash from the chopper blades. Bending over, reaching out. Then, *boom!* No matter how many times the moment has come flooding back to me, it always ends the same way, always in utter catastrophe. The memory is still there today, buried deep inside the ancient, reptile part of my brain. It hunts me in life, always there, always threatening to leap back into my consciousness. When it finds me again—sometimes in dark, quiet moments, sometimes at moments of great stress—I am right back there again on that hill, dying. I remember lying there asking myself the same questions over and over again.

Why?

Why did I bend over to pick it up?

Why did it go off?

How did the pin come out?

Grenades have a small, removable cotter pin in the firing mechanism. Pull the pin out, and the grenade goes off in a matter of four seconds. I always bent the pins back on my grenades, curling them back on themselves so that it was impossible to accidentally pull one out. Everyone was trained to do that. So what went wrong? How did the pin come out?

Inevitably, I was left feeling like I had fumbled the ball. Game over, and I lost. No one had shot me. No one had thrown the grenade at me. I had blown myself up and ruined my life. It was all my fault.

LZ Home

THE ARMY AMBULANCE rattled through the streets of Yokohama headed for the airfield. After one week in the hospital in Japan, and almost a year into my tour of duty, I was going home. My war was over. There were two stretchers in the ambulance. I was on one, and another soldier lay across from me. He didn't look like he could have been more than 18 and was so thin he almost wasn't there. A corpsman knelt next to him, feeding him a soda through a straw. His eyes were big and lost. I recognized the look. It was in my eyes too, I imagined. His body was covered by a white sheet, just his head poking out. I gazed at him and sized up his injuries. After a moment, I realized why someone was holding the Coke for him. The young soldier had no arms. Judging by the way the sheet collapsed along his lower body on the side closest to me, I could tell he had just one leg. He was the only other triple amputee I'd ever seen.

I thought he had it worse than me. As the bus bounced through the jumble and bustle of Yokohama traffic, I ran off a list of all the things he'd never be able to do: dress himself, go to the bathroom by himself, feed himself, hold a book or a girl, and who knows what else. With an arm, and a fully functional hand, I knew I would be able to do a lot more than he would. A doctor in the hospital had suggested I even had enough of my right arm left to get fitted with some kind of prosthesis back in the States. And a nurse said I might be able to walk on artificial legs. But the body of the kid next to me seemed beyond help. As terrible as it was, I had finally found something to be thankful for. I wasn't him.

More than a year later, I came across this young man once again. He had gained almost 100 pounds. He was walking with artificial limbs. And he was married. Wow, I guess he made it back too!

As we pulled onto the air base, I realized I was anxious about going back to the States. How could I explain what had happened to me? At least in the hospital, everybody had been shot up some way or another. They had seen the horrors I had seen. I didn't have to explain anything to them. Heading home meant going back to the real world, the normal world, back to a place where everyone would seem normal but me. And it meant seeing my parents. God, how I dreaded that. What would my mother say when she saw my destroyed body for the first time? How would she react? Would she still love me? Would anyone ever love me again?

The medics bearing my stretcher snapped it into place in a rack on the plane. I could hear the click of dozens of other stretchers getting locked down. I felt a new kind of sadness. It was grief for all I was leaving behind in Vietnam, grief for the life I would never have.

Going home so broken had not been in the plan. War was supposed to make me stronger, not weaker. I was strapped down on my back and naked except for a thin sheet covering my mangled body. Why the hell was I so dead set on volunteering for Vietnam anyway? I asked myself. I could have finished out my time working for the general at Fort Monmouth. I would already be out of the army if I had stayed stateside, and presumably I would be all in one piece. I probably could have gone back to Washington and gotten a job on the Hill. I could have gotten married. What was there for me to do now? I gripped the metal rail next to me with my hand as the jet engines throbbed up to takeoff speed. We sailed out over the Pacific Ocean and headed north for the polar ice cap. Trapped in my stretcher, unable to move, unable to do anything for myself, I had a vision of what lay in store for me. I began to sob.

A nurse came to me and asked what she could do to "help me adjust." How could anyone adjust to this?

"Give me a shot," I said, asking for Demerol, the only thing that seemed able to numb the pain. I had quickly fallen in love with the opiate dream haze that Demerol put me into. It meant I didn't have to think anymore. I didn't have to cope. I didn't have to hurt.

After touching down in Alaska at Elmendorf Air Force Base, we made one more hop and arrived at Andrews Air Force Base, outside Washington, D.C. It was nighttime, around 9:00 p.m. The flight from Japan had taken 16 hours. I knew we were landing on the runway used by the president and Air Force One. A year earlier, that thought would have tickled me beyond measure. Now it just served to isolate me further, to send me deeper into sadness. Because I was an officer, and probably because I had such severe wounds, they loaded me into an ambulance all by myself. As it carried me from the airfield to Walter Reed Army Medical Center, I couldn't believe I was back in the nation's capital, the place where I had had so much fun. I couldn't see how I would ever get to work in politics again. One didn't see a lot of one-armed men in wheelchairs in the halls of power. We traveled up Fourteenth Street, the action center of Washington in those days, where I had once partied my rear end off dancing to the Rolling Stones song "Satisfaction."

When I arrived at Walter Reed, a woman in a Red Cross uniform offered me the chance to make the traditional call home given to soldiers returning from overseas. My mother answered. I talked to my father too. They said they would come to D.C. as soon as it could be arranged. They said they were proud of me. Part of me was longing to see them, and part of me was terrified of looking into their eyes as they saw the new me. I felt the same way about seeing my friends. I didn't want to feel their eyes upon me, their pity for me. I didn't think I could stand the silence that would fall between us.

A nurse soon wheeled me into a dark room with eight beds spread in a U shape around the edges. It was a classic old-fashioned hospital ward. The glow from a couple of small black-and-white TVs provided the only light. Several men were snoring.

"Welcome to the Snake Pit," came a gravelly voice from out of the dark. "Looks like you got it pretty good."

The voice belonged to Harry, a heavyset guy with a crew cut who was watching as the orderlies helped me shift onto a bed. There was a small television attached to the bed, and a lamp. Looking around in the dark, I could tell the other guys were missing parts of their bodies as well. But nobody was missing as many as me. I met a few of them. Some had been blown to hell like I had, and some of them had just been shot to pieces. In the dark, I could see a big coiled snake painted on the linoleum floor in the center of the room. It was gold and worn from people walking across it. The Snake Pit, Ward 1, Officer Amputee Ward, was reserved for young officers who had lost limbs. The men there would become some of the most important friends I would ever have.

In the morning, I woke to find a thin, middle-aged woman striding toward my bed. She was Major Baker.

"Mornin', Cap'n Cleland," she said in a sweet Southern drawl. Her voice was high and shrill, but she had a great way about her. I liked her already.

She announced that the dressings on my wounds needed changing. I hated to hear it because it hurt so damn bad. But I knew she was right. My arm was beginning to smell.

I hadn't bathed in more than a month, since before Khe Sanh. It had already been three weeks since the grenade went off.

"How long am I going to be here, ma'am?"

"In the hospital? Can't say, Captain. It'll take a while."

A month ago, I had never spent a night in a hospital for any reason. Now it was beginning to seem like I might end up living in one. She said I would be going to the cast room after she finished with me, so the doctors could check me out.

"Not much to see," I said, glancing at my legs as she worked at cutting off the soiled gauze.

Major Baker scowled at me.

"Don't talk like that, Captain Cleland. You're a good-looking young man, and you are going to make it out of here just fine." She smiled, and for a moment I believed her.

The next day, I was pushed on a gurney to the cast room. It was where dressings were changed and casts were applied. It was filled to overflowing. The wounded waited their turns in wheelchairs, on litter beds, or stood along the wall if they were able to do so. The guys in line were missing arms, legs, eyes, ears, whatever. I didn't see anybody as bad off as I was, but all these fellas were pretty banged up by normal standards. The room itself was big. Half a dozen doctors moved about from patient to patient. Stainless steel sinks, IV racks, and the waxed linoleum floor gleamed under a harsh fluorescent glare. You had the feeling that serious medicine was practiced here. When it was my turn, my gurney was pushed across the smooth floor toward a young doctor. He grabbed my chart and studied it.

"Man. They really got you, didn't they?" He started reading from it. "Traumatic amputation of right arm below elbow with multiple contusions, residual shrapnel, and drainage. Surgical amputation of left leg above knee. Amputation of right leg above the knee. Tracheotomy. Superficial shrapnel in lung, stomach, and groin area. Shrapnel and scar tissue on left side of neck."

As he started to unwrap my stumps for his examination, I braced for the coming pain and asked for a shot of Demerol.

He said no.

"But Doc, it hurts."

"Your Demerol days are gone." He continued pulling away the gauze even as I winced and squirmed. He said they didn't want to turn me into a junkie.

That didn't sound like such a bad idea at that moment. The doctor said my right leg was healing up nicely, but my arm and left leg were probably going to need a skin graft from somewhere else on my body to help them heal over.

More operations. More pain.

"We're going to need to clean your wounds once a week, and change the dressings daily until we can do the skin grafts. I'd like to get you started exercising in bed to get your strength up. After that, some physical therapy. Then, once we see how the grafts are doing and healing up, we'll look at fitting you for some limbs."

My heart skipped.

"Artificial limbs? Will I be able to walk? I mean, will I be able to walk out of this place?"

He looked up from his clipboard and studied me. He frowned slightly and squinted.

"No one can say." He laid his hand on mine. "You have no knees."

He explained that knees were the one thing they couldn't replicate with artificial limbs. They were too complicated, and were the key to the balance required for walking. The limbs the doctor was talking about were made of wood in a little tool room right there at Walter Reed. He said I would have to use crutches in order to use the limbs, and I would have a hard time with crutches because I only had one good arm. What was left of my right arm extended to just below my elbow. More to the point, he said he didn't know if my still-healing stumps would ever be able to take the pressure and stress put on them by the clunky limbs available at the time. I said I wanted to try and that I wasn't afraid of pain. I told him I would do whatever was required to be able to walk again.

"I know," he said, his tone softening, his gaze falling to the bottom half of the bed, the half where my legs should have been. "But even if you manage to walk, you won't be all that independent. What if you fall down?"

"I'll get up."

"Not without knees. You won't be able to." A sad smile played across his face, and then he turned and walked away.

I felt that brief moment of joy slip out of me like life itself as an orderly wheeled me to the elevator for the ride back to the Snake Pit. I had never really considered that the U.S. Army's premier hospital would be unable to get me walking again. Being able to walk, even on artificial limbs, was the difference between living and dying in my reckoning. As the elevator doors slid shut, I imagined being stuck in a wheelchair. I'd probably spend the rest of my life sitting in front of the television in my parents' living room.

Like hell I would!

I resolved to walk, no matter what. Screw the doctor and my missing knees.

But I went nowhere fast. The weeks it took to heal up enough to get the skin grafts crawled by. Every day I couldn't try on legs was torture. The guys on the ward were the only thing that saved me. The camaraderie we shared ended up being the only psychological help I got the entire time I spent at Walter Reed. There was plenty of therapy for my body—physical therapy, occupational therapy, corrective therapy. But there wasn't anything for my mind. There was no such thing as post-traumatic stress counseling or readjustment counseling back then. It was just me and my "band of brothers." I remember an air force doctor, an orthopedic surgeon, walked by me and asked, "How you coming along?" I said, "OK." I meant, *I want to be OK. I don't want to fall apart.* So I didn't tell him I was falling apart.

There was one guy asleep in the ward when I got back from the cast room. I lay in my bed and stared at the ceiling. I heard him stir after a while.

"They call me Jack—Nasty Jack."

I grunted at him, not much in the mood for talking after my discussion with the doctor.

"What did he say?" Nasty Jack persisted.

"Who?" I asked, looking at him for the first time.

"The doctor, you jackass."

Jack was in his late twenties. He had close-cropped black hair that was already receding. His eyes were engaging, darting all around when he talked. He was a ball of energy, but he looked like he was in one piece. He had all his arms and legs, though he had a cast on his right arm. He even had all his fingers. What was he doing in a room for amputees?

I told him what the doctor said. Nasty Jack started cussing.

"Anybody who says you won't walk out of this outfit—the hell with them!" Nasty Jack kept on cussing. Now I knew why they called him "Nasty Jack." He was just a string of expletives directed at anything and anyone. I liked him right away. We were both Airborne, and became great friends.

I asked about his wounds, which weren't visible to me in the nonregulation, civilian clothes he was wearing. Turns out Captain "Nasty Jack" Lawton was a hero. While on patrol with his unit from the 101st Airborne near Tam Ky, he and his men were ambushed. The North Vietnamese opened up on them with rockets, mortars, and automatic weapons. Jack was shot 22 times in his right arm with an automatic weapon. He took bullets in the arm, leg, and shoulder. Jack kept fighting and actually ended up rescuing several other wounded men. He was awarded the Distinguished Service Cross. He had almost healed by the time we met.

Jack was in better shape than a lot of us. He had all his limbs. Muscles in his arm had gotten torn up pretty badly, but to the world at large, he looked as fit as a fiddle. He was the ward cheerleader, cussing at anybody who started to wallow in self-pity.

I was feeling pretty much at home at Walter Reed by the time my parents announced they were coming for a visit. I had some friends, and was fixated on walking. That gave me something to focus on other than the fact that I thought I had accidentally blown myself up. But I was still dreading seeing my folks. They knew by that point the shape I was in. Some family friends, Dewitt and Winnette Buice, who were living in Arlington, Virginia, had come to see me right after I arrived at Walter Reed. I was glad for that because I thought it might diminish the shock when my parents saw me for the first time. The day my parents came, I asked for a visiting room where we could be alone. I was still weak and in a bed when they came into the room. I could tell they wanted to cry when they saw me. I did too.

"You're looking good, son," my dad said, almost inexplicably. He said it over and over during the half hour we were together. My mother said I looked thin. I tried to sound cheerful. There wasn't a lot for us to say, and we fell into the silence I dreaded. All of our lives had changed forever when the grenade went off, and this was the moment my parents were learning just how different things would be. One of my doctors stopped in for a minute to say hello, and my mother followed him out into the hall when he left. I knew her well enough to know she would be asking him a thousand questions about my care and my future. I asked Dad questions about home. Then out of the corner of my eye, I saw my mother asking a doctor if I would ever walk again. He lowered his head and shook it from side to side, "No." I watched as she started sobbing. I was exhausted after almost an hour with my folks. My parents said they would come back in the morning and take me to lunch. It was to be my first trip back into the real world.

The next day, the Buices came with my parents. It took a while to figure out how to transfer me from the wheelchair to the car. I enjoyed the car ride, just being out of a hospital and back in the States, but I had to wear my seat belt because I couldn't use my feet to brace myself when the car stopped. What I remember from that day were the stares. It was my first time in public since the grenade. We sat at a table covered with a white cloth and I felt every eye in the room staring at me. If I looked back, people would avert their gaze and look at the ground awkwardly. I knew those self-conscious moments would follow me for the rest of my days, no matter what I did, no matter where I went.

But I was up against other challenges too, particularly within my own head. I entered Walter Reed in April 1968, just around the time Vietnam really went to hell. For the first few months, I was pretty much restricted to my bed. I didn't have a wheelchair that I could operate with one hand yet, and my wounds were still so tender I wouldn't have been able to use one anyway. Mainly, I read, watched my little black-and-white TV, and brooded. The Tet offensive, which had begun two months before I was wounded, had put the lie to Johnson's claims of imminent U.S. victory. We weren't winning, we were losing, and badly. Johnson had dropped out of the presidential race and his defense secretary, Robert McNamara, had resigned in disgrace. I remember tasting the bitter bile that welled up inside me in 1995 when McNamara's book *In Retrospect* came out. He tried to duck the blame and allowed that the massive war he single-handedly escalated might have been a mistake. He had sent 58,000 men to their death for a mistake. He had blown my life to hell, along with the lives of the 350,000 wounded. Was it all just a mistake?

I was feeling that way about Vietnam as early as 1968. I didn't need another 30 years to come to that conclusion. I had that sickening sinking feeling those first few months in the hospital watching the news on my little black-and-white TV—a growing sense of meaninglessness about my sacrifice. I felt like I had given almost everything for a big national question mark.

The peace movement had really exploded in America while I was overseas. I remember seeing a few hippies before I shipped out in May 1967, but that was it. It was before Woodstock, before bands like the Doors, the Jimi Hendrix Experience, and the Beatles started preaching peace to a hungry world. Lying there in my bed watching protest after protest around the country in 1968, watching draft cards burn, I began to feel like I had been on the wrong side of history. I read a comment in some magazine from a soldier who'd lost his foot in Vietnam. "Maybe for some other war, fighting it would be worth losing my foot, but not this war." Right! That was how I felt. Also, I read an interview where an army major was quoted saying about a Vietnamese town, "We had to destroy the village to save it."

Unbelievable.

Looking back, I can see that the most hellish 90 days in my life were among the most hellish days in the nation's history as well. I went into combat at Khe Sanh on April 2 during the largest battle of the war. Martin Luther King was assassinated on April 4. I was blown up on April 8. Bobby Kennedy, perhaps on the cusp of winning the presidency, died on June 6, 1968. Riots erupted regularly. African Americans rioted over race. College students rioted against the war. Campuses were taken over. Buildings were burned. My little TV showed me a nation on fire. It seemed like everything was happening in the blink of an eye. MLK was gone. My body was gone. Bobby was gone. The America I knew was gone. I no longer recognized the country. Everything I stood for, everything I believed in, it seemed, had turned to dust. The Lone Ranger kid from little Lithonia had stepped out into the big world and gotten his ass kicked.

The student-friendly, positive, peaceful, make-the-world-safer country that I loved wasn't there anymore. There were now machine guns on the steps of the Capitol Building, and the U.S. Army was on alert to repel any kind of student assault. My former battalion commander from Vietnam had been reassigned to Washington. He was now the commander of the ready-reaction force tasked with defending the capital.

Against what?

I learned he was sitting in a command helicopter with blades rotating in charge of units armed with sticks and clubs ready to move in case of rioting students. I was lying in Walter Reed thinking, That's my battalion commander! That's my army! Wait a minute! The army is supposed to be fighting the bad guys, not American students protesting the war! I felt like the world was collapsing around me as I tried to recover from the most massive trauma of my life. Much of the time, I didn't feel like I was going to make it.

★ 9 ★

Walter Wonderful

"CAPTAIN CLELAND, YOU use it or you lose it."

It was my first session of physical therapy, and it seemed pointless. The therapist wanted me to press my stumpy arm against his hand as hard as I could, over and over. Why would I bother to exercise what was left of my arm? It wasn't good for anything. Exercising it just seemed pathetic. It couldn't grip a tennis racket anymore, or throw a baseball. I didn't even have a hand. The therapist pushing me to use it just made the loss all the more obvious. Same with my legs. I wasn't ever going to be an athlete again. Why would I lie on the ground doing leg lifts for legs I no longer had? I was just going through the motions with this guy to shut him up, and he could tell. He stared at me hard for a minute.

"If you don't use your right arm stump, your shoulder will become frozen in place. If you don't exercise your leg stumps, the muscles in your thighs will shrink."

He told me I would end up stuck in a bed, unable to do anything for myself. Sorry, bud, but I'm already there, I thought. Then the therapist said that walking on two heavy, wooden legs would probably be among the most physically demanding things I would ever do in my life. Suddenly what he was saying mattered to me. He was talking about my dream of walking. He likened it to tying a log to each thigh and dragging them around while I tried to balance on top. With that epiphany, I realized he was right. I had to become an athlete again. Only this time, my playing field would be a very personal one. Just a month before I got to Walter Reed, before the grenade, I had been a 215-pound, six-foot-two army paratrooper. I was in the best shape of my life while I was in Vietnam. I had a head start. But the therapist had already made clear that it was going to be hard to stay in fighting trim without legs to run on. I dedicated myself to the task.

Just trying to dress myself turned out to require moves worthy of an acrobat. Once my wounds had healed up enough to where I could wear clothes, I was flummoxed by the task of putting on a shirt. With just the one hand, little things like buttons, especially the little ones on the sleeves, became almost insurmountable obstacles. I tried putting on a shirt one-handed. It was tough. Pants were a whole different ball game. How do you put them on one leg at a time without legs? In my case, it involved spreading them out on the bed, lying on my back next to them, and shimmying one stump in, then the other. Then I would rock them up toward my waist by lifting first one side of my body, then the other, and pulling the pants up inch by inch. I could get them fastened easily enough, but zippers remained a source of frustration. Things might not have been so difficult if I had lost my left arm instead of my right, as I was right-handed. To this day, neither I nor anyone else can decipher my left-handed chicken-scratch writing. But, with each week came a little victory. I began to reject help with things I could do myself. I began to see a way back into the world. If I could figure out how to get dressed with one hand, maybe I could find my way outside after all. I began to imagine living in an apartment of my own. That became my focus, to become independent. Key to that effort, at least in my mind, was walking.

Coming to terms with my new body and its limitations was unfortunately not as easy as learning to get dressed. We were on our own
in terms of the mental stuff. I tried not to let myself sink into self-pity
and came up with tricks to pull myself out of it. I'd turn on the TV,
or engage one of the guys in conversation, call somebody I knew—
anything to distract my mind from my desperate situation. But those
things only worked when they worked. When they didn't, there was
no helping me. I could usually feel the sadness coming on before it
happened. It would start with, Cleland, you are dumb. You've screwed
everything up. You blew yourself up. You've ruined your life and your
body. You're just a dumbass.

It was maddening lying there in Walter Reed for those first months,
not knowing how things were going to turn out. The doctors hadn't
agreed to let me try artificial legs. They were still worried about my
stumps. I didn't know if I was going to be able to walk ever again. And
what about driving a car, getting a date, finding a job? Nobody could
tell me anything. So I just kept going. I was like the mule that puts its
head down and just plows on to the end of the furrow. That was how
I got through my days. If it was a bad day, I cried until it was over and
tried again in the morning. The only alternative was death.

One of the things I liked to distract myself with was girls. Certainly
it would be a challenge to find one who could see past my missing
parts, but I had come to believe it could be done.

We had a guy named Dave on the ward who we called "No Way
Alligood." He was from the 173rd Airborne, and his legs had been
shot all to hell. The doctors wanted to take one of them off, but Dave
fought them. He agreed to an excruciating regimen of operations and
skin grafts as a last-ditch effort to save his leg. To do the graft, doctors
planned to grow skin from his stomach to his arm. Then, once it was
established and healed onto the arm, this large flap of skin would be
cut loose from his stomach and sewed to his calf while remaining attached to his arm. He would have to remain doubled over for months,

trapped in a body cast while the skin grafted from his arm to his leg. His calf muscles were all torn up, and the doctors hoped the graft would fill in the missing muscle mass. Well, just before they started the graft process, Dave fell for a physical therapist. He asked her to marry him and I'll be damned if she didn't say yes. They set the wedding date just before Dave was to be bent over and wrapped in a body cast. After the wedding, once they'd put him in the cast, we started calling him "No Way" because there was no way he was going to physically reach his woman while he was in that big body cast. We would chant it at night in the room sometimes, just to rib him. "No way. No way. No way." That was the big joke in the Snake Pit, "No Way Alligood." Nasty Jack coined it. But before long, Alligood found a way, even in his cast. His new bride became pregnant. I never did figure out the precise mechanics of the accomplishment, but I learned something that has proved itself time and again in my life. If you've got your brains and your sex life, you're in business. You will find a way.

That was the thing about all of us. We were young, 25, 26 or so, and had been to war. We all still had a mind-set that said we were still at war. Walter Reed was just another battlefield, and in our fight to get our lives back, the Snake Pit was like our personal officers' club. We had fun all the time, despite the fact that we were all living, breathing tragedies. Our camaraderie was therapy in its purest form. We were heaped in there together, and couldn't help keeping an eye on each other. At first, sharing a room with so many guys bugged me. But, looking back, if I had been put in a private room, I think depression would have swallowed me whole. Instead, I would show up at the real officers' club inside Walter Reed with my new best friends and enjoy the booze and the girls.

At my first cocktail party as a triple amputee, I learned that my stumps throbbed relentlessly if I got lit on rum punch and that women besides nurses would still laugh at my jokes. We used to have "Pit parties" occasionally with a blousy redhead from Baltimore named

Wilma Clark. She'd show up with a gallon of bourbon and a big laugh. Sometimes she'd bring a handful of *Playboy* bunnies with her. One Saturday, Wilma showed up with two army buses and took a load of us to Baltimore to meet Blaze Starr in all her redheaded 1968 glory. Except for the pasties, she was like a statue of a Greek goddess come to life. She started drawling in her West Virginia accent before she danced and I was putty in her hands. Especially when she said she invited us up just to remind us that we were still men. Hi-ho, Silver! I still have the photograph she signed for me.

The Snake Pit was buzzing when I talked an old girlfriend into coming to town for a date. The guys were as excited as I was. This was a landmark moment for me. The main thing all of us wanted to do was get with a woman. Any activity that carried even the slightest chance of some romance was a major deal. I didn't care that I was missing arms, legs, whatever. I still wanted to be a silver-tongued devil and talk my way into a lady's arms. I was still a man, just like Blaze said. I talked a girl I will call Darlene into coming from New Jersey with promises of fun in the big city. She and I had kept up over the time I was away in the army. She knew about my wounds. I liked Darlene and figured my best shot for a real, live date was with someone who knew me before the war.

She said she'd come.

On the appointed day, I was waiting in the lobby of the Hilton in Washington. With combat pay from Vietnam, I had saved up quite a bit over the last year. I reserved the largest, most expensive suite at the Hilton with a bedroom for each of us. She was flying in. We were going to have a ball no matter what happened. I sat in a corner of the lobby pretending not to stare at the front door. I was so nervous I could feel my heart beating in my stumps. Darlene sauntered in, and my heart fluttered. She looked beautiful, just like I remembered. I, of course, didn't look the same as the last time she had seen me. When we first met, I had been a newly commissioned second lieutenant working for a general at Fort Monmouth. She remembered a swinging dance partner who knew how to show a lady a good time.

She saw me heading for her in the lobby and started chatting to me like old times as soon as I rolled over. I fought for her bag but a bellhop got it first. The three of us rode the elevator to the suite. We caught up on each other's lives for about 20 giddy minutes, and then the conversation began to sag. I could feel her staring at my stumps. Her eyes darted away from mine when I looked at her. The air in the hotel room became heavy with expectations. I saw Darlene eyeing the door. I tried to rescue the moment with outsized levity. I tried telling her about the dinner reservations. I tried everything I could think of until she stood abruptly and said, "It has been good seeing you, Max." She told me her plane was leaving at 4:30 that afternoon, even though she'd only arrived an hour before. She was running away, really fast. I felt like some kind of monster. It wasn't the first time I'd been brushed off in my life. Just the most painful.

With her gone, I went to the bar and ordered a whiskey sour. I drank five in a row. I made passes at every waitress in the hotel restaurant during dinner. Then I hit on the cashier. Stone drunk, I worried that maybe love wasn't in the cards for me anymore. Maybe nobody but my mother would ever be able to love me. Not even Nasty Jack picked on me when I rolled into the Snake Pit hungover and a full day early from my weekend leave. The guys could tell what had happened to me. They had all been there too. They had been where I was—so low that all you could do was hope that tomorrow would hurt less.

After a few months, I was healing nicely. I got word that I was to be fitted with legs. I had gotten an arm with a hook about a month before. That was great. I could pick things up like I had another hand and even made a wooden doorstop in shop therapy. But I wanted those legs. I dreamed about them. One of the guys in the pit, Carl Nunziato, had gotten his—beautiful, flesh-colored plastic that filled me with envy. That was the state of the art at the time, plastic instead of wood. They didn't bend or anything, but they didn't really need to, as Carl still had both knees. At the end of the day, he would take them off and stand them up next to the bed like they were just waiting to walk somewhere with him. They had heavy leather straps that reached all the way up to a sturdy belt that cinched around Carl's waist. I was glad for Carl, but I would get so jealous watching him put them on that I could barely stand it. With his pants dropped down over them, you couldn't even tell he was wounded, except for the crutches. I thought he looked like a million bucks compared to me in my wheelchair.

He had to use the crutches to keep from falling over, as he didn't have any ankles—another key part of the balancing mechanism. It took him a couple of minutes to get them on each day, with all the straps and everything he had to buckle. I knew that would be more of a challenge for me, as I didn't have two hands like he did. But I was undaunted. No amount of cautionary mumbo jumbo from the doctors about not having knees or about my stumps not being able to take the pressure could discourage me. I could tell it was hard work, though. Carl would be sweating from the exertion of just crossing from one side of the room to the other. He didn't look graceful. He lurched. At night, he rubbed his stumps like they hurt.

After a little while, Carl was discharged from Walter Reed. He was living on the outside in a real apartment, one all his own. I was in awe. Once I had legs, I would do that. I'd live on my own. Then, about a month later, Carl was back. He moved right back into his old bed. He seemed defeated.

One afternoon, with just the two of us in the Snake Pit, I asked Carl about the legs and what had happened. He said the pain was getting better, but the sockets still rubbed his stumps almost raw. Being on the outside had just taken too much out of him. He decided he wasn't quite ready for independence. I hadn't really been out much yet. My wounds were just getting to the point where I could start taking leave for a few hours to roll around in my wheelchair. Carl talked about how much harder it was out there.

"As long as you're in the hospital and around the guys, it'll seem pretty easy. But when you leave, then it'll get tough." I followed Carl's gaze out the open window to a bird soaring against the blue sky.

This was a long time before the Americans with Disabilities Act mandated that new public places be made accessible. The world he was talking about was definitely designed for people on two legs. Oddly, the more worries he laid in front of me, the more optimistic I was that I could make it once I had legs. I wasn't scared of toilets or stairs. I was scared of spending my life on the sidelines or as a lifelong patient.

I was given a one-arm-drive wheelchair, which had two rings on the left-side wheel. One wheel turned me right, the other left. Both at the same time and I went straight. I had become a hallway terror with it, whizzing down the halls at Walter Reed, frequently knocking into the nurses while rounding corners. Motion felt good. It was freedom and I loved it. But I wanted legs.

I was bursting with excitement when they gave me an appointment to get fitted for legs in the limb shop. I was of a mind that if I could stand face-to-face with people, they would be more able to see past my missing limbs. Going to the limb and brace shop to get fitted had become the focus of my recovery. I was exercising constantly and with the same vigor I used to employ in sports. If it was going to be harder for me to walk than it was for Carl because I didn't have knees, I was going to work twice as hard. Rolling into the limb room was the biggest moment in my four months of recovery. But when they set my new limbs down in front of me, I nearly cried.

Instead of long, flesh-colored legs like Carl had, I was getting stubbies. I had heard the doctors talk about getting me started on stubbies, but I had no idea what they actually were. They said I should think about them like training wheels.

"You won't be able to walk on them right away. No one does." The limb maker pointed toward my new limbs as he spoke. He gave me a talk about balance and how to use my back, not my thighs, to lift the stubbies, but I didn't hear a word of it. I was dumbfounded and couldn't take my eyes off the abominations he pointed at.

They looked like torture devices—short, squat hunks of wood a little wider than a man's thigh resting atop sturdy wooden rockers like you'd see on the bottom of an old-fashioned rocking horse. The stubbies had sockets in them that my stumps were supposed to fit down into. Thick steel bracing rose up from the wood sockets. Heavy leather strapping and a thick belt were supposed to tie the monstrosities to me. The doctor said if I could handle stubbies, I *might* get to try legs. My dream was in danger of being crushed.

Jim Cloud, the limb maker, put thick wool socks on my stumps to protect them from wear. He was an amputee himself with one leg missing from above the knee. That's what drew him to the limb-making profession, which he had been practicing for a long time. I felt ridiculous as he and one of his guys lowered me down onto the rocking horses while I wiggled my stumps, trying to aim them into the sockets. They buckled me in. I leaned back and found myself tipping unsettlingly. Then my legs started itching. Like mad. Jim said it was the blood rushing back into the ends of my stumps and the new sense of pressure where the bones rubbed my skin grafts. They said I would get used to it. I looked down. The stubbies were ugly and crude, not the lovely legs of my dreams. Wood cut into either side of my crotch.

I couldn't believe what was happening to me. One moment I was a six-foot-two army captain, a paratrooper. The next second—literally, the next second—my legs and my right arm were gone. My identity was gone. I came back to the States and Walter Reed ready to get going and get out of there. Then I got rocking-horse legs and stood about four feet high, like a midget. I was a little rocking-horse man. I was about ready to give up on the whole enterprise. I didn't want to go through life looking like a bizarre creature from the land of misfit toys. I had imagined my first moments on legs for so long. It was comical how far off-base the reality was.

They set me up to walk between a set of parallel bars that were about four feet off the ground, roughly even with my head. I reached for the bars and prepared to take my first step.

"Now hold on to one bar and swing one leg forward. Then rock onto the other side and bring the other leg forward. You'll walk as long as you stay between the bars so you have something to hold on to. And, remember, no one does it right away. It's going to take practice, but it will get easier. Just keep hold of the bars so you don't fall over."

Jim Cloud looked on attentively.

I shuffled forward like he said, rocking and swinging my legs. I was huffing by the time I had made it to the end of the bars. I turned and faced him and started back. It took all I had to move the big hunks of wood with legs that hadn't walked in five months. Halfway back toward him, I stopped. I pivoted away from him, ducked under the bar, and took a first lurching step out into the open room. I rocked forward precariously, but I had done it. I had taken my first step unaided.

"I can do it!" I called over my shoulder to Jim.

"I'll be damned," he said, grinning.

I took a second step, but disaster struck. I overbalanced and pitched forward on my rockers. I was falling onto my face. Instinctively, I thrust my one good arm out in front of me to break my fall. Just as my face was about to smash into the linoleum, my hand hit. In one smooth motion I pushed off from the floor with a one-handed push-up and swung back upright, rocking back and forth for a moment like one of those blow-up punching bags for kids. My heart swelled. I was walking! I set off across the room, waddling up to everybody in the limb shop with a grin as big as a slice of watermelon. I swelled with the same sense of pride and accomplishment I had felt when I won that first band medal, or beat Edgar for the city tennis championship. I could do this. If I had managed to walk on the stubbies unaided on my first try, there was no stopping me.

Little did I know, the U.S. Army was about to stop me and my recovery cold.

Three months after I walked those wobbling few steps, before I was ever fitted for proper legs, I was told that I was being retired from the army and released from Walter Reed. I would be transferred to the VA hospital system. I couldn't believe it. I was bereft as the guys gathered out front to see me off. I was leaving "Walter Wonderful" for good.

Or so I thought.

★ 10 ★

The Hopeless

LEAVING WALTER REED was like getting blown up all over again. It meant leaving my eight best friends, almost all fellow amputees who understood what I was going through. I was losing the little world that had gathered around me in the better part of the last year, a world where I had rediscovered how to be myself again despite my injuries. But more than anything, I was losing the 24-hour-a-day companionship of those who helped wrest me back from the barest edge. They were the bravest men I've ever known. By the time I was discharged, Walter Reed had become my home in the truest sense.

Apparently, my transfer into the VA system was my own fault. I tried to fight it all the way up the chain of command, but my fate had been sealed months before. Nearly a year prior, during the druggy twilight of my first few days at Walter Reed, I had agreed to allow the army to move me to a VA hospital. I didn't realize that I was signing away some of my rights as a combat-wounded soldier for further treatment at an army hospital. Originally, they wanted to send me to the Atlanta VA. I didn't want that. I didn't want to go home until I could stand on my own two feet, figuratively if not literally. When I went back to my hometown for good, I wanted to be able to function on my own. I figured the VA hospital in Washington, D.C., would be better for me.

Boy, was I wrong.

Now, once again, I found myself alone and drifting into an uncertain future, my fate completely out of my hands. On the short ride to the VA hospital in Washington, I was as nervous as if I were headed halfway around the world to Vietnam again. I kept thinking, Cleland, get a hold of yourself. You're just going to a new hospital. It's going to be fine. But I didn't feel that way. I felt like the life I had so carefully cobbled together in the Snake Pit was the only thing I had to hold on to. Now it was unraveling like a half-finished sweater, every stitch pulled loose leaving me a little closer to the brink of desolation. And it was my precious army doing the damage. I felt like the army was kicking me out the door to the VA, where the rest of yesterday's warriors rusted away like so much unwanted junk.

If I had not been a patient in the VA system in 1969, I would never have believed that such a surreal whorl of bureaucracy could exist. The VA is the second-largest part of the federal government. Only the U.S. Postal Service has a greater physical presence in America. Only the Department of Defense has more employees. The VA is larger than five cabinet-level departments combined.

Once I was inside the VA hospital, an orderly wheeled me into the registration office in my chair. The woman behind the counter glanced at me but didn't stop what she was doing. After a few minutes, she approached the counter, picked up her clipboard, and addressed me.

"What's your claim number?" she asked brusquely.

"I don't have a claim number," I said under my breath.

She told me that a person doesn't exist in the VA system until and unless he has a claim number.

She pointed to a corner and told me to wait. I sat there for two hours before an orderly brought me a pair of pajamas in institutional green and told me I should put them on so he could take me to my ward.

"I can't just wear my clothes?"

"Not in here."

Not only could I not wear my own clothes, I wasn't allowed to *have* clothes. Or personal effects, food, TV, or radio. I had a nasty feeling that my life had just taken a turn for the worse. This hospital didn't feel like Walter Reed. It wasn't a place to get better. It was eerie and silent, with long, empty halls. It seemed like a place for rotting away, for being controlled, for being forgotten. No TV? No radio? I felt like I was checking into prison. By the time I went upstairs to my ward, I had a claim number. I was told that I would be identified by that number for the rest of my life. My name, rank, and serial number— none of those things mattered anymore. I was a number now, not a soldier. In two hours, I had lost my rank, my identity, and my friends. I felt abandoned by the army and abandoned by my country.

The ward itself was a study in institutional living. I was given a bed in a room with over 30 other men, most of them more than 20 years older than I was. Gone were the semiprivate cubicles of Walter Reed. There were just four guys from Vietnam in the whole ward. Two of them were totally paralyzed. The rest of the residents were from World War II and Korea. One guy across the hall was dying from mustard gas poisoning from World War I. His low moans echoed in our ward. I realized that the VA hospital was full of the hard cases and old people, many of whom were never going to leave alive.

I knew I couldn't let that be me.

I decided that first day that I would get my legs as soon as possible and get the hell out of there.

The next day, I met with the doctor who was the head of the Physical Medicine and Rehabilitation Service. Short, stocky, and bossy, she was the gatekeeper when it came to getting legs. In our first meeting, before she had even asked about my progress with the stubbies, she said, "I don't know whether I'll be able to fit you with limbs or not."

"You've got to let me try," I insisted.

She didn't respond. She just looked down at her desk and started writing. The message was clear. The meeting was over and there was nothing I could do about it.

I was on the verge of tears as I wheeled to the elevator, but at the same time I felt like I might explode in a screaming rage.

The doors slid open, and a patient wearing a blue VA robe over a pair of the same green pajamas I was wearing stepped out. He looked at me for the briefest of moments, reached into his pocket, and handed me a little white card, like a business card, then shambled off down the hall without a word. I studied his gift. There was a cross on one side. On the other, these words: "Saint Jude, Patron Saint of the Hopeless. Pray to him."

Hopeless. That's how I was beginning to feel.

Even that first day, I could see that the culture within the VA was different from that of Walter Reed. More than a hospital, the VA seemed like an old folks' home peopled with doped-up, spaced-out guys, many of whom seemed to have no hope of making it in the outside world. That wasn't me: I still had some fight in me. Sure, I was blown to hell, but I still felt like a soldier. I was one of the young lions, trained to fight for my country or die trying. I wasn't looking to fade away in a room full of broken men.

From the moment I arrived at the VA, I was plotting my escape. I was already trapped in a body that had been betrayed by life. There was no way I was going to spend the rest of my days trapped inside that wretched hospital.

The lobby in the VA hospital was nice, but it was really just a façade. I imagined that it was used as a place for pretty pictures when members of Congress or other visiting dignitaries came by for a photo op with a wounded veteran to show they were "supporting the troops."

The hospital itself was among the worst in the VA system because it was without a champion in Congress. The District of Columbia had no voting members in the House or the Senate to make a stink if conditions were unacceptable.

Whereas we had been treated with respect at Walter Reed, at the VA we were treated like mental patients who needed to be controlled and supervised. We weren't even allowed to play Ping-Pong after 4:15 p.m. It was a big comedown from life at Walter Reed, where I could play Ping-Pong in the Red Cross Hall until midnight or hang out at the officers' club anytime I wanted. I was still a captain in the U.S. Army at Walter Reed, and as such was accorded the respect due to a returning warrior. At the VA, we were treated like people looking for handouts, expecting the government to take care of us. Partly, that attitude reflects a truism about the VA: 80 percent of the patients in the system when I entered in 1969 were there for health problems totally unrelated to their service in the military. Only about 20 percent of the patients in the VA back then were in the hospital due to illness or disability obtained in military service. In essence, the VA's largest mission was, and still remains today, to care for aging veterans who can't afford better health care. A large portion of the older patients were in for psychological reasons, alcoholism, or drug addiction. I discovered that the system wasn't ready for guys coming back from Vietnam like me. The VA hadn't had to deal with combat casualties since Korea in the 1950s. By 1970, it had been 20 years since the last influx of war-wounded. There were few people on the staff who had any experience with soldiers fresh from the front lines. That was also partly why the VA was such a lonely experience for me. Conversation at lunch was nil because so many of the patients were on heavy psychiatric drugs. Those early medications so blunted the mind that the people on them could never seem to hold a thought longer than a sentence or two.

Seeing all those lost men trapped inside themselves taught me a lot about war. They seemed like the zombie staff at the field hospital I almost died in. The most catastrophic war wounds are often the ones that don't leave a visible scar. It took decades for me to realize the same was true about me. An arm and two legs seemed to me to be the only things I had lost. Those losses seemed to be pretty easy to get over. I moved past them. But in time, I realized I had lost something else. I had lost my sense of personal identity, my confidence, and my sense of safety and justice. The thing I have never gotten over is the fear and anxiety that all hell could break out at any moment, that I could lose everything in the blink of an eye.

I've never forgotten the difference in the care I received at the two institutions—Walter Reed and the VA. They were both run by the same federal government and they were less than 10 miles apart. However, they were separated by an unfathomable space and time. That education informed me when I later became head of the VA, and it guided me as a member of the Senate Armed Services Committee.

But the VA did give me Big Jon. At 230 pounds, Jon Peters was the only guy on staff they thought was big enough to handle me personally and professionally. My first physical therapist, Dee, was a small lady. She took one look at me and cried. Big Jon was next in line. He wasn't scared of my disabilities or of hurting my feelings. He consistently pushed me to do more, be better, and get stronger. Jon and Dee ultimately married. Maybe talking about me helped bring them together.

Jon's influence didn't end with my physical rehabilitation. He talked to me about my head and my heart, where I was inside. He became my friend, just like the guys in the Pit.

One day, after listening to me complain about the crappy care within the VA and the lack of personal freedom, Jon called my bluff.

"You don't have to stay here, you know. Why don't you get an apartment of your own and just come in for therapy as an outpatient?"

That stopped me cold.

Move out? My own apartment? Why the hell not?

Suddenly, after Jon's suggestion, I realized I didn't owe anybody anything anymore. I had been summarily retired from the army effective on Christmas Eve, 1968. Merry fricking Christmas! The VA had to care for me for the rest of my life. That was its mission whether I lived there or not. The very thought of moving out filled me with pure joy. It was also terrifying. I didn't want to end up like Carl, who had been so glad to move back into Walter Reed after only a short time on the outside because he just wasn't ready for its obstacles.

The more I thought about it, the more it seemed like getting out of the VA hospital was the right path. After a few months in the VA, I longed to get back to the land of the living. I wanted away from waxed linoleum. I wanted to wake up someplace where morning didn't smell like antiseptic. I wasn't in danger of dying anymore. My body was, for all intents and purposes, as healed as it was ever going to get. Staying in the hospital meant having my meals fixed, my laundry done, and my bed made, but it didn't mean getting any healthier emotionally or any closer to living some semblance of a normal life. For the first time, I truly imagined jumping back into the river of life and letting chance and fate sweep me toward my future.

Jon said all I had to do to actually be discharged from the hospital was prove I could care for myself. That was easy enough. I could dress myself, get around on the street in my wheelchair, bathe myself, feed myself. I knew I could do all this. Within days, I had rented a tiny studio apartment near Walter Reed in a building with elevators and wheelchair ramps. My place had a kitchen, bathroom, and a small bedroom. My windows looked out onto Rock Creek Park, not a bad view in Washington. There were no accommodations for my handicaps in the apartment, though I found I didn't need them. Using my good arm and my stump, I could lower myself into the tub just fine. I could even climb back out. Getting on and off the toilet was no problem.

The apartment was like magic. I went from being a victim and a patient to being a person overnight. For the first time in a long while, I didn't have to answer to anybody. I wasn't living with my folks. I wasn't in a college dorm. I wasn't in the army. And I wasn't sharing a hospital ward with more than 30 strangers. I felt like I was getting my life back, and I loved it. I went to the movies and to dinner. I invited the girl who lived upstairs to come over to listen to records. I threw parties. It was great.

I commuted to the hospital by cab. Every day, I ate breakfast in a coffee shop in the building, lunch on the chow line at the VA, and dinner out of a blender filled with Wild Turkey whiskey, ice, and daiquiri mix—the only food I had in my apartment refrigerator.

As I made the daily commute and spent more and more hours away from the hospital, I began to feel like I could really make it on the outside.

One of my neighbors in the apartment building had been paralyzed from the waist down as a young Special Forces officer in Vietnam. He was the executive director of a Washington veterans' rights group, the Paralyzed Veterans of America. His name was Pete Lassen. He asked me to testify with him before a Senate Veterans' Affairs subcommittee hearing in December 1969. Although I had moved out of the hospital by that point, I was still under the care of the VA. He wanted the committee to hear from someone with firsthand experience in the VA system. The subcommittee was chaired by Alan Cranston, a freshman senator from California.

In my testimony, I told the committee that I thought the Vietnam veteran was a different animal from veterans of earlier wars, primarily because those who served in Vietnam did not feel like they sacrificed for a noble or just cause. The TV lights glared down upon me, hot and white on my face, but I was determined to finish reading the speech I had written.

"To the devastating psychological effect of getting maimed, paralyzed, or in some way being unable to reenter American life as you left it, is added the psychological weight that it may not have been worth it, that the war may have been a cruel hoax, an American tragedy that left a small minority of young American males holding the bag."

I told them that these doubts continued to explode within the minds of the wounded for months and even years after their return home, going off like "secondary explosions." I didn't know it at the time, but I was describing PTSD—post-traumatic stress disorder—exactly. I used the term "secondary explosions" because that's what it felt like to me.

I got a taste of being at the center of the action in the Senate that day. I liked it. I also got acquainted with Senator Cranston. We hit it off instantly and became lifelong friends.

By March 1969, I had been on my stubbies for eight months. I walked all over the hospital with them in an effort to impress the doctors, but nobody would authorize a fitting for limbs. I demanded yet another meeting with the head rehab doctor, the one who wrote the orders for limb fittings. She said she didn't think I'd ever be able to walk and didn't want to waste money on a lost cause. I wanted to throttle her. The primary factor behind her decisions, according to the physical therapists working under her, was her desire to bring her department in under budget every year and so improve her chances for a promotion.

Instead of a chance with limbs, I was sent to the swimming pool inside the hospital for therapy. I'm sure part of the reason was to calm me down. But I wanted my limbs, not a dunk in the pool. I could tell I was getting the brush-off again, and this time in a way that wouldn't impact her precious budget. Still, I was excited by the prospect of getting in a pool. Swimming was one of my favorite activities as a kid, and I even swam on a team for a while. Maybe getting in the water would feel liberating. I knew Franklin Roosevelt loved being in the water because he felt light as a feather and could move around even without the use of his legs at Warm Springs.

The air in the indoor pool area was humid and heavy with chlorine. A group of men were playing volleyball in the shallow end. The warm air, the yelling, and the smells reminded me of being a youngster again. A young man named Branch became my therapist. He had shoulders like a linebacker. He helped me into a special chair next to a ramp that led into the pool and rolled me backward down the slight incline like I was a boat getting launched from a trailer. I started moving my good arm through the water in a swimming motion as soon as it got wet. I felt the familiar resistance of the water and squirmed off the chair thinking I would just float around on my back for a minute. I sank like a stone. I tried to kick off the bottom but had nothing to kick with. Flailing my one arm just spun me in a circle underwater. Rolling on the bottom of the pool, I tried to propel myself upward by frantically wiggling my stumps. Nothing happened. Just as panic was taking me, I looked toward the surface. I could see Branch's face through the clear water. I could tell he was leaning over me, then hands slipped under my armpits and I was borne up. I came sputtering to the surface, minus both my dignity and my short-lived dream that I might find some kind of grace in the water.

"Got a little ahead of us there, Max," said Branch. "Try these under your arms."

He handed me a pair of empty Clorox bottles, their handles tied together with a short length of rope. With a set of bottles under each armpit, I was able to float. I started kicking my stumps and moved forward. Then I added the arm. I liked it.

Over the next few days, I figured out how to tread water without the Clorox bottles. It was all about breath control. Then I started actually swimming, doing a sort of modified, one-armed, no-legged breaststroke. They had sent me to the pool ostensibly so I could practice standing on my stumps in the shallow end without all of my body weight pressing down on them. No one expected me to be able to swim. Branch couldn't believe it when I swam an entire lap unaided. Within a few weeks, I had worked up to swimming 20 laps without stopping, nearly a quarter of a mile.

One morning, I rolled up to the edge of the deep end of the pool. I waited there for a minute. One of the head therapists, someone who might have a little say in whether or not I got a fitting, was watching me. I jumped out of my chair into the deep end. I sank for a minute, then bobbed to the surface just in time to see the panicked therapist tearing off his coat as he ran toward the pool to jump in and save me. I laughed at him, squirted a jet of water out of my mouth, then swam three lengths of the pool to show him what I could do.

I loved that moment. It was fun to beat the odds. But when I left the VA that afternoon and got back to my apartment, I felt deflated. Sure, I could swim. But that didn't change the broken thing I had become. It didn't change how alone I was. Snow began to fall. I felt the walls pressing in on me. I wheeled over to the refrigerator and mixed a strong daiquiri. I set a Beatles record on the turntable and listened to Paul McCartney's "Yesterday."

> *Yesterday, all my troubles seemed so far away,*
> *Now it looks as though they're here to stay . . .*

That song said it all for me then. I did feel like I was half the man I used to be. I had spent the last year longing for yesterday. While I had made progress, and—miracle of miracles—was still alive, I was still a one-armed guy in a wheelchair going to rehab every day. I didn't have anything else in my life. Didn't have a car. Didn't have a job. Didn't have a girlfriend. Didn't have a future. I saw the Snake Pit guys regularly, and had them over to the house for parties, but all we did was get drunk. That's what life had become for me. Rehab all week, then drink with the guys on the weekend to forget my life. I wanted more. I needed more. I knew I was wasting away.

The next day, I went to see the doctor in charge of rehab and again demanded a fitting for limbs. I had been on the stubbies for eight months, and I had walked on my first try. I had learned to swim with one fin, which should have been nearly impossible, and could now swim more laps than a lot of people with two good arms and legs. I had moved into my own apartment and was taking care of myself in the world. I told her it was time for my limbs. I had been home from Vietnam for a year and I wasn't going to be put off any longer. Maybe it was my determination, or maybe it was the anger in my voice as I talked to her. Whatever it was, she finally relented. A meeting was arranged with representatives from the three limb-making companies who did contract work for the VA in Washington.

I wheeled into the meeting room in a pair of shorts and a T-shirt for a thorough going-over by the arm and leg guys. There was a lot of tut-tutting, a lot of measuring, and a lot of head shaking.

"He's just too great a risk," one of the men said. "Those stumps are too hard to fit."

I'd heard that before at Walter Reed. I'd also heard what the next guy concluded.

"The effort really wouldn't be worth it," he said, looking away from me and toward the doctor. "I just don't think it would work."

The doctor smiled at me, so smug I wanted to strangle her.

Then the third guy spoke.

"I'll take him."

My hero.

I took a cab to his shop a few days later for my fitting. He cursed the head doctor for only authorizing wooden legs, the most archaic and physically demanding type of limbs available. They relied on technology dating back to before World War II.

"I'm sorry this is all we can do. They won't authorize me to make some real legs for you out of plastic with the new hydraulic knees," he said, holding out a crude-looking puppet leg made of wood. "These legs, it's going to be hard for you. Really hard."

The leg he held out looked just like one of Pinocchio's legs before he becomes a real boy. There were screw heads and putty smears all around the top, where a stiff metal rod joined the wooden thigh socket. Heavy leather straps and a girdle like the one from the stubbies topped off the legs. A swinging wooden hinge joined the calf to the femur.

The limb maker explained that instead of knees, the legs had a lower half that swung on locking hinges. Swing one leg forward, the knee hinge locks, then you swing the other leg forward. He warned me that every step would require complete concentration on my part. I learned that as a triple amputee, if I took one step on artificial limbs it would take nine times the effort of a normal person. These old-style legs were dangerous because the knees could lock up—or give way—unexpectedly. If that happened, I would end up falling on my face without two arms to break my fall, or falling backward and hitting my head. I didn't care. I'd take the chance. If the rehab doctor was going to make this as hard as she possibly could for me, I'd beat her at her own game. I'd work my ass off, learn to walk on the worst legs they made and then force them to give me better ones.

I was positioned between parallel bars just as I had been with the stubbies while they tried to attach the limbs to my stumps. The first time I put my full body weight on them and stood up straight, two things happened: One, standing six feet tall again showed me what an awfully long way I had to fall if something went wrong; and two, I realized how horribly uncomfortable artificial legs were going to be. I took a tentative step. My stumps screamed in pain, but everything seemed OK. I took another step. God, the legs were heavy. It was just like my first physical therapist at Walter Reed had told me—I was essentially dragging a log that was tied to each of my stumps. As I made my third step, a crack rang out like a rifle shot. It turned out the snapping sound was the wood socket fitted around my right thigh splintering under my weight. A knot in the wood had given way. This was going to be harder than I thought. The limb maker cussed the rehab doctor and told me what a breeze the whole process would have been if the hospital had just agreed to fit me with plastic limbs that couldn't break and hydraulic knees that couldn't give way.

I almost started crying when he said it would take another two weeks to rebuild the shattered right leg. Two more weeks stuck in legless limbo. I didn't know how much more I could take. I had built so much of my recovery around the day I got fitted for limbs. Instead, my trip to the limb maker sent me spiraling down.

The one-year anniversary of the explosion was fast approaching. I found myself sinking more and more often into the sodden world of daiquiris and "Yesterday." My rehab was losing momentum and I didn't see how much more progress I would be able to make. The two steps I had taken on the legs had been incredibly painful, much worse than the stubbies for some reason. The brash confidence I lived off at Walter Reed was gone, replaced with bitterness and resentment directed at the army, the VA, and, most of all, at myself for picking up that damn grenade. I drank myself to sleep that night and dreamed again that I had my real legs back. I loved that dream. It came to me about as often as the dream where I had no legs and an unspeakable danger from which I couldn't escape was bearing down on me.

A few days later, I woke up feeling awful. By nightfall, what I thought was a cold had become so intense I was scared to be alone. I went to see a doctor at the VA, and he had me admitted, saying I had a fever "of unknown origin." He told me to cancel my planned Easter brunch with friends. I slept fitfully and woke at dawn Easter morning in a nearly empty ward. Weak light filtered in from the windows. Dark clouds scudded low against the horizon. It was quiet, as most of the guys were home with family or out on leave. I started taking stock of the cold realities of my life. I would forever be separated from all I loved by my injuries. I would never again be an athlete or an imposing army paratrooper. I would never have an easy friendship. I might never have a girlfriend again. I might never have the exciting life in politics that seemed mine for the taking just one year ago.

Instead, I would keep on pulling it together every morning to ride to the VA to go through the torturous and tedious work of rehabbing the half a body I had left. And what would that get me in the end? Nothing but more pain. What was left for me? I realized I wanted to die more than at any point since the grenade.

Sobs came quickly. My body quaked as I gave vent to the primal misery inside me. I thought of my parents and kept thinking the same thought I had on the battlefield when I first saw my missing hand: Why, God? Why me?

By nightfall, something had clicked inside me. I realized I wasn't sad anymore. I was furious. I was mad at the army, mad at the president, the VA, myself, my situation. I felt this kind of rage build inside me, but it was a rage to live! Though I didn't see it as such for years, I had my own resurrection that Easter. I had rejected death as a way out. I decided to quit thinking of all the things I couldn't do. I began to figure out how to do all the things I could do and how to accomplish getting the things I most wanted—legs, a job, and a girl.

The legs were on their way. A job seemed a reachable goal for a guy with a college education. But a girl? That one had me stymied. At least for the time being.

I got my legs about two weeks after Easter. They were wood, and they were clumsy, but they were mine. I learned to walk the first day. I needed a crutch strapped to my artificial arm to stabilize me. It was hard, physical work. Walking the length of one of the VA's long halls left me as winded as if I had run a mile. My heart thumped, my lungs wheezed, and my stumps ached. But I was getting stronger every day. I was walking farther every day. I could feel my chest muscles growing. One of the first things I did was walk by that rehab doctor who had stood in my way for four months. This time *I* had the smug smile. It occurred to me that I probably could have walked on wooden legs the same day they started me on stubbies back at Walter Reed. That had been 10 months ago.

Within two weeks I could handle a flight of stairs by holding on tightly to a handrail. I was awkward and unsteady going up them, and slightly terrified going down, but I could do it. My first real test came about a month after I got the legs. I was visiting a friend who had an office in the VA hospital. He was a World War II veteran of the D-Day invasion. His name was Eddie Griggs. He had been to hell and back and had lost a leg in the process. I enjoyed talking to him. I would often strut down to his office on my legs, visit for a minute while I caught my breath, and then clump back to the therapy room, where Big Jon was waiting. This particular day, I slipped and fell down on the floor for the first time since I had gotten my legs. It happened as I was heading out the door of my friend's office. The tip of one of my crutches slipped on the waxed floor. The knee I had swung into the locked position as I prepared for my next step suddenly gave way. There was nothing holding me up. I toppled over like a toy soldier.

Collapsed in an embarrassed heap on the floor, I saw my friend's hand reaching down to help me up. I had a flash of my first day at Walter Reed, the doctor saying that artificial limbs probably wouldn't do me much good because if I fell down I wouldn't be able to get up without knees. I waved my friend away. I'd already done the "impossible" several times since the grenade. I might as well try again. I began this latest trial by leaning all my weight on one of my crutches. Then I locked the knee on one of my legs with my good hand and braced it against the floor. Jamming the other crutch against the ground, I started pushing myself upward with my arm and my stump, trying to physically lift my bulk and the wooden legs with my arms. It was working, sort of. I found myself inching higher and higher as my other leg clattered against the linoleum. It sounded like a hollow bone. My arm muscles quivered under the strain. Beads of sweat dripped off me. As soon as I was high enough off the ground, I dragged the other leg under my body and locked the knee. I was up! And it had only taken me about a minute to figure out how to do it. The swelling pride felt just like that long-ago day when I brought the first-place medal home from the state band competition. I thought of No Way Alligood getting to his woman. Now I could walk. I was good to go.

I've come to believe that a lot of recovery, both the physical side and the mental side, has to do with believing you can do it. I've seen it time and again in my life. The trick is finding the will and holding on to it even when confronted with an army of people shouting, "No way."

Something I expected to be a piece of cake proved to be the most daunting thing I faced on my new limbs—the curb at the street corner. Getting up or down a curb was a whole different ball game compared to a flight of stairs. I couldn't figure out how to do it. Obviously, I was going to have to master the curb or I would never be able to leave the hospital. It was my last obstacle before discharge. I had to conquer it. A little curb on the street just five inches high might as well have been the Great Wall of China. With the stairs, I could brace one wooden foot against the bottom of the step I was about to climb up and use the handrail, which provided more support than my crutches. That way that foot couldn't slip out from under me during that critical and vulnerable moment when I placed all my weight upon it to pull my other leg up. But the curb gave me nothing to brace against for that tricky transition, especially going down. It took six weeks for me to figure it out, and that was with Big Jon helping. Once I did, though, the world was my oyster. I was allowed to wear my legs home to my apartment. I was a proud puppy.

I spent plenty of time in front of the mirror. I'd try on different pairs of pants with my legs to see how they looked. I was like a teenager trying on outfits before a big date. I bought several pairs of new shoes as well. It was amazing the difference it made in my heart to see myself standing up again. The wheelchair was the symbol of my infirmities. In it, I was crippled, a problem, a useless lump that other people had to deal with. It wasn't so much that there were places I couldn't go in the chair; it was more that I didn't think anyone would ever see past such a glaring symbol of my handicap. But on the legs I was a man again. I could walk into a room full of ladies and be my old charming self. It was like magic. The legs turned me back into Max.

A few weeks after I'd gotten my legs, my handlers at the hospital declared that I had nothing left to learn. I was discharged to the VA Prosthetic Center in New York City. It was there that I finally got the latest in artificial limbs I had needed for so long. It was there I finally got the new plastic, laminated legs with hydraulic knees.

In December 1969, more than a year and a half after being blown up in Vietnam, I was discharged by the VA. I was headed back to my hometown in Georgia, facing the rest of my life.

★ 11 ★

The Candidate

THE FIRST THING I did after being released from daily rehab was arrange a meeting with Senator Dick Russell.

We had been friends since I first met him during my semester in Washington in the fall of 1963. He had followed my rehab closely, and kindly offered to help me any way he could. Looking back, he might have been able to help me stay in Walter Reed, though I would never have been so presumptuous as to bother him with what I considered my petty complaints. He was too important. By late 1969, Russell had been chairman of the Armed Services Committee, chairman of the Appropriations Committee, and had served in the Senate longer than anyone else on the Democratic side. He was now president pro tem of the Senate, making him third in line for the presidency after the vice president and the Speaker of the House. He had become the ultimate U.S. senator.

I wanted to pay a courtesy call on him to thank him for his concern for me during my recovery, and ask him for some personal guidance as I returned to Georgia.

By then, the *Atlanta Journal-Constitution* had published the notes I had taken during the informal briefing we had with Russell while

I was serving as a congressional intern for Georgia congressman Jim Mackay, my political mentor. The senator's remarks from 1965 looked remarkably prescient at the end of 1969. The war in Vietnam had gone to hell just as Russell had feared. During the briefing in 1965, Russell had said about Vietnam, "It is the most frustrating and complex situation ever to confront the American people. We are there, but don't want to be. We want to get out, but can't. It is one of the great tragedies of our history."

He talked about President Johnson that day as well, saying, "He knew how to use every means of persuasion known to man. He knew how to cajole and when to threaten. He knew how to handle men."

But Johnson's powers of persuasion weren't cutting it when it came to Vietnam, according to Russell. He had said that Johnson had "almost humbled himself to get the leaders in Hanoi and Peking to come to the conference table. They will not come as long as they are winning . . . and they are still winning. Vietnam is the problem that is the obsession of Washington today."

Having the senator's words published in an article with my name on it in his hometown paper cemented our friendship. Russell agreed to see me. It had been four years since I had seen him. I looked a lot different, but stood eye to eye with him, proud and tall on my new legs. I was worn out from walking the long corridors to his Senate office, but I made it. We shook hands.

His physical appearance had changed also. The old warhorse looked haggard and ashen. It took him a full minute to cross his office, a distance of about 30 feet, to greet me and say hello. He was wheezing the whole way. I didn't know it at the time, but his lungs were eaten up with emphysema. He would be dead within a year and a half.

I told him I was headed back to Georgia.

"What are you going to do when you get there?" he asked.

"I was thinking I might run for public office," I said, trying to sound casual.

He smiled.

I hadn't told anybody else I was seriously thinking of running for something. I didn't know how Russell might take it when I told him of my plans. I thought I had lost the dream of public office when I lost my legs and right arm. Who would elect anybody in that shape? But, as time went by, I thought more and more about running anyway. I wanted to live a productive life, the life of my dreams. That meant politics.

As we visited, I gazed around his office. Out of the corner of my eye, I could see photos with presidents and little models of the planes and ships he had helped win Senate approval for—all the perks of power. I remember thinking, I'd give just about anything for an office like this. The senator was tired, but I could tell he liked my plan.

Russell looked directly at me, eye to eye, and said, "That's good. Just remember to take your job seriously, not yourself."

I never forgot that piece of wisdom from one of my personal heroes.

So it was that I moved back to Georgia with nothing but my artificial legs and the good wishes of a dying man.

By early 1970, I was back in Lithonia. I was 27 years old, totally disabled, living on Social Security and VA compensation in my parents' house. I had no car, no apartment, no job, no girlfriend, and no future. My political aspirations—all my aspirations—were fast disappearing as I dealt with the reality of being a handicapped man in small-town Georgia. Sure, I could walk around on my legs, but they would only carry me so far. To really get back out there in the world, I needed a car.

As much as I was built up in the newspapers as a hometown hero, no one came forward to give me a job. It was painfully obvious to me that I was on my own. With each passing day that I sat in the living room watching TV, that desire for a job became a little more desperate.

I grew more and more frustrated. I remembered seeing pictures of FDR driving a car around Warm Springs, Georgia, when he stayed at his famous "little White House." His legs didn't work. Sure, he had one more hand than I did, but maybe something could be done for me so I could drive.

As the good Lord would have it, I met Ralph Coley around this time, another Vietnam veteran in the same boat I was in, meaning a triple amputee with no legs and one arm. But he had something I didn't—a car! It had a specially modified hand-control mechanism that allowed him to operate the gas and brake with his artificial arm.

After growing frustrated with the care at the VA hospital in Arkansas, his home state, he had transferred to the rehab facility in Warm Springs, the same facility that President Roosevelt had put together. Originally chartered to treat people with polio, the Warm Springs facility made its name helping the president but had since moved on to treating people with handicaps of all kinds. A couple of guys working in a machine shop there had equipped Roosevelt's car so he could operate it without legs. They had done the work on Ralph's hand controls too. My mother and father soon drove me to Warm Springs, 100 miles south of Atlanta. The same limb and brace shop that had installed hand controls for the president and Ralph installed mine. A system of homemade and hand-welded levers and rods connected the gas pedal and brake to a shaft on the steering column. My artificial arm fit into two holes on a steel rod. Pushing forward on the rod pushed on the brake. Pulling back on the rod activated the gas pedal. I could steer with my left hand.

Being able to drive a car was like a miracle. Since then, I have installed hand controls on every car I've owned, including the car I drive now. I've been driving for 41 years. I was amazed at the time that a couple of guys with a rudimentary machine shop could get me driving when the VA, one of the largest employers in the United States, couldn't come up with legs made of plastic for a year and a half!

Once I got wheels, there was no stopping me. I felt like a million bucks. That was the moment I finally felt rehabilitated. A car is freedom, and freedom was the primary thing I had lost in the explosion. From the moment the grenade went off until the moment I got behind the wheel for the first time, I had felt trapped—trapped in my broken body, trapped in my wheelchair, trapped forever at the mercy of others.

Driving the family car to downtown Atlanta alone for the first time was sublime. To be able to walk up to the car on my artificial legs, get in, and drive myself anywhere I wanted to go made me feel like I had learned to fly. I went to bars, parties, anywhere and everywhere. I was especially partial to drive-in movies and drive-through eateries. Soon I was ready to buy a car of my own. I used a $2,700 onetime car allowance from the VA to make a down payment on a gold Oldsmobile Toronado with front-wheel drive. The car allowance was something created to help veterans get back on their feet after service in World War II. Back then, $2,700 would pay for a car outright. The onetime grant went to disabled veterans who had lost their legs, or lost use of their legs. The VA and Congress somehow never got around to raising the allowance during the ensuing 30 years, one more example of an agency and a country that was out of touch with the needs of newly wounded combat veterans.

Even with the wheels, I was no closer to getting a job. Sitting in my parents' living room for the rest of my life collecting my VA check and a Social Security disability check sounded like living death. I was only 27 years old. I still wanted a real life.

That was the thing that pushed me into running for public office. Running, even without legs, was at that time my only option for a job. I still wanted to be elected to the Congress, but it seemed out of my reach then. The Republicans were in charge in Washington and an incumbent Republican was deeply entrenched in my congressional district.

I looked at other options for a race.

Using my old precinct analysis techniques from my time in Mac-kay's campaign, I researched the local races in my neck of the woods. Mackay had lost his seat in Congress just before I went to Vietnam, providing me with an early lesson in political warfare—savor every victory, for it may be your last. His seat had gone firmly Republican in the election of 1968, when Nixon's tidal wave swept across the country and put an end to the idealism of the '60s.

I began to focus on a state senate seat that covered my district in Lithonia. The seat was held by a one-term Republican, but the vote totals from the 1968 election showed that he had barely scraped by on Nixon's coattails. I drove myself through the different neighborhoods in the district and found it was pretty mixed in terms of class, race, and income. The seat was "marginal" in the sense that it did not lean heavily Republican or Democratic. Much like the Fourth Congres-sional District I had analyzed for Mackay, it had an urban left flank, a fat suburban middle, and a rural right flank. My town, Lithonia, was a small city in the rural part of the district. I figured if I could take the urban areas and the small towns, and split the middle suburbanites, I would win. The trick, of course, would be getting people to vote for a disabled Vietnam veteran they had never heard of.

In April 1970, two years to the month after I had been wounded, I told my parents I was running as a Democrat for the state senate against an incumbent Republican. The odds were against me, but I didn't care. It felt so good to be finally moving on from a year and a half of recovery. I was getting my life back on track.

I had no Democratic primary opposition, since Democrats basi-cally conceded the district to Republicans after '68. That meant I was automatically on the November ballot, which I considered tan-tamount to being halfway to victory. I set up my campaign office in the den of my parents' house. I used the house phone, kept my own calendar, and ran the campaign myself. I wrote everything on little 3 x 5 cards while sitting at my mother's desk.

Somebody had given me a framed copy of a quotation attributed to Calvin Coolidge, although I can't believe he was smart enough to have said it. I kept it above my desk the entire campaign. It read:

> *Nothing in this world can take the place of persistence. Talent will not; nothing is more common than unsuccessful men with talent. Genius will not; unrewarded genius is almost a proverb. Education will not; the world is full of educated derelicts. Persistence and determination alone are omnipotent. The slogan "Press on" has solved and always will solve the problems of the human race.*

The quote resonated with me because that was all there was left for me to do, press on. "Press on" was also the motto on our company flag in Vietnam. So I pressed on, despite obstacles and opposition at every turn. I put on my artificial limbs and drove myself around town asking for donations. I raised a total of $10,000, which enabled me to buy the first-ever batch of "Cleland, State Senate" signs. Pretty soon I graduated to bumper stickers.

One of the best ways for me to campaign was the old-fashioned Southern tea party. Standing on my limbs for more than a few minutes at a time was tough, and hurt more and more the longer I stayed on them. That meant that going door to door and shaking hands at the grocery store were techniques that weren't going to work for me. I didn't want to be wincing as I tried to give people my campaign pitch. Teas and coffees put on by hosts in their homes became my way of communicating to people and campaigning. The hosts would invite their neighbors and I would be the entertainment.

I held my first political event in the spring of 1970. It was a tea at the home of a woman I knew. She invited her friends over to meet me. I showed up wearing a coat and tie and walking tall on my legs. I remember my stumps were already sore and raw from campaigning that morning when I sat down among the women. I talked. I answered questions. I did my best to charm them out of their votes. Things seemed to be going pretty well. Then someone asked me about the war in Vietnam.

My opposition to the war had grown in proportion to the increasing death there. I had seen the casualties pouring into Walter Reed after I was wounded and said to myself, Stop this insanity. But Nixon was only continuing it, expanding the war by invading Cambodia. He was trying to play George Patton, and I was angry.

"We're losing our ass to save our face," I replied forcefully. The sweet middle-aged woman who had asked the question winced and put her hand to her mouth in shock.

Oops!

These were small-town, churchgoing women meeting a young politician and veteran at a friend's house and they were scandalized to hear such language. No one talked to these ladies that way. Not only that, they were the sort of people who supported the military through thick and thin. I sounded like a turncoat to them. They started clucking at each other right away. The hostess was mortified. She burst into tears and said I had embarrassed her and used foul language in her home. She asked me to leave. She was right, of course. My mouth had become unconscionably dirty after three and a half years in the army and a year in VA facilities. My anger and frustration just came out there at the tea party. Now I was afraid I'd already cost myself the race.

So, as soon as I got home from my first political event, I sat down and wrote a letter of apology to everybody who was there. That's how I got started in politics. My first event was a complete bust, but I went on to have similar tea and coffee parties in all 24 precincts in the district. I didn't cuss at any of them. And, I left the subject of Vietnam alone. I had learned my lesson. Unfortunately, like too many politicians, I also learned how to hide my true feelings for political gain.

No one I talked to thought I would win. I knew I was a long shot, but the campaign made me feel alive. It was the first real-life nonrehab activity I had had since the war. I felt like I was at least stepping back into the stream of life, putting myself out there where chance and fortune might find me.

One of the people who helped me politically was a young peanut farmer from Plains, Georgia, who won the Democratic primary for governor that year. Jimmy Carter and I would both appear on the general election ballot as Democrats. I'd never met him, seen him, or really even heard of him, but he had a little buzz going in 1970.

The Carter campaign saw me as an asset in my home county. Lithonia was located in the second-largest county in the state, and I was a wounded Vietnam veteran. I was invited to introduce Jimmy Carter at a campaign rally near Lithonia. I really didn't know anything about him. I certainly didn't think he had a chance to win. So when I introduced him at the campaign rally, I didn't give the normal, rousing sort of buildup his staffers were expecting. I told the audience that Carter had taken his campaign to the people and that he sought to restore trust in government. I said I admired him and that we needed leaders in America who trusted the people. Then I barked, "Now, ladies and gentlemen, Jimmy Carter." I should have introduced him as "the next governor, Jimmy Carter." But I didn't. I didn't think he could win. Plus, I was fond of the candidate he was running against, former governor Carl Sanders, and was thinking I might back him instead of Carter.

Carter seemed to me like a good ole farm boy, not a governor. He gave one of the most god-awful political speeches I had ever heard. It was dry, boring, and hardly the sort of thing that would make you excited to vote for him. He had zero stage presence. If you told me he would be president six years after that rally, I would have laughed in your face.

I was dead surprised when he won the office of governor. He had none of the poise or gravitas of Dick Russell or Herman Talmadge, the two senators I had met. He's always credited the fact that he shook over 400,000 hands in 1970 with delivering the victory. Perhaps that was the ticket.

Over the years, however, as I've gotten to know Jimmy Carter, I've come to discover his magic. He has a smile and a personal touch that pull you in. In small groups, he is devastatingly charming. He makes you feel like you matter. Jimmy Carter is totally sincere, honest, and loyal. He genuinely cares about people. These qualities carried him to the Governor's Mansion in Georgia, the White House, and the Nobel Peace Prize.

As for my campaign, I was terrified waiting for the results on election night. I had poured every hope and dream into the campaign, and I didn't have a backup plan if I lost.

We had a party in Lithonia to wait for voting returns. Just about everybody I'd ever known growing up came. Back then, it was always a little bittersweet for me seeing the people I'd known all my life. It was the worst with the mothers of my childhood friends. They'd tell me I looked great, sometimes with a little catch in their voice or even a tear in the corner of their eye. I'd thank them and ask about their loved ones. But every time, such meetings served to remind me of the yawning chasm between what I had once been and what I had become. I knew I was the embodiment of their deepest fears, of the worst that might befall their own children in the big, wide world.

I stood on my artificial legs for five hours straight that night. It was the longest I had stood up to that point. It was important to me that everyone at the rally see me as an able-bodied man standing on his own. I made a point of greeting everybody who came to the reception. This was it. This was everything.

When the returns showed that I had won, I was stunned into silence. I had a friend who played in the band at the Playboy Club in Atlanta. He brought the whole group to the reception. We danced and hollered for hours. I was somebody! I was State Senator Max Cleland! I felt like I had come back from the dead.

★ 12 ★

State Senator

I WASN'T FULLY sure what got me elected as the youngest member of the state senate at the age of 28 with 57.5 percent of the vote, but I wasn't about to look a gift horse in the mouth. I was the only Vietnam veteran in the upper house of the state legislature.

The senate is housed in the Georgia State Capitol, a fabulous edifice built after the Civil War and capped with a dome covered in gold leaf mined from the mountains of north Georgia. Gazing up at the glistening dome as I pulled up for my first day at work, I felt like I was going to Oz.

During his four years as governor, Jimmy Carter and I struck up a friendship that has lasted a lifetime. There was no way to know in the early '70s that my friendship with him would carry me all the way back to the Oval Office. In those early years, I came to admire his courage, his integrity, and his tenacity in going after the things he believed in. He is the second most intense man I've ever met, just slightly more relaxed than Bobby Kennedy. The younger Kennedy was wound tight as a drum, totally focused on whatever he was doing. Carter was like that too. He just talked a little slower than RFK, thanks to his thick south-Georgia drawl.

When Carter won the governorship in 1970, the outgoing governor, Lester Maddox, was elected lieutenant governor. That set up a battle royal between Carter and Maddox. Whereas Carter had courted the black vote as part of his winning coalition, Lester Maddox was famous for wielding an ax handle, a symbol of segregation, as he marched around his restaurant in Atlanta. He also campaigned for governor carrying the ax handle, a pretty charged message when set against the backdrop of the newly passed civil rights acts of 1964 and 1965.

Maddox presided over the state senate, of which I was a freshman member. In those days, the lieutenant governor, if he played his cards right, could stymie a governor completely, even to the point of just about running the state. Maddox understood that fully and cozied up to the power structure in the senate right away. Good ole boys still ran things in the state capitol and Maddox became their number one boy.

He and the senate's old guard went after Carter relentlessly. Maddox opposed Carter's plan to reorganize state government. He opposed Carter's support for an expansion of Atlanta's bus system, and the creation of its subway system. He opposed a planning mechanism to manage the rapid growth of Atlanta. If Carter was for it, Maddox was against it.

Soon it came to a showdown. There were a number of us in the state senate who were sick of Maddox's dictatorial ways. The only hope we had was to change the rules of the senate so the lieutenant governor could not appoint the members of the various committees or the chairpeople of those committees. So long as Maddox had those powers, he could completely control the legislative process. My little band of rebel senators attempted a coup, proposing new rules that would have stripped the former governor of his senate powers. We lost, and badly.

Maddox consigned us to the basement of the capitol. All our desks were removed from our normal offices on the second and third floors and taken to the basement. We were dumped together in an open area that had formerly been the capitol stables and given one secretary to share between 24 senators. This was political Siberia. Ironically, in this same area of the capitol basement, there was a group of offices set aside for the governor's staff. Unbeknownst to me, Young Turks like Hamilton Jordan and Jody Powell were already planning Jimmy Carter's run for the presidency, even though it would be four years away. I became friends with those guys, unwittingly stumbling onto the ground floor of the future Carter administration.

The first thing I did in the senate was to team up with a fellow Vietnam veteran who was over on the house side. His name was Walt Russell, Senator Dick Russell's nephew. He was also the hero of Pork Chop Hill during the Korean War. In the movie *Pork Chop Hill,* Lieutenant Russell, played by Rip Torn, leads the relief effort and rescues everyone. Years later, Walt was wounded in Vietnam. He took a machine-gun round in his head. Half of his body was paralyzed. He was elected to the state house from my home county of DeKalb the same year I was.

He saw the Vietnam War the same way I did. It had to end. We put forth a resolution that called for the withdrawal of American ground forces in exchange for our POWs. This was in 1971, when Nixon was still riding high and still pouring men into the meat grinder of Vietnam. I knew the war was going south fast, as did the majority of the people in the country. By then I believed the only thing we could really get out of Vietnam were our prisoners of war.

Our resolution passed the senate. Of course, we knew it would have no effect on the war itself, but it did generate a bit of hate mail for me. I even got a call from the local VFW post commander, who shouted into the phone, "Cleland, your political career is over!"

But what we had proposed was exactly the same deal that Kissinger worked out two years later in 1973. More than 9,000 men died between when we submitted our bill and when Kissinger worked out the exit.

For my next bill, I proposed that all buildings being built with public money in Georgia be made handicapped-accessible. This was pretty radical stuff in the early '70s. It was years before the Americans with Disabilities Act was made federal law. My bill was one of the first of its kind in the nation and served as one of the models for the federal law. I was honored to have Jimmy Carter sign it into law in 1972.

Midway through my first term, Senator Dick Russell died of emphysema at Walter Reed. They brought his body back to Georgia, where he lay in state at the capitol. I stood my watch as an honor guard, sitting in my wheelchair next to the casket for a few hours. President Nixon flew down to pay his respects to Russell at the capitol. When it was my turn to shake his hand, I was so excited that I clutched his hand much harder than I meant to. A reporter from a local paper was at the occasion and printed a story that described how my handshake had caused the president to visibly wince.

My own reelection campaign was gearing up at the time. I had some decisions to make.

One day, one of my dear friends, a lady I had known for a long time, noticed how much my artificial legs were bothering me. I explained why I thought it was important that I wear them, all that stuff about standing eye to eye and not being seen as a man without legs.

"Max, honey, we all know you don't have legs anymore and we love you anyway. You don't need those things."

In truth, I wasn't sure how much longer I could wear them. I'd been using the legs for three years, and the pain came quicker each time I wore them. I had long since quit wearing them when I went to the capitol for work. In fact, I seldom wore them if I could avoid it. Essentially, they came out for public appearances or nights on the town. As it came time to campaign, I dreaded the hours I'd have to spend in my legs. I'd bleed. I'd ache. I'd be miserable.

I made a decision.

"I'm running without my legs," I told my parents at the dinner table. They knew how the legs wore me out. They could see the pain etched in my face with every step. I had become somewhat expert at hiding the grimace, but mothers always know.

Mine did.

In truth, the legs had been a psychic crutch for me. When I wore them, I could imagine that I was almost whole. I believed my legs elicited less pity than the wheelchair. Campaigning without them for the first time was very scary. I felt absolutely naked. Going up to a potential voter in a grocery store in my wheelchair, holding out my left hand, and saying, "I'm Max Cleland and I'm running for the state senate," took every bit of courage I could muster. I couldn't have felt more vulnerable if I hadn't been wearing a stitch of clothing. I had no confidence whatsoever, and was shaking as I reached out to grab that first hand.

Nobody in those days really knew me. I'd say my name and people would say, "Who?"

Campaigning for reelection was tough. I was terrified of losing, of being rejected at the polls. Nixon was at the top of the Republican ballot and I was running in a Republican county. I put out a campaign brochure touting the things I had done during my two-year term. That was the main media, along with billboards. Billboards had helped me the first time in 1970. That's when I met Ted Turner, then just a young Atlanta businessman with a few radio stations and a billboard company. Ted offered me six billboards for next to nothing and told me I could take my pick of locations. We've been good friends ever since.

When the results came down, Nixon swept my district, Georgia, and the nation. I was narrowly reelected, but I knew it was time to move on. After two more years battling it out with Lester and his boys, I was ready to move up politically, or get out of the game altogether. The state senate had been a great training ground, but I could tell I was going nowhere fast. Georgia and the country seemed to be swinging harder to the right as Middle America tired of hippies and the antiwar movement.

I decided to run for lieutenant governor in '74. Carter was limited to one term by Georgia's archaic term-limit system in place at the time, so Maddox was running for governor again, thus leaving the lieutenant governor spot open. The race seemed winnable, so I announced. Almost immediately, one of Maddox's protégés, Zell Miller, announced his intent to run. Zell had been Maddox's executive secretary when Maddox was governor, and would ultimately become a U.S. senator. Miller ended up winning the 1974 race for lieutenant governor; I came in third in a field of 10 in the Democratic primary, missing out on a runoff by one percent. I thought my political career was over. What was I to do now?

Back in my parents' home in early 1975, I tried to figure things out. Being a defeated candidate for lieutenant governor didn't magically result in job offers. It seemed I was right back where I was after I got out of the hospital—in my parents' living room looking for work.

I thought, How could God be so cruel as to save me on the battle-fields of Vietnam, help me endure unimaginable pain and misery for two years, see me get elected to my chosen profession, and then yank away the one bright spot in my life?

I lost the race, but I hadn't lost everything. I hadn't lost my home, because I was living with my parents. I wasn't engaged or married, so I hadn't lost a fiancée or a wife. I hadn't lost my precious car. I had lost a political race. I cried a little, but that was it. I decided to get on with my life any way I could. I called Senator Alan Cranston out in California and offered to volunteer for his reelection effort. His campaign flew me out to the West Coast and put me to work introducing him at various campaign events aimed at veterans. We had kept in touch in the years after my testimony before his committee, and he was glad to have my help.

A few weeks after he kept his seat, his office offered me a job on his staff. I was to visit and inspect VA hospitals around the country and report back to the Senate Veterans' Affairs Committee.

On March 2, 1975, I put everything I owned into the back of my gold Oldsmobile Toronado and set out for Washington, D.C. Mother made me some pimento cheese sandwiches and a thermos of iced tea for the drive. I was driving through a rainstorm along a dark stretch of Interstate 95 in Virginia. Everything began to close in on me. I felt the familiar arms of depression and grief reaching out for me. I should be happy, I told myself. I was headed for a job making $12,500 a year, more money than I'd ever made in my life. I was going to be working in a U.S. Senate office at a job I was more qualified to do than almost anyone else. I was going to be in a position to shine a light on all the dark corners of the VA. I didn't have any reason to be sad.

But as the miles ticked by, not a car in sight, the sadness of my life just washed over me. I started crying, then sobbing. It was like everything that had happened since the grenade exploded welled up all at once. All my travels, all those flights around the world, all the military stuff, all the operations, all the pain, and all the things I would never do again overwhelmed me for the first time since I left the netherworld of hospital life five years earlier. For the first time in a long while, I found myself wanting to pray. The unconditional faith of my childhood, a faith born in a lifetime of Sunday school and church, had vanished. I thought God had turned his back on me. As I cried, I reached out and asked God to forgive me and help me. I knew my life was all played out. I had come to the end of my string. I had nowhere else to turn. There was nothing inside me but bitterness at my lot. Driving through a blinding rain, my hook clamped on to the hand controls of my car, I whispered out into the darkness, "God help me."

I meant it.

And he did.

The next day was Sunday. I was staying with the Buices, my god-parents, while I looked for a place in Washington. They invited me to go to church with them. I was ready. They said I'd feel right at home because we were going to hear a minister who was a Southern Baptist preacher from Georgia.

Oh no, I thought. The last thing I need is hellfire and damnation. I've had all the hellfire one man can stand. I need some love. I went with them anyway. Much to my surprise, the minister's prayers touched me. I don't remember the sermon. I remember the prayers. More specifically, I remember the loving, gentle way in which they were prayed. That was what I needed. Love and gentle acceptance.

I went back to that church every week for the next six years. I sat in the front row, the sinners' bench, I called it, with this elderly man, Zack Massey. He became a great friend. If I fell asleep, he'd lock his arm through mine so I wouldn't topple forward, smash my face on the floor, and embarrass myself. Ever since, that's been one of my measures of friendship: someone who sits next to you in church and holds you up if you fall asleep.

My job with Cranston turned out to be wonderful. I loved being a part of the Senate. And I loved being back in the swing of things in the nation's capital. I found a girlfriend shortly after I got to Washington. We had a lot of fun kicking around town, and it did wonders for my general well-being. I liked her, but periodically she would go through spells of heavy drinking, which was starting to take a toll on the rest of her life, professionally and personally. My own drinking, while not nearly in the same class as hers, wasn't doing me any favors either.

One night, she invited me to go to an open Alcoholics Anonymous meeting. We sat and listened while everybody told their stories. They talked openly and intimately about what was going on in their lives, the things that were getting them down. These people were hurting, and they were talking about it. It was a remarkable thing to me. I had never been in such an honest situation.

It felt good to listen to other people who were struggling with crosses of their own. No one was quite like me, but everyone was supportive and warm. I felt like I was among friends that first night. It was clear to me that I was taking to the program better than my girlfriend was. Eventually we split up. She continued to have her fight with alcohol, but I quit drinking that year, 1975. I ended up going to Al-Anon meetings, which is the counterpart of AA for friends and family, for about two and a half years. For the first time since leaving Walter Reed, I found real friends who could help me deal with everything that was going on in my life. It was the first "counseling" I had received since the war. It helped me just to be able to give voice to all that was going on inside me. The program provided a sense of fellowship and grounding as I worked through the twelve steps with people who cared about me. I made amends to some people that I needed to make amends to. But most of all, I tried to make amends to myself. Forgiving myself was the biggest challenge. My decision to extend my service so I could go to Vietnam, my desire to see combat, the individual decisions that led up to the grenade explosion, all of that had gnawed at my soul for the last eight years. I had no one to blame but myself, so that's what I had been doing. For me, the Twelve Step program was an exercise in dealing with grief, massive loss, and a soul in chaos.

One day, sitting in the Senate Veterans' Affairs Committee hearing room, I heard that Saigon had fallen. That's it, I thought. The war is over. No more excuses. No more bullshit press releases from the president touting victories that don't exist. No more of the ridiculous "Five O'Clock Follies" military briefings from Saigon. No more "Peace with honor."

It was just over.

Finally.

A history of the Vietnam War written by Neil Sheehan called *A Bright Shining Lie* captures the war in a nutshell. With each passing

year, it has seemed more and more meaningless to me. I once heard
General Hal Moore—who with Joe Galloway wrote about his experience in Vietnam in a book entitled *We Were Soldiers Once . . . and
Young*—say quietly to a small group that Vietnam would have turned
out the same way "had we not lost a man." That was so very powerful
for me to hear. It's the way I feel about the war too.

The sense of meaninglessness came home powerfully to me in the
early '70s when I saw Senator Edmund Muskie on television. He said,
"We must come to the conclusion that Vietnam has been a mistake."

What do you mean, a mistake? Where's the meaning? Where's the
purpose? What does that do to a guy like me, who lost so much? What
does it do to all those who lost so much in Vietnam? Those are questions I'll be trying to answer for the rest of my life.

I once asked my mother why I hadn't grown up, gotten married,
and had kids like everyone else.

She said, "Son, your life was interrupted." After World War I,
20 million people were dead. Gertrude Stein described *le génération
perdue*—the Lost Generation. F. Scott Fitzgerald wrote that the world
had "grown up to find all Gods dead, all wars fought, all faiths in man
shaken." That was how I felt after my war. All the political theories
were empty; American diplomacy was dead. For me, Vietnam meant
loss: lost legs, lost arm, lost youth, lost innocence, lost war. Those of
us who fought there were victims of history, just like the soldiers in
Iraq today.

★ 13 ★

To Care for Him Who Has Borne the Battle

JIMMY CARTER WAS the only president during the Vietnam era with a son who served in the war. None of the men who put America on the battlefield—Eisenhower, Kennedy, Johnson, or Nixon—had such a personal stake in the battle, although Lyndon Johnson had a son-in-law who served as a marine officer there. Johnson's son-in-law, Chuck Robb, later became governor of and U.S. senator from Virginia.

Carter had been a submarine commander in the navy. A graduate of the U.S. Naval Academy, he understood the trauma that the Vietnam War had brought to a generation of young American men.

He wanted to help them heal. He had campaigned on that promise.

In keeping with that, I was Carter's first official appointment as president on Inauguration Day. He had been in office for exactly five hours and 20 minutes. As I wheeled across the carpet bearing the Great Seal of the United States toward Carter behind his desk, I realized it was *the* desk, the same desk I had seen in Kennedy's Oval Office so many years before.

"This is only my second time in the Oval Office, sir," I said, feeling faint with excitement that my friend was now the most powerful man in the world.

The president flashed that famous grin and replied, "It's only my second time too."

A few days after Jimmy Carter was elected in 1976, Senator Alan Cranston sent him a letter suggesting he appoint me head of the Veterans Administration. I was just 34 years old. The biggest thing I'd ever been in charge of was a platoon of 50 guys in Vietnam. The VA, in contrast, was one of the biggest bureaucracies in Washington, with 226,000 employees in 1976. There were 172 hospitals, 106 national cemeteries, and 81 nursing homes and outpatient clinics within the VA system. Just seven years prior to being considered for the top job at the agency, I had been at the absolute bottom of the system as a triple amputee. The experience was still fresh in my mind. The memories of my time in that hospital were not fond.

Despite that, I told the president that I was thrilled to be nominated for the job. I felt like I had worked my way up the chain and earned the right to try to fix the agency. I understood being severely wounded in combat. After a year in VA hospitals and rehab facilities, I knew what soldiers needed to recover, and I knew where the system was lacking. I had worked as a staff member on the Senate Veterans' Affairs Committee for a year and a half investigating VA hospitals. On top of that, I knew the key players in the Carter administration, and they knew me. Carter was elected just two years after I left the Georgia senate. Jody Powell and Hamilton Jordan, who became my friends after Lester Maddox relegated me to the political Siberia of the capitol basement, were now Carter's press secretary and chief of staff, respectively. I honestly believed that I was the best man the president could have picked.

It was time for the nation to focus on the new veterans coming back from Vietnam, and to fix a broken bureaucracy. For instance, in the years before I arrived, the VA had a 43 percent error rate in the computer system for the millions of checks sent every year to veterans on the GI Bill. Imagine a system that had a 43 percent error rate! On top of that, the hospital system was drastically short on nursing personnel. A *Life* magazine exposé in 1970 revealed deplorable conditions at a VA hospital in the Bronx. Images of paralyzed veterans fighting to recover amid slime and rats caused a national scandal. The magazine even ran an image of a dead rat caught in a trap set by a partially paralyzed patient. Ultimately, Congress appropriated money to raze that building and construct an entirely new one, which I dedicated in 1980.

Unfortunately, few in the upper echelons of management at the VA felt there was a problem. As a young whippersnapper, I ran up against a senior staff that had been there since the end of World War II. They were known as the Class of '46, because they had come to the VA as youngsters during the Truman administration. They were all about World War II and Korea. They had not dealt with genuine combat casualties fresh from the battlefield since the early 1950s. I remember learning that the VA's public information shop, which was supposed to reach out to the young veterans of the early '70s, was sending out Guy Lombardo records as morale boosters. Guy Lombardo for kids like me who had been raised on rock and roll? Are you kidding?

Right away, I was seen as a kind of pariah within the VA—the smart young kid from the Vietnam War trying to tell everybody how to do their jobs. Worse still, in their minds, I only got the job because I was from Georgia, like the new president. But the main reason they disliked me involved Carter's first official act.

Jimmy Carter views the world through the lens of his religious conviction—forgiveness and love are his guiding ideals. When he made good on a campaign promise his first day in office and granted a pardon to all who had dodged and evaded the draft rather than go to Vietnam, the veterans' groups, and some of the staff within the VA, went nuts. Carter called the move a "pardon" and said it was part of the nation's reconciliation with the war. Leaders of the veterans' organizations called it "amnesty for draft dodgers" and swore to fight him every step of the way. Since I was his proxy in the VA, they took it out on me. I personally didn't have any problem with the pardon, even though I had answered the call and volunteered for duty. I could understand how people had come to a different point of view about serving and fighting in Vietnam. I was coming to a different point of view about the war myself. The pardon issue made for rough sailing for me right from the start.

"There are two dead ends in Washington," a friend from the U.S. State Department once told me. "They are the VA and the Bureau of Indian Affairs." Being head of the Veterans Administration was not considered a choice appointment by Washington standards. And it's true: It's pretty much a thankless task. But I wasn't doing it to get thanked. I was doing it because I thought I could help.

There is a great legend about how General Omar Bradley got the job of heading the VA under Truman. Bradley, known as the soldier's general, was still on active duty in 1945, fresh from leading the D-Day assaults in France, when Truman appointed him. The president said he wanted him to take care of the soldiers he led in battle. Later a Missouri politician asked Truman, "Why didn't you give that VA job to a good Democrat?"

"I wouldn't do that to a good Democrat," Truman responded blithely.

But for me, leading the VA was a moral obligation, a spiritual calling almost. Etched in stone on the front of the VA headquarters is a magnificent quote from Abraham Lincoln's second inaugural address. It is the mission statement for the VA. It reads simply, "To care for him who shall have borne the battle and for his widow, and his orphan."

I believed I had been saved to do just that—to care for those who have "borne the battle."

First, I had to battle for a decent budget. No matter how many congressmen yelled, "Support the troops!" at the top of their lungs, the VA always ended up a redheaded stepchild at budget time. The wreckage of all of this country's foreign policy mistakes winds up on the VA's doorstep—yet in wartime, the VA is usually the last agency to get funded. It should be first, but the Department of Defense is always at the head of the line. Wars fought with jets and tanks and million-dollar missiles provide a dramatic need for funding. Broken soldiers lying in hospitals don't.

The Johnson administration did not plan or budget for the massive casualties coming out of the Vietnam War. No one expected 350,000 wounded. Yet, like a tidal wave, those men and women wound up on the VA's doorstep during and after the war. Three and a half million young Americans served in Southeast Asia during the Vietnam War. Nine million young Americans served during the Vietnam era, which lasted from August 4, 1964, until May 1975. All nine million of those people earned the right to a lifetime of health care from the VA, and they started rolling through the door by the millions on my watch.

There was a push, beginning with some of the doctors within the VA, to label and treat long-term mental trauma resulting from war. They were calling the problem post-traumatic stress disorder (PTSD). When I started hearing talk of emotional disorders brought on by the stresses of combat, I was a believer. Hell yes, I thought. Combat can traumatize you. Living on hyperalert with the knowledge that death is imminent, as soldiers do, takes a toll. Seeing death firsthand takes a toll. Killing takes a toll. I had seen the empty eyes of those doctors and nurses in Vietnam. I had heard the boys in the Snake Pit wake screaming from war dreams. I had had such dreams myself. Sometimes those visions of horror came even when you were awake. It was the VA's responsibility to treat all the changes war wreaked on those who had borne the battle—whether mental or physical.

Every one.

In 1978, psychiatrists in the VA finally admitted to themselves and to their fellow professionals that there was, indeed, something called post-traumatic stress disorder. That year, PTSD became an official psychiatric diagnosis in the VA. For the first time ever, such a diagnosis meant you could get combat-related disability pay even if you came back without visible wounds.

As for me, I never once thought I had any kind of PTSD problems back then. I was clicking along like gangbusters. I was head of the VA. I was attending cabinet meetings by executive order of the president and developing relationships with the top leaders of our country. I was running the VA and trying to help all these other poor guys who were all screwed up. I didn't think I had any sort of problems at all.

I was dead wrong. The excitement of a cabinet-level position during those turbulent days thrilled me, but I was also eaten up with stress. It began to manifest itself in subtle ways. I felt an increasing sense of concern about my personal safety. I would double-check the door locks in my apartment repeatedly and study the knobs on the stove again and again to make sure they were all off. On occasion, these little routines made me late for work. Looking back, I can see that that feeling of imminent danger, even in my own home, was one of the first manifestations of my PTSD. I was feeling the first flush of a condition now known as obsessive-compulsive disorder (OCD), which is part of the suite of symptoms commonly seen in combat veterans. From time to time, my OCD still crops up today, though I've become much better at coping with it over the years. It is another invisible scar left inside me by war.

On my recommendation, President Carter agreed to push Congress to fund a new psychological readjustment counseling program for the VA. Senator Cranston had been fighting for years for such a program, modeled after storefront counseling centers that popped up in communities all over California during and after the war.

In pushing for the counseling clinics—what we decided to call Vet Centers—we ran up against some resistance in Congress. Olin "Tiger" Teague, a World War II hero and one of the most decorated soldiers to ever serve in Congress, was chairman of the House Veterans' Affairs Committee. He once referred to Vietnam veterans as "crybabies." There was a lot of that same sentiment even within the VA, especially among the Class of '46. We fought through it, and in 1980, with the help of President Carter and Senator Cranston, we launched the new Vet Center program. Because Vietnam veterans were so alienated from the VA by then, we disguised the Vet Centers as just another community outreach program. In those days, the term "VA" did not appear on any of the Vet Center literature or on the signs in front of the clinics, although all the centers and their staff were funded by the VA.

I opened the first Vet Center in America in Van Nuys, California, on a beautiful, clear day in 1980. Since then, over 200 Vet Centers have been added to the system. The need is only increasing. Veterans from the Iraq War and Afghanistan are pouring into the Vet Centers already. Often they provide just what struggling veterans need most, a place to talk with people who understand what they've been through. Their creation is one of the things I am most proud of.

The day after Jimmy Carter lost to Ronald Reagan in 1980, I got one call of thanks for being head of the VA from a midlevel staffer in the American Legion. That was it. The Reagan White House gave me the boot on February 25, 1981. My tour of duty as the youngest VA chief and its first Vietnam veteran was over.

I was on my way back home to Lithonia, again. I was unemployed, again. And like my earlier return to my parents' home, I had no apartment, no money, no job offers, no future, and no girlfriend.

The VA had been a dead end, after all. But I had done what I could do. To this day, my time as VA chief is the public service I cherish most.

★ 14 ★

A Job for Life

AFTER I GOT my marching orders from the Reagan administration, an old friend from my Stetson University days came and moved my furniture out of my one-bedroom apartment in D.C., and dropped it off in my father's basement in Lithonia. I was spent by the time I got back to Georgia. The last year of the Carter administration had been an exercise in frustration. Bad news kept getting worse—the Iran hostage crisis, a tanking economy, the energy crunch. None of those things were really in my bailiwick as VA head, but the way Washington works, if you're on a team that is in trouble, then you are in trouble too. As Carter lost clout with Congress, his ability to help me push for changes at the VA essentially disintegrated.

There were plenty of things I wasn't going to miss about the job itself, but the perks had been grand. The president had been particularly gracious to me during my time in his administration, inviting me to White House get-togethers and strategy powwows. I loved rubbing elbows with history.

Back in Georgia, however, eating pimento cheese sandwiches with my mother in the kitchen, it was like none of that had ever happened. I was right back where I started from before the VA, before I was a

135

state senator. I was an unemployed triple amputee with no prospects. Once again, politics seemed like my only option for finding a fulfilling job. Public service was the only thing I had ever known, and since the days of JFK's presidency, it was the only thing I had ever really cared about.

I began to think about running again—this time for the office of Georgia secretary of state. While I was in the state senate in the early 1970s, I had gotten to know Georgia's venerable secretary of state Mr. Ben Fortson. Everybody just called him "Mr. Ben." He had served as secretary of state since World War II and had been confined to a wheelchair most of his adult life due to an automobile accident in his youth. I can still remember seeing Mr. Ben rolling around the capitol pushing his wheelchair with both hands. It was one of those old-fashioned, high-back chairs straight out of the nineteenth century with a wicker back and wooden frame.

Mr. Ben was loved by everyone. He had been the number one vote-getter in Georgia for years. Around the capitol, he was thought to have "a job for life," meaning no one would ever be able to unseat him. But by the time I got back home in February 1981, Mr. Ben had passed away. The governor, George Busbee, had appointed a state employee to fill the position until the next election in 1982. That man, David Poythress, had never run for office before. While I had never won a statewide campaign before, I believed I could beat Poythress in the Democratic primary in August 1982.

Living at home with my parents again, I ran hard in 1981 and 1982, without my artificial legs. It had been years since I had worn them. I won a runoff against Poythress in the primary and beat the Republican candidate handily in the general election even though he had changed his middle name to "Reagan" on the ballot.

At the age of 40, I was elected the youngest secretary of state in Georgia's history. As the years went by, I too became the biggest vote-getter in the state, just like Mr. Ben. I appointed the first black assistant secretary of state in Georgia's history and opened up the political process by registering one million new voters. Like Mr. Ben, I kept an open-door policy in my office in the state capitol. Anybody could walk in to see me, no appointment necessary.

I won reelection in 1986 and again in 1990. During my 12 years in office as Georgia secretary of state I was able to get an apartment on my own, get a new car rigged out by the boys in Warm Springs, pay off my campaign debts, and for the first time in my adult life be generally safe, secure, and happy.

Politically, however, I was getting antsy. I was in my early fifties and feeling restless. Zell Miller had been elected governor and said he wouldn't run for a second term. I began to think seriously about taking a shot at the governorship, although, as my friends and parents often pointed out, I already had a "job for life" as secretary of state.

"Why would you risk that, Max?" was something I heard a lot.

But I wasn't another Ben Fortson. I didn't want to just wait out my years sitting in the secretary of state's office. I was itching to move on to something more challenging. Zell continued to say he wasn't going to run, so I made the necessary preparations and began planning a rally to announce my candidacy. Then I came across the first Republican dirty trick of my political career.

I liked to date beautiful women. That sounds like the beginning of many a political scandal, and it was the beginning of mine.

I was single by choice, but I loved to flirt. I stayed on good terms with my girlfriends, even after we broke up. One day a former girlfriend sent word by a male friend that I should give her a call. I did, and the conversation got pretty steamy.

Unbeknownst to me, she was working for the enemy. Two Republican men set her up with taping equipment and she recorded a phone sex conversation I had with her. Within days, the men had distributed the tape to radio, TV, and the newspaper. Copies of the tape made the rounds of the Speaker of the House's office, the governor's office, pretty much every office in the state capitol. I became the butt of jokes. The Atlanta paper did a piece and a TV station interviewed me. A local radio station interviewed me, played the tape, and asked if it was me. I said yes.

With that admission, I gave up my fledgling bid for governor. I considered dropping out of political life altogether, mostly because I was so embarrassed to be caught up in a sex scandal. I was mortified by the thought that my sweet mother was hearing the tape, never mind that it was just me and a lady on the phone. In the end, I retreated to the safety of running again for my "job for life." Even that was no sure thing in the aftermath of my stunning publicity.

The people of Georgia, however, took my side. With their votes, they showed that what a single woman and a single man did in private was their business. As a matter of fact, supporters of mine from south Georgia said it probably helped me down there. The tape had become statewide news by that point, embarrassing in the extreme, but it had an unexpected effect the Republicans hadn't counted on. It not only raised my profile in the state in a way that no amount of political advertising ever could, it also showed that I was, despite my handicaps, a full-blooded American male. Although I had been grievously wounded in Vietnam, I had not lost my sex life or the requisite machinery. The tape proved it.

Zell Miller ran for governor again. At the next general election, he was reelected governor and I was reelected secretary of state. I figured my aspirations for higher office were essentially over. I would take Mr. Ben's place as an icon in state politics. I would die as "Mr. Max." If a new door to a new political future was to open, the good Lord would have to do it.

He did.

In the fall of 1994, Sam Nunn upset the political applecart in Georgia by announcing he would not run for reelection to the U.S. Senate in 1996. I announced for his seat a week later. All along in my political career, Washington, D.C., and federal office had loomed in the background as the great dream. Congress had always interested me more than state and local government. I spent 16 years in Georgia politics, but my real love was always in the Capitol of the United States. I had never really had a shot at running for the U.S. House due to popular incumbents, but now I had a real chance at winning a seat in the Senate. The seat had been held by a Democrat for more than a century. A popular Democrat, Bill Clinton, was in the White House and would be running for reelection at the same time I would be running. I knew I would never have a better chance.

After the VA, I had promised myself that I would never go back to Washington unless it was to take Sam Nunn's seat on the Senate Armed Services Committee and look after the troops. To me, being in that slot in the Senate—which was also Dick Russell's old seat— was the ultimate coronation. Russell and Nunn had set the standard for unselfish public service, both in Georgia and the nation. Between the two of them, they had occupied that seat on the Armed Services Committee since 1933. Now someone else was going to fill it. I wanted that person to be me. I imagined myself in Russell's fabulous office, just the way I had last seen it circa 1970. In an odd way, the sex scandal that kept me from running for governor had become a blessing. If I had been in that job, I would not have been able to reach for what I considered the brass ring.

I resigned from the secretary of state's office in January 1995 and began my campaign in earnest. I hired a campaign manager, a fundraising team, a media firm, and an office staff. I ran hard for two years, clearing the field of any Democratic opposition within the state even before the primaries. Though I was the best-known and best-supported candidate in the race, Republican or Democrat, I had little support from Washington, D.C., political action committees (PACs). I guess I wasn't sexy enough.

That was too bad, because even in 1996, elections were all about money. I spent the major portion of every day locked in a "call room" dialing for dollars. My Republican opponent, Guy Millner, was a self-made multimillionaire. He was pouring millions of his own money into the race, and I was clearly going to need more money than I had. I sent out SOS calls to the PACs in Washington, but all I got was the brush-off.

"We have you on our radar screen," they'd say, but they never sent me anything. I came to hate the phrase "on our radar screen." The Democratic Senatorial Campaign Committee was really no help to me either.

I was on my own.

In the waning days of the campaign, President Clinton offered to campaign for me for a day in Georgia. I rejected my friend's generous offer. I hate to say it, but I had a feeling the president would hurt me more than help me in my conservative state. I was told that Clinton was offended.

Election Day in November 1996 was cloudy and overcast. Rain always meant deep trouble for Georgia's Democrats, as it decreased the urban voter turnout, something I was counting on.

I held my breath.

I had waited all my life for this moment. The first political event I had ever attended was a "Dick Russell for U.S. Senate" barbecue held in a Georgia pasture in 1954. If I were to win his seat, some kid might one day remember being taken to one of my rallies. It was almost too much. Even the day of the vote, it seemed almost preposterous to think that I had a fifty-fifty chance to become a U.S. senator. I felt like I was living someone else's life. The morning I saw my name on the ballot and cast my vote had the gauzy unreality of a dream.

But it was real. I had raised and spent $3.5 million, a stunning amount to someone from my humble background. Meanwhile, my Republican challenger, Guy Millner, had spent $13.5 million, most of which was his own money. He outspent me more than three and a half to one. With Millner's expenditures, the race went down as the third most expensive Senate race in American history up to that point. I had been swamped with negative TV ads. I knew the race would be close even though Millner was a political neophyte. If I lost, I would be political roadkill. And, as in every race I'd run before, I didn't have a backup plan.

Early on election night, the networks reported I was winning. My heart soared and I began to imagine that victory was possible. Then, as the night wore on, the race fell into the "too close to call" category. I started sweating. Everything I had ever dreamed of was on the line. My heart was thumping, but my fate was out of my hands. It was all I could do to master the panic and excitement swirling inside me.

By three o'clock the next morning, the race was still too close to call. My campaign manager said I should go ahead and declare myself the winner because I was slightly ahead and that might not be the case for long. I did, but it seemed more political theater than anything else. There were just a few counties in Georgia where the vote totals were still out. They all leaned Republican, and I knew it would take a miracle for my slim lead to hold up in those red counties. I left for my apartment. It looked like it was all over. As I crawled into bed at about 4:00 a.m., I tried to make peace with losing.

I tossed around for about an hour, but sleep wouldn't come. I got out of bed and made for the TV. Better to learn I had lost while I was all alone at home in my apartment than in front of anybody else. I surely didn't want to hear the news over the phone from one of my staffers. I wasn't sure I'd be able to hold it together. I turned the TV on at 5:00 a.m. and was astounded to see that I was still ahead! My heart started pumping. At the same instant, the phone rang. I almost didn't pick up. I was afraid the news on the other end would be bad.

"Congratulations, Senator." It was Jennifer Wardrep, my campaign press secretary. She was the first person to ever call me Senator. "You've won!"

"Are you sure?"

She was. The giddy rush of euphoria I felt was so intense I feared I might have a heart attack. I simply couldn't believe it. We decided to get together in a few hours and have breakfast with our small campaign team.

I hung up the phone and cried.

By breakfast time, Millner still had not conceded. My team settled in at a place called the Flying Biscuit for my idea of a victory party— eggs, bacon, and homemade biscuits with gravy. After breakfast, we got in the car and turned on a news radio station. At 9:40 a.m., Guy Millner conceded the race to me.

I was officially the new senator-elect from Georgia.

It was the biggest political victory of my life, the biggest personal victory of my life. I was numb. I was dazed at how far I had come and all I had overcome. I told my staff to get the whole team together for lunch. I wanted to celebrate.

Mary Mac's Tea Room is the most popular place in downtown Atlanta for home cooking. It's been in business since 1945 and has become famous in Georgia. I have always loved it there. I hung out in Mary Mac's a lot during my 12 years as secretary of state. The waitstaff, most of whom I knew by name, clapped when I came in. My campaign team was already there, about 20 people whooping it up as I arrived. We all hoisted glasses of iced tea for our victory and I gave a prayer for the table. I ate my fill of fried chicken, squash, mashed potatoes, collards, black-eyed peas, all my favorites. I was giddy. I had made it. All of us had made it. In January 1997, I would become the junior senator from Georgia. I was 54 years old.

Almost 30 years before, I was as close to being dead as a person can be.

After lunch, I just wanted to drive around and see the neighborhood in Atlanta where my parents lived when I was born. We passed by the old apartment building, which dated to the beginning of the twentieth century. Down the street was the newly created Jimmy Carter Library. Passing it brought back so many memories of my last time in Washington. In a strange way, I felt like I was going home by going back to Washington.

I thought of my parents and the wonderful people of my hometown. They had watched me grow up and gathered close around me when I got blown up. When the world had broken me, when I was reduced to half the man that I had been, those small-town folks donated the $10,000 that launched my political career. They resurrected me. Now, here I was, leaving home again to go to the United States Senate. I would take them with me in my heart.

I was exhausted, but thrilled out of my mind. Little did I know that I was headed for the most trying time of my life.

★ 15 ★

A Splendid Misery

THOMAS JEFFERSON ONCE called the presidency "a splendid misery." That's what the U.S. Senate turned out to be for me.

"A lot of people come to the U.S. Senate to make an impact on the institution only to find out that the institution makes an impact on them," observed Senator Robert C. Byrd, the great, white-haired statesman from West Virginia, in my first week as a member of that most exclusive club. Byrd had served on Capitol Hill longer than any other American, and gave our small group of incoming freshman senators an orientation to the Senate that included lessons in both history and the fine art of senatorial decorum.

As promised, the Senate did make a great impact on me from the very first day. Although I had been sworn in to important posts before—second lieutenant in the U.S. Army, Georgia state senator, head of the VA, and Georgia secretary of state—nothing moved me like being sworn in to the U.S. Senate. Being there caused me to sit taller, think straighter, and be more committed to doing my job than ever before. I remembered what Senator Russell had told me. I tried to take my job seriously but not myself.

I knew everybody would be watching—it was hard to miss the C-SPAN cameras all over the Senate. I loved everything about the institution, from the regal carpet in the great chamber itself to the dark wood paneling and the white-shirted pages scurrying to do our bidding. From time to time, I would pass by the directory of Senate offices on the wall of the lobby in the Dirksen Senate Office Building, where I had my office. I liked to look up my name to reassure myself that I was actually meant to be there.

The great American historian Robert Caro devoted an entire chapter in his Lyndon Johnson biography *Master of the Senate* to "The Desks of the Senate." Unbelievably, I was going to have one of them. Even members of the House of Lords in London do not have their own desks in the main chamber. Nor do the members of the U.S. House of Representatives. It is a senator's prerogative.

Each Senate desk is chock-full of American history. The senior senator from New Hampshire always has dibs on Daniel Webster's desk. Ted Kennedy still sits behind the desk that both his brothers used when they were members of the Senate. Tradition dictates that when you leave the Senate, you carve your name in your desk's drawer. I would often open my desk to see the names of former senators carved in it. Mine bore the whittlings of Spessard Holland of Florida, Estes Kefauver of Tennessee, Bennett Johnston Jr. of Louisiana, Dennis DeConcini of Arizona, David Pryor of Arkansas, and Henry M. "Scoop" Jackson of Washington. When Maria Cantwell won Jackson's seat, I gave her my desk as a victory present.

She loved it.

Being in a wheelchair presented interesting challenges in terms of access to the Senate floor and to the men's room off it. Initially, in order to get to my seat on the back row where the freshman Democrats sat, I had to come up the "Stennis elevator." The small, hand-operated elevator lifted former Mississippi senator John Stennis up a few steps so he could access the upper rim of the Senate floor. For about a year, I used that elevator routinely to reach my seat. One of the doorkeepers of the Senate ran the elevator for me.

The Senate rules were amended to allow a staff person from my office to push me around the Senate floor. After my first year in the Senate, a ramp was installed up the middle aisle of the Senate floor to make the area more accessible, and also to make it conform accurately to the design of the old Senate chamber, which had been turned into a museum in the Capitol.

One evening, Tom Daschle, the Democratic leader at the time, and his lovely wife, Linda, took me out to dinner. During the meal, Tom leaned across the table and asked, "What do you like best about being in the Senate?"

"Being in the Senate," I replied easily.

Tom smiled. "And what do you like least about being in the Senate?"

"Trying to stay in the Senate."

In the years I was there, the drive to win reelection never stopped. That meant I was defending myself from Republican attacks all the time, raising money all the time, and after the first year, traveling back to Georgia nearly every weekend to stay in touch with my constituents.

It all began to wear on me. I would work all week in Washington, capping many of my days with hours spent in a call room trying to drum up money via the telephone. Then, come Friday afternoon, I would rush to National Airport to try to make a Delta flight back to Georgia. Arriving in Atlanta, I would be handed a briefing book about the schedule for that weekend. Many times I was so tired I couldn't even open the briefing book. When I eventually did, I always dreaded the schedule before me. In the final couple of years going into the campaign of 2002, I did not spend a single complete weekend in Washington, D.C. I was always on the road. And that wasn't just my story. That remains the story of just about everybody in the Senate. I fear that the insidious influence of money in politics and the incessant, year-round campaigning required to hold on to power are among the greatest threats to our democracy.

That's why the first speech I made on the Senate floor in 1997 was about the corrupting influence of money on campaigns and to announce my support and cosponsorship of the McCain-Feingold campaign reform bill. Years later, after I left the Senate, the bill passed. But the law did not, by itself, change the fact that getting elected to the Senate and staying there requires a mountain of money.

The beginning of my Senate tenure was marvelous. Even though Democrats were in the minority (45–55), Bill Clinton was in the White House and drove the train. He was so masterful at stealing Republican issues and recasting them as his own, we often felt like we were the majority party. My first year in office, Clinton was riding high after beating Bob Dole by a substantial margin in the election. The economy was humming, people were working, and it seemed like he was untouchable. Nothing good lasts forever, though, and Clinton gave the Republican machine an opening soon enough. In France there is a saying, *Cherchez la femme.* That translates in English as "Look for the woman."

Clinton found one.

A young man who later worked for me in my Senate office in Georgia was in the same White House intern class as Monica Lewinsky. His name is Trey Ragsdale. After my Senate years were over in Washington, Trey told me the full and startling story of Monica and Bill.

Shortly after Trey and Monica's group of interns arrived in Washington, they started gathering at a local bar for drinks. One night, the bunch started talking about what they would most like to do while they were in the nation's capital. Some wanted to make connections for the future, some wanted to pad their résumés, some hoped to visit each of the museums that make up the Smithsonian. Monica's desire was unique among the assembled.

"I want to earn my presidential knee pads," Trey quoted Monica as saying. He was aghast.

"You can't say that, Monica! You don't really mean that, do you?" Trey sputtered in disbelief.

But Monica really and truly *did* mean it.

A short time later, Monica started to call Trey regularly for snacks in the White House mess. Trey worked in the White House itself, while Monica worked in the EOB, the old Executive Office Building next to the White House. Trey had a pass to the White House. Monica did not. She wasn't allowed into the West Wing of the White House unless someone escorted her in. She began calling Trey at least once a week, sometimes more often. The first time she came for snacks with Trey, the president made an appearance in the mess. Mysteriously, President Clinton was always there in the mess on the days Monica asked Trey to bring her for snacks. And each time, the leader of the free world visited this pair of lowly interns. After this scenario played out several times, Trey became suspicious. He ultimately came to realize he was only being used as a cover to set up meetings between Monica and the president. In effect, Trey was being used to get Monica signed in to the White House without involving anyone on the president's staff.

As they say, the rest is history. I lived through that history, but it was excruciatingly painful. When the Drudge Report broke the story of the White House assignations, it spread like wildfire around Capitol Hill. Soon the mainstream media picked it up and the Republicans had a field day. Sex in Washington was really big news. Sex in the Oval Office between a sitting president and one of his interns was literally the biggest news in the world.

Every day seemed to bring new revelations about the president's peccadilloes. The cigar, the stained dress, the kiss in the rope line—the national and international appetite for all things Bill and Monica seemed limitless. The media swarmed over the Senate press area like flies. The television cameras set up a permanent encampment in an area just off Capitol Plaza, next to where senators park their cars. The area is usually called the "Senate Swamp" because it gets muddy when it rains. But once the TV cameras were set up, with those big white reflectors designed to bounce light onto the faces of TV reporters, everyone began calling the swamp "Monica Beach," as the reflectors looked so much like beach umbrellas. It was surreal.

As Washington got bogged down in the scandal, the business of the public came to a screeching halt. The business of the Senate hit a wall. Reporters only wanted to talk about Monica and the impact of the scandal on the presidency, the Senate, the Congress, and America. It was futile to try to talk about things like unemployment or a pay increase for our troops when there was such a salacious topic ready at hand.

Ultimately, Republican Speaker of the House Newt Gingrich went after Clinton. Gingrich, the no-holds-barred, bare-knuckled brawler, had cut his teeth running for office in Georgia around the same time I had. He practiced smash-mouth politics from the beginning, and he had shown himself capable of hunting large game early in his House career. One night, with no one in the House chamber watching but the C-SPAN TV cameras, Gingrich attacked Democratic House Speaker Jim Wright from Texas on a supposed "ethics" violation regarding a book deal. At that moment, Gingrich carved out an ideology of the Republicans as "ethical" and the Democrats as "unethical" that would shift the balance of power in Washington for years.

Newt found his mark with Wright, and the Speaker was ultimately forced to resign. By 1994, with the Republican takeover of the House, Gingrich was named Speaker. With Clinton in his sights over what appeared to be a stunning lapse of both ethics and common sense, Newt went for a bill of impeachment in the House just before the State of the Union address in January 1998.

The night of the speech, Monica Beach was aglow with klieg lights and Congress was atwitter with dirty jokes. The tension was palpable

Basketball was my favorite sport in high school. In 1960, my
senior year, I was the team's leading scorer.

A break from the action in Vietnam with the 1st Air Cavalry Division, 1967.

As a platoon leader in 1967 with Sergeant Pete Green.

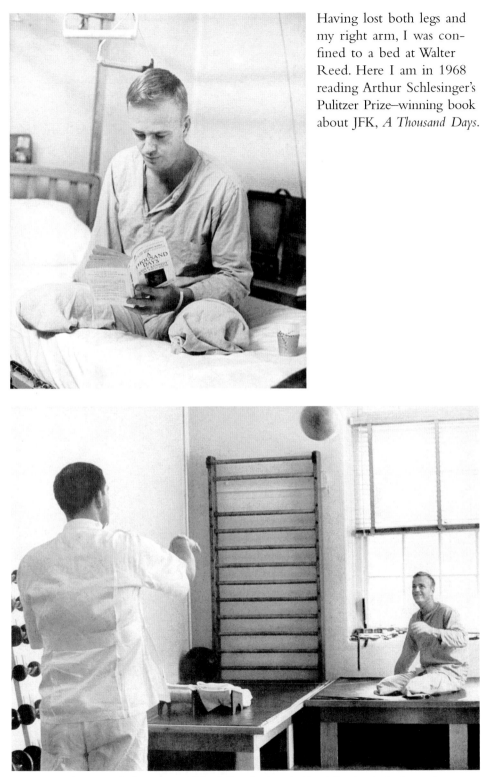

Having lost both legs and my right arm, I was confined to a bed at Walter Reed. Here I am in 1968 reading Arthur Schlesinger's Pulitzer Prize–winning book about JFK, *A Thousand Days*.

Learning how to balance myself while playing ball with physical therapist Steve Miller at Walter Reed in 1968.

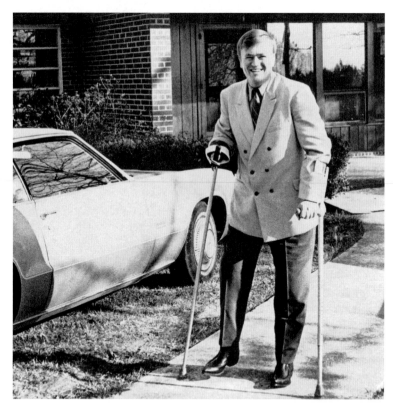

Campaigning for the Georgia senate on my artificial limbs in 1970, my first political race as a candidate. I am about to get in my car in front of my parents' home.

President Carter gave me a hug at our first Veterans Day ceremony at Arlington National Cemetery in Washington, D.C., after he appointed me Administrator of Veterans Affairs in 1977.

With my parents, Hughie and Juanita Cleland, at the VA headquarters in Washington, D.C., in 1977. I was the youngest head of the agency and its first Vietnam veteran.

Surrounded by campaign signs at a rally during my Senate reelection effort in 2002. I ran harder than ever to hold on to the job of a lifetime.

Al Gore, my fellow Vietnam veteran, and I in 1998. We were headed on Air Force Two to view tornado damage in south Georgia while I was in the U.S. Senate.

President Clinton and I shared a laugh in the Oval Office after he signed legislation that I had cosponsored in 2000.

I voted for the invasion of Iraq, which Secretary of Defense Rumsfeld led.
I came to regret that decision.

In 2004, John Kerry, also a Vietnam veteran, asked me to introduce him at the
Democratic National Convention in Boston.

President Obama appointed me Secretary of the American Battle Monuments Commission. We celebrated the sixty-fifth anniversary of the invasion of Normand in France at the American cemetery there on June 6, 2009. That cemetery is one o the twenty-four abroad run by the commission.

as I followed the procession of senators that wound through the Capitol Rotunda past the press gaggle and into the House chambers. The usual suspects were hanging over the rail looking down on us, longing to get their faces on TV. The Big Game was on. I remember thinking that Clinton would either find a way to salvage his presidency or go down in an ugly heap right before our very eyes.

Once in the well of the House, I peeled off to the right of the podium. I rolled past the justices of the Supreme Court and moved toward my seat near the Joint Chiefs of Staff.

The House clerk's loud voice boomed out the traditional "Mr. Speaker, the president of the United States." Clinton came in to loud applause. He did his fair share of shaking hands and ultimately followed the same path I had used when I came in. When he got to me, he gave me a great big bear hug. That's how we have greeted each other every time we've been together since we first met.

The first time I met him, he was governor of Arkansas and I was Georgia secretary of state. That was in the late 1980s. I was in Little Rock as the guest of the Arkansas secretary of state. I called Governor Clinton and said I wanted to drop by and meet him if he had time. Instead, he offered to have breakfast with me in the lobby of the hotel where I was staying. I was already at my table in the morning when the governor came in alone. Before he sat down, he walked up to me and wrapped me up in a big hug. I was astounded to see he had no aides or state troopers with him. That was not how the other governors I had known operated. Most of them seemed to enjoy being surrounded by the largest entourage they could round up.

In the early 1990s, before he decided to run for president, Clinton came to Georgia and spoke at the annual Jefferson-Jackson Day dinner. At that dinner, Clinton was introduced by then-governor Zell Miller, who would later introduce Clinton at the Democratic National Convention. Zell did Clinton quite a favor around the time of the dinner by introducing him to James Carville, the "Ragin'

Cajun" who masterminded Clinton's improbable campaign for the presidency.

I spoke to Bill privately at the dinner that night just a few months before he was to announce his campaign for the presidency. He told me he didn't know whether he really wanted to run for president or not, that he enjoyed being governor and he was just getting some of his programs through the Arkansas legislature. He sounded like a man who knew he had it pretty good as governor, and wasn't at all sure that he should give it up.

Now everything was on the line with his State of the Union speech. The early rumblings of the Monica Lewinsky scandal were afoot, although the nation had not yet heard the president ruminate on the meaning of "is." No doubt about it, the Comeback Kid was under tremendous pressure to perform. He mounted the steps to the podium, gave a copy of his speech to the House clerk, and launched into one of the great orations of his life. It was an incredible performance under the most adverse of circumstances.

Bill Clinton is the best politician I've ever known. I had seen that firsthand in 1992, when Clinton brought his presidential campaign to Georgia. Forty thousand people packed a football stadium. I was on the stage as secretary of state along with a handful of other Georgia dignitaries. After his speech, I went down the ramp to the football field to get out of the way so the people on the podium could exit without running me over. As Clinton came down, he saw me over to the side, out of the way. He moved toward me and gave me a big hug. Standing up—amid 40,000 people cheering for him—he had tears in his eyes as he looked at me. That's the kind of guy he is. You can't forget him.

It was especially painful for me to watch how the Republicans made hay out of the mess Clinton was in. The Monica scandal gave the Republican Party a true gift: the rise of the "moral voter." This new group became the base of the party and handed the Republicans unprecedented power for the first decade of the twenty-first century. Much like Prohibition voters in the 1920s, moral voters were concerned about a perceived decline in societal values. For them, politics was all about abortion, gays, and God. With the country at peace and experiencing record prosperity, the question of a politician's personal morality became paramount, trumping all the usual ideological issues that define liberal and conservative, Republican and Democrat. George W. Bush and the Republicans courted the moral voter heavily. Bush promised to "restore honor to the White House." By the end of Bush's tenure in Washington, those words would ring hollow, with the country stuck in a quagmire of wars in Iraq and Afghanistan and the economy in shambles. But in the late 1990s, with Clinton's personal failures laid bare, the Republicans found a ready-made staircase to the higher ground.

For those of us watching from the Senate, there was little to do but lie low. In our weekly Tuesday luncheon, some members of the Democratic caucus actually began to give voice to the idea that we would all be better off if the president resigned. Nobody dared ask him to do it publicly, but the idea was on the table. I don't think Clinton ever really considered resigning. He wanted to fight Gingrich and the radical Republicans all the way. Yet he had lost the moral authority to govern. That put those of us in the Senate in a difficult position.

The president had clearly done an egregious thing and lied to the American people about it. I didn't think it was an impeachable offense, but it certainly deserved a censure motion, which I wanted to support in the Senate, even against my old friend.

The Republicans never gave us that chance. They wanted blood and they went after it like a school of sharks. On a cold day in the winter of 1998, a vote was taken in the U.S. House. The Gingrich-led body, backed by former federal prosecutor Bob Barr—also from Georgia and a member of the House Judiciary Committee—passed a bill of impeachment. Such a process was so unusual and so difficult to grasp, few of us understood what would happen next.

The last time an article of impeachment had passed out of the House had been after the Civil War and the Lincoln assassination. President Andrew Johnson was impeached there by the Radical Reconstruction Republicans. The issue came to the floor of the Senate in 1866. When President John Kennedy was a senator from Massachusetts in the late 1950s, he and his terrific research assistant, Ted Sorensen, wrote a book about politics entitled *Profiles in Courage*. One of the chapters was devoted entirely to the seven Republican senators who ultimately voted against impeaching President Johnson in 1866, thus saving Johnson and the presidency. One of those senators, Edmund Ross from Kansas, had criticized the Johnson administration severely. People felt he would surely vote for impeachment.

According to Kennedy's tale of the event, the charges against Johnson were trumped up, designed to shift the balance of power in the leadership vacuum created by Lincoln's assassination. When the time came to vote, the Senate was split down the middle. It came down to Ross to decide the fate of Andrew Johnson and the future interpretation of the presidency under the U.S. Constitution. Such a vote would change American history. According to Kennedy's story, Ross rose, looked at the august body in which he served, and voted, "Not guilty." People in the gallery were stunned. Johnson's presidency was saved. The institution of the presidency was intact, and the Constitution was strengthened. By one vote, Andrew Johnson missed being the first president to be convicted in an impeachment trial. Today, Ross is credited by many historians with saving America from descending into a de facto dictatorship, where a handful of senators could control who is president, regardless of whom the people voted into office.

As was the case with Johnson, the impeachment of President Clinton had a tawdry, political stink to it from the beginning. There's an old saying that seems fitting: "When they say it's not about sex, it is about sex." The Republicans always said it wasn't about sex. But it was. The facts were an embarrassment to President Clinton and to Democrats nationwide, and they had the potential to take down the president of the United States. That's what Newt wanted.

Once the impeachment bill was passed in the House, the ball was in the Senate's court. No longer could anyone there pass the buck. The trial of the president of the United States in the U.S. Senate was on.

The chief justice of the United States came to the Senate and sat in the presiding officer's chair. Only twice in the history of the United States had that ever happened. I sat at my desk in the Senate watching this second time, one of only 154 Americans ever sworn in as judge and jury for an impeachment trial of a president. It was unreal. The Senate, in Senator Robert Byrd's phrase, was definitely making an impact on me.

The question before the Senate was whether the president should be convicted for "treason, bribery, or other high crimes and misdemeanors." More to the point, did getting a blow job in the Oval Office by a woman not your wife and then lying to the nation about it afterward constitute "treason, bribery, or other high crimes and misdemeanors"? That was what I had to decide. Certainly, it was distasteful, but was it treason?

The scary part for me was that each member of the Senate was to find the answer to that question in his or her own heart. Once the Senate ruled, that was it. If two-thirds of the Senate voted guilty, on that vote the president of the United States was impeached. At that moment, the vice president of the United States became the president. There was no appeal to a higher authority after the Senate voted. Not even to the Supreme Court. It was the most important decision I would ever make on behalf of my country.

In order to make a good decision, I consulted constitutional experts. They all told me that I alone was judge, jury, and evaluator of all the evidence. In addition to rereading Kennedy's *Profiles in Courage* chapter on Andrew Johnson's impeachment, I talked to historians. I reread parts of the Federalist Papers, which at the dawn of our country made the argument for adopting the Constitution we now have.

Back home in Georgia, black citizens thought it was terribly unjust that a president they had overwhelmingly voted for—not once but twice—might be removed, while the state's Republicans backed impeachment. I could find no solace in the advice of others.

Finally I turned to the most authentic living voice of history in terms of the U.S. Senate and its role under the Constitution, Robert C. Byrd, the senior senator from West Virginia. Byrd had, in fact, written an award-winning history of the Senate. But the senator said he had not come to a final conclusion on how he would vote.

"You don't have to roll up your pants until you get to the creek," Byrd was famous for saying in his rolling, hill-country drawl.

He knew off the cuff the details of the first impeachment in British history. It was that of a clerk in London. He also knew how the concept of impeachment had come down from British law to the U.S. Constitution. A short while later, Byrd wrote an op-ed piece in the *Washington Post* rejecting the idea of convicting the president. That was where my heart was as well. I came to believe that by setting the highest of standards for tossing out a president, the Founding Fathers made clear the Congress should not take a vote of impeachment lightly.

It takes two-thirds of the Senate, 67 votes, to convict.

Just around the time of the Clinton trial, I began to feel sick physically. I sensed that my body was going down, and fast. I couldn't figure out what was wrong with me. I later learned I was fighting mononucleosis—the infamous "kissing" sickness of youth. Early in the trial, I found myself so cold I thought I would freeze to death. I wrapped a green scarf around my neck, trying to keep warm. Pete Domenici, the senator from New Mexico, insisted I remove my scarf, as it "violated the decorum of the Senate." I took it off and asked a page to fill up a glass with the warmest water he could tolerate. When he came back with the glass, I held it up to my cheek just to keep warm. Here, at the most momentous moment of my political career, I could barely hold my head up.

The mono morphed into a massive sinus infection on the day of the impeachment vote. In Kennedy's *Profiles in Courage* chapter about Senator Ross, I remember reading that one of the seven Republican senators who voted against impeaching Johnson was sick with cancer. He made it to the chamber, however, and, using all of his strength, managed to stand up and cast his vote. I considered doing the same by "standing up" on my stumps to cast my vote, just to make a point about how outrageous I thought the whole thing was. Ultimately, I decided that would seem like grandstanding. This was a deadly serious moment. Better to get it over with and be done with it. I called out my "not guilty" in as loud a voice as my raging sinus infection would allow and retreated to Georgia and a heavy course of antibiotics. In the end, the vote wasn't close to the 67 members needed to toss Clinton out.

As for Gingrich, the failed impeachment served as a mortal wound in political terms. His approval rating dropped to 28 percent in national polls. Even his own party turned on him, threatening a coup against him in the House. It was like a pack of young dogs finally getting together and tearing up the oldest one.

★ 16 ★

Turning Point

AFTER THE U.S. Senate voted to retain the president of the United States, Democrats actually picked up five seats in the U.S. House in the '98 election. Gingrich was thrown out as Speaker and resigned from Congress, even though he had just been reelected by the people of Georgia. Conventional wisdom at the time held that Newt didn't want to return to Washington unless he could be in charge. I think he was nervous that some skeletons in his closet might be fixing to come to life. As it turned out, Gingrich did admit in 2007 that he had been cheating on his own wife throughout Clinton's impeachment, even as he attacked the president daily for having low morals. To top it off, Bob Livingston, the Republican Speaker who replaced Gingrich, was found to have failed Ethics 101 as well. Within days of bashing Clinton on the House floor for his dalliance with Monica, it was revealed that Livingston himself had a mistress.

The radical Republicans had gone too far, and now they were paying the price. But the Clinton affair with Monica Lewinsky did take a toll on the Democratic Party, ushering in the rise of the moral voter and of the right-wing media. Those two things, particularly the creation of Fox News, began to make a difference in American politics.

They were Bill Clinton's parting gifts to the Republican Party. Sadly, it was Al Gore during the campaign of 2000 who would ultimately pay the price for Clinton's sins in what turned out to be one of the nuttiest elections in the nation's history.

By the end of the summer, Al Gore had the Democratic nomination locked up. His extralong kiss at the convention in Los Angeles was an extralong reminder that he *really did* love his wife and he *really was* faithful to her. It was a showboat of a kiss, and said in no uncertain terms that Gore was trying to distance himself from Bill Clinton already.

At his base, Al Gore was different from Bill Clinton, but it became mandatory that he prove it. He had to distance himself from certain aspects of the Clinton legacy or risk making the election a cakewalk for Bush II. Of course, Gore could only walk so far away from one of the most popular and successful presidents of the last 50 years. He needed to convey the message that he shared Clinton's perceptive political compass, but not his defective moral compass. Clinton's two terms represented the greatest period of prosperity in the history of the United States. His administration had won a war (Kosovo) and helped bring a tyrant (Milosevic) to justice at the World Court without losing one man in combat. Any vice president would want to align himself with a legacy like that.

Unfortunately, the rise of the moral voter meant complications for the Gore campaign. From my perch in the Senate, I was privy to the latest internal polling data, information not generally shared with the public at large. Moral questions and questions of character had taken center stage over pocketbook issues and international diplomacy. This transition was most pronounced among core Democratic voting groups, such as the elderly and those with young families. In survey after survey, voters of both parties said they would be voting for the candidate they felt would help restore dignity to the White House. In each poll, these voters were shown to be leaning toward Bush. Still, the Democratic National Convention in Los Angeles was a blast. After a week of high-fiving and doing the Macarena for the TV cameras, everyone, especially me, believed Al Gore would beat "Dubya" come November.

Visiting L.A. as a Democratic senator in the company of Bill Clinton was like traveling in the king's royal court. We hit the highlights of Beverly Hills, ate at Wolfgang Puck's restaurant, and were wined and dined by top-line Hollywood producers and stars, such as Michael Douglas and David Geffen. Los Angeles was a Democratic town big-time, and Bill Clinton was welcomed as a conquering hero everywhere he went. But as much fun as I was having sitting in the midst of the convention center watching the confetti float down upon a newly crowned party nominee, I could feel something was not right inside me still. The next few months would help put my heart at peace.

After the convention, I left on a trip to see the troops in Korea as part of my work on the Armed Services Committee. On the way, I took a side trip to Japan. I hadn't been to Japan since I left the hospital in Yokohama. I saw the historical sites that interested me, particularly the underground headquarters of the Japanese imperial fleet in World War II. Their command center was dug deep into a mountain range near Yokohama and was filled with crisscrossing tunnels. It was considered virtually impregnable. If we had invaded the islands of Japan like we stormed the beaches of France on D-Day, the carnage among Japanese and American soldiers would have reached into the hundreds of thousands. Perhaps my own father, who served at Pearl Harbor after the attack in 1941, would have been among the dead.

After my sightseeing, I made a pilgrimage to the site of the old U.S. Army 106th General Hospital. I had waited a long time for that rendezvous. When I left the hospital in April 1968, I vowed to return. At the time, that vow had been a way of saying I was going to live. That hospital was the first place that I began to believe I would survive the explosion. It was there that I realized I had some life left in my body after all. To my surprise, I discovered that the old hospital had been torn down after the Vietnam War.

The site was now a park.

I was glad.

Sitting solemnly on a bench watching an elderly Japanese lady sweep the sidewalk, I was overcome by a sense of peace. The place I had come to see, a place that had treated hundreds of thousands of wounded American boys like me from both the Korean War and the Vietnam War, was no more. There was no longer a need. Thank God. Between World War II, Korea, and Vietnam, more Americans had been killed in the Pacific theater than anywhere else in the world. And now there was peace. Still, my mind dwelled on all those bodies and all those wounds from the past. I couldn't really absorb it all. I said a prayer for myself and all the others hurt so badly so far from home. More parks, less war, I thought. That's what the world needs.

After I left Yokohama, I set out for Korea and the DMZ—the Demilitarized Zone. What an odd name for one of the most heavily armored and booby-trapped spots on our planet. There are one million mines buried in the ground separating North Korea and South Korea along the DMZ. I spent my birthday, August 24, 2000, on the border there with American troops. Rolling up to the actual line between the two nations, I had the distinct feeling that North Korea was really a giant Potemkin village—all bluff and gruff but with no substance. The country couldn't even afford to feed itself, for goodness' sake. As a member of the Senate Armed Services Committee, I was occasionally shown satellite photos of the world's trouble spots. The thing that always struck me about North Korea was the absence of light.

North Korea is a black hole on earth, both literally and figuratively. The stark contrast visible on the Korean peninsula in the nighttime satellite images says it all. On the South Korean side of the DMZ, the free side, the entire nation is full of light. And above North Korea in China, the image is also aglow. But in between the twin seas of light, there is just darkness and the mad world of Kim Jong Il.

I enjoyed being with the army troops in the DMZ. Sensing the electrified air that always surrounds combat zones, I felt like an old platoon leader again. Being around all those bright-eyed, eager young men reminded me of my days as a young lieutenant in my early twenties. I have some old 16-mm movies I shot in Vietnam during that period and get them out to watch every now and then. There are just a few images of me in the films, as I was mostly operating the camera, but to see myself again at that age always reminds me of how engaged and hopeful I was. It also reminds me of the nurses I was chasing and filming. The films seem to capture someone else's life, not mine. After 40 years, it is almost hard to remember myself whole. I've had this body for much longer than I had the original one.

But seeing those young men in the DMZ reminded me that I was still a soldier at heart. The same sense of duty and love of country that drove me toward military service coursed through these men as well.

Something else happened around this time that helped slay much of the bitterness inside me. I participated in a documentary about combat medics, relaying how they had saved my life after I dropped the grenade getting off the helicopter and got blown up. The day after it aired, I got a phone call at my Senate office.

"My name's Dave Lloyd and I saw your program on TV about combat medics. I just want to let you know it wasn't your grenade," said the man at the end of the line.

"How do you know?" I asked skeptically.

"I was the first guy to you. I was the guy who cut your uniform off and made a tourniquet out of my weapons belt."

My chest got tight. I knew right away that this wasn't a hoax, that he was telling the truth. Even in those first seconds after the explosion, I had remained conscious. I remembered someone doing exactly what this man had just described. Only someone who had been there would have known that was what had happened.

I told him we needed to get together. After we hung up, I realized I hadn't thanked him for saving my life.

Dave came to see me at the Capitol a few days later. We ate in the Senate dining room. He even showed me pictures of the hill where it happened. It was my first contact with anyone who had been there when the grenade went off, and the news he gave me was stunning.

Dave told me that another soldier getting off the helicopter with me had dropped the grenade. I realized he was probably the FNG (Fucking New Guy) on the chopper. Apparently, this poor kid had loosened all the pins on his grenades because he was afraid he wouldn't be able to pull them out during a firefight. That was exactly the opposite of what they taught soldiers to do. We all bent our pins back over themselves so that they would be harder to pull out accidentally. This fellow had turned himself into a walking bomb. When the grenade fell out of his gear as he jumped from the chopper, the pin just fell out. I jumped out next and saw the grenade on the ground. The timing was such that it exploded just as I reached for it.

For the first time, I realized it wasn't my fault! For 30 years, I had been beating myself up thinking it was my grenade. The relief I felt was extraordinary. It changed everything for me. After decades of calling myself a dumbass, the truth was that I had just been unlucky.

Dave introduced me to another marine, Charlie Wolden, who had tended to me as well. The two of them, along with a navy corpsman named Steve Johnson, were the first to me on the battlefield. The three of them tended to my wounds and put me on the medevac chopper to the division aid station. I called the other guys and thanked them for saving my life.

With the presidential race gearing up, the Gore campaign asked me to hit the road on Al's behalf. How could I refuse?

The Gore folks sent me to West Virginia. The state was reeling economically, but Karl Rove was still able to peddle the holy triumvirate of

Republican wedge issues—God, guns, and gays—to the people there. The Bush team handed out brochures that had the Bible crossed out and said that if Democrats were elected, the Bible would be no more. The National Rifle Association warned that Democrats would take their guns away, and alleged that the Democratic Party was shot through with gays and lesbians. That kind of message seemed to resonate in Appalachia, and—little-known fact—actually cost Gore the election just as much as losing Florida in the Supreme Court. Despite all the hanging chads in West Palm Beach, if Gore had won West Virginia, he would have been president of the United States. But God, guns, and gays cut for the Republicans in a big way that year. Specifically, the election year of 2000 marked a little-noticed turning point in terms of the NRA's power in national politics. For the first time, the group showed it had the muscle to deliver entire states for the Republican Party.

Over dinner with John Kerry in 2004, just before he announced for the presidency, we discussed the NRA and its devotion to spreading the great untruth that Democrats were trying to take everybody's guns. Kerry said he thought he could deal with the NRA because he was a hunter and he ate what he killed. But John was being naive. With the NRA, it doesn't matter whether you eat what you kill or not. If you're a Democrat, they're going to try to kill and eat *you!*

I knew we were in for dark days when the 5–4 decision by the U.S. Supreme Court handed Bush the presidency. He had lost the popular vote, but he had won where it counted, in the governor's office in Florida, in the secretary of state's office in Florida, and in the Republican-leaning U.S. Supreme Court.

The results of the election set up one of the most tragic and shameful eight years in American history. It changed the course of our nation for the worse, and was about to change the course of my life for the worse too.

★ 17 ★

The Bush Era

INAUGURATION DAY, JANUARY 20, 2001, was wet and dreary with the temperature hovering just above freezing, perhaps the worst weather recipe Washington has to offer. It was not cold enough for snow, but if you found yourself sitting outside in the spitting rain, it was plenty cold enough to make you miserable. I sat on the VIP platform with the other members of Congress wearing a huge peacoat my father had given me, his navy-issue watch coat from World War II. It was one of those touching gestures fathers make to sons, and he was tickled when he heard I would be wearing it to see the inauguration of a new president. What better for a member of the Armed Services Committee to wear than one of the finest products ever made by our military? To keep the drizzling rain off our heads, the Senate staff had given each member a clear plastic hat, sort of like an oversized beanie. As I looked around the crowd and saw everybody with the little soft plastic tops on their heads, the wife of a dear Senate colleague, a former nurse, whispered to me that it looked like the entire congressional delegation had shown up with giant condoms on their heads. It was fitting, I told her, because the whole nation was about to get screwed. I was more right than I could have imagined, and the Bush folks made sure I was first in line.

When I got elected to the U.S. Senate, I never imagined that I would get beaten for reelection. I was so fiercely dedicated to doing a good job and was so well recognized in Georgia that I thought I was in pretty good shape politically. I wasn't naive. Politics is rough, and I had already been knocked around pretty well. But I had also been Georgia's number one vote-getter for a time. Talmadge, Russell, and Nunn all served long terms in the Senate, faithfully reelected by a loyal Georgia electorate. That's what I was banking on too.

Taking my job seriously meant getting deeply involved in committee hearings and learning my craft as a senator. It meant touring the world, visiting the troops, and finding out what our armed forces really needed. I wanted to become a nationally recognized expert on defense issues and a voice for the kind of levelheaded foreign policy that Dick Russell and Sam Nunn exemplified when they held my seat.

When I took the job, one of my staffers found Dick Russell's desk in the archives and pulled it out for me. It was right out of the 1930s. The desk had a leaf on each of its four corners so that multiple secretaries could sit and take dictation. There was a locked door on the bottom left side of the desk. A friend told me that was where Russell kept his stash of whiskey. Apparently, every six months or so, a lobbyist for the Taiwanese government would come by and give Russell his whiskey, and each night after work hours Russell would unlock the door in the desk, pour himself a shot, and sit back and watch the evening news. To me, the desk and office were part of a most exquisite history, one that I wanted to live up to, with the single exception of indulging in the whiskey. The office still had Dick Russell's phone number. Sam Nunn had never changed it. I didn't either. I tried to keep things as traditional as possible in the office, so as to preserve the sense of history that went with the seat. I added a big blowup of a photo of Dick Russell and me to the main wall in my office. It was taken in the summer of 1965 when I was an intern. I looked like the proverbial deer in the headlights. Russell had signed the photo, "Best of luck in your career, Dick Russell, USS." The USS abbreviation stood for "U.S. Senate." I remember looking at an official book of biographical sketches of all the senators published in the mid-1960s. The senators listed the various things they had achieved en route to the Senate. Several of them had gilded the lily a bit. Not Russell. The man was a former governor and a former speaker of the Georgia house, but all he had listed in his biography was "Dick Russell, USS." U.S. Senate. That's the thing he was most proud of. Likewise, it was one of my proudest moments when I first wrote "USS" after my own name.

I loved my Senate seat like I've seldom loved anything on this earth and was determined to keep it. I began raising money for my reelection campaign at a furious pace. For the campaign in 1996, I had raised only $3.5 million and had been outspent more than three and a half to one. I knew I needed to do much better than that for reelection in 2002.

Senator Harry Reid, then minority whip, promised me, "Tom Daschle and I are never gonna let you be outspent again." I felt like I had made some strong allies and would have my fellow senators on my team in '02. That was comforting and I was glad to have their best wishes, but my mind kept drifting back to what Herman Talmadge said to Jimmy Carter, namely, "When the water starts coming over the deck, it's every man for himself." I became a fund-raising machine, even if calling people up and begging for money felt just god-awful.

Regardless of my personal distaste for the task, by mid-2001, I was on my way to raising an eventual total of $13.5 million for my reelection race in 2002. If it came down to every man for himself in my race, like it did the last time, at least I wouldn't be broke. I thought I had all my ducks in a row.

September 11, 2001, started off as a beautiful day. For me, the fall of the year is always the most wonderful time in Washington. The heat of the summer begins to subside, the kids are back in school, and the tourists are at a minimum. When the leaves begin to turn, Washington settles down to the one thing it does best—politics.

That morning, I arrived with my driver and parked in my designated spot underneath the Dirksen building. I got out of the car and moved toward the underground entrance. As I approached the door, the female guard looked at me and said, "A plane just hit a building in New York!" An image flashed in my mind of a small plane, a private plane, hitting a big building, as had happened in the 1930s when a small plane flew into the Empire State Building.

I rode the elevator up to my office, chastising myself for running 15 minutes late for a private meeting with the newly designated chairman of the Joint Chiefs of Staff, General Dick Myers. As I passed into my office through a private entrance directly off the hallway, I asked my secretary, Elaine Iler, to bring the general in. He sat down and we started talking. Ironically, we were discussing how best to defend the nation. Suddenly Elaine burst in and said, "You've gotta see the TV." She was clearly agitated. We followed her out to the television in her office. Almost as soon as we got into the room, we saw the second plane hit the tower at the World Trade Center. For a moment, I thought it was a replay of the first plane hitting the tower, but it quickly became apparent there were two planes involved, and neither of them was little.

The phone rang. Lorrie, one of the office assistants, answered. She was a sweet, small-town girl from south Georgia. It was unusual to see her get ruffled by a caller. There was an edge to her voice as if someone was shouting at her. Then she said firmly, "I'm sorry, sir, but you'll just have to wait. The general is in a meeting with Senator Cleland."

The general's aide snatched the phone out of her hand and began nervously scribbling. She read what he wrote on the notepad: "New York under attack. Washington next."

Myers abruptly bolted out the door without another word. I still remember seeing his heels clear the door just as it slammed shut.

The top commander of the nation's military had just learned that the Pentagon, his headquarters, had been hit with a plane and was on fire. A friend of mine who lived in Arlington happened to be outside on top of a hill near his home smoking a cigarette just before the attack. He said the plane flew over him so low that he could feel the heat from the jet exhaust. He followed the plane across the horizon and watched it smash into the Pentagon and erupt in a ball of fire. Many months afterward, General Myers and I mused to each other that it was a good thing that he was in my office that morning rather than walking around the Pentagon. He might have been one of those who lost their lives there.

After he left, I looked out the window of my office in the Dirksen building. I could see smoke billowing up across the Potomac at the Pentagon. I assembled my staff in the conference room. I remember vividly turning toward my secretary and saying, "I'm back in Vietnam." That's exactly how I felt. The smoke, the images of the planes on television, and seeing the general and his aide dash out of the office in their uniforms triggered memories of being rocketed and mortared. Feelings I hadn't felt in decades enveloped me.

We *are* under attack! I thought. I looked out the window at the Capitol dome and thought, That's the next target. Then, realizing my personal proximity to the Capitol, which was just outside my office window, I thought, Good God! *We* are the next target!

The plane that went down in the fields of Pennsylvania was targeted at the White House or the Capitol. It is amazing to think of the heroism of the people on that flight. Who knows how many lives they saved in Washington that day by taking on the hijackers.

With my heart pounding in my chest, I felt like I was in charge of my platoon again. We had already discovered that the telephones had quit working, both landlines and cell phones. Panicked voices and clacking heels filled the hallway. People poured out onto the Capitol lawn and into the street, moving away from the building as fast as they could. Bill Johnstone, my top policy adviser, looked at me and calmly said, "Senator, I think you should dismiss the staff now." I agreed. I told them to go home. Five minutes later, as we were trying to figure out what the hell was going on and what I should do, Bill looked directly at me and said, "Senator, I think it's time you left the building."

Abandoning my post was not something I was used to in war or politics. It felt strange to leave my office knowing that America was under attack. I wanted to stay, but the old signal officer in me knew that staying put in a likely target with no communications was just plain dumb. Reluctantly, I prepared to leave. I didn't have anyplace to go to, except my apartment in Arlington. I grabbed my driver, Daniel Barton, got in my car, and pulled out of the Senate garage. There I saw a solid wall of people on the sidewalks and in the streets, all slowly moving out of Washington. It was a mass exodus the likes of which I had not seen since watching two million refugees abandon the cities in Vietnam after the first wave of the Tet offensive. My car inched at a snail's pace down Constitution Avenue, toward my apartment in Virginia. At that time in my life, I had a girlfriend whom I will call Liz. She had just moved to Washington a few days earlier and now found herself in the midst of a terrorist attack. I figured she was bound to be freaking out. I tried to raise her on the phone. Nothing. I tried stopping by her workplace. No luck there. She was out somewhere among the masses trying to get to me. It seemed like a scene from the movie *Doctor Zhivago*—two people struggling to make contact with each other through a chaotic mass of humanity.

Steve Leeds, my campaign chairman, was traveling with us in the car fiddling with a newfangled gadget called a BlackBerry. As we traveled with the slow-motion wave of refugees fleeing Washington, I looked over my shoulder again at the smoke rising steadily from the Pentagon. It is hard to describe the full effect of a war flashback to someone who has never had one, but that's what I had right then. I felt oddly removed from the happenings around me. The voices of my companions faded out and I found myself awash in all the old sensations of war. Back in Vietnam, there were two constants that defined every soldier's days: the potential for death to strike at any moment, and the ever-present smoke plumes on the horizon that rose from whatever one side or the other had blown up in the night. The fire and smoke of battle felt familiar. So did the tingling nerves. The fact that I was sitting in the front seat of a Cadillac in Washington, D.C., did nothing to cut the feeling that I was back in Vietnam. For me, I was back on the battlefield and back in mortal danger.

Although I wouldn't know it for years, that moment was the beginning of the end for me personally, the beginning of my great descent into the abyss. War—the great nemesis of my life and soul—was back on the nation's front burner and it was about to boil over.

By the afternoon, I was back at my apartment with a small cadre of my staff. We were glued to the television with the rest of the nation. Liz turned up shortly after I did, which was a great comfort to me. While we stared in shock at the TV, the buildings in New York collapsed with people still in them. Weeks later, Liz and I would go to Ground Zero and inspect the damage. We stared into the gaping hole in the earth, the one that swallowed thousands of people forever like some horrible mine disaster. It seemed as if the smoke still wafting from the smoldering wreckage carried the spirits of those who had been killed.

How could this happen? Spending more than a quarter of a trillion dollars annually on defense, how could this happen to America?

Who did it?

By late in the afternoon of 9/11, FBI officials were on television showing photos of people connected with Al Qaeda who were known to be on those planes. I was amazed. It seemed an incredible bit of sleuthing. How did they get those photos? How did they have a sense so quickly that these people were the attackers? Yes, Al Qaeda had blown up the USS *Cole*. Yes, there had been attacks on American facilities in Saudi Arabia. Yes, there had been an earlier attempt to blow up the World Trade Center years ago. But how did the FBI know these people were Al Qaeda? And if they really were known terrorists, why the hell were so many of them able to get on airplanes all over the country?

Ultimately, I learned as a member of the 9/11 Commission that Al Qaeda had declared war on the United States in 1998 and the CIA had been tracking them for quite a while. But the FBI and the CIA were not really swapping information about Al Qaeda like they should have been. Intelligence, just like at Pearl Harbor, had been "stovepiped." Agencies had it, but they didn't share it completely with each other.

At that time, there were more than 16 different agencies in Washington involved in intelligence. Those agencies as a whole had information that clearly suggested there was a potential threat to the nation's airlines months before the actual attack. The problem was, each agency protected the separate bits of intelligence its spies and analysts had discovered regarding terrorist activity in the United States. It was only when you put all the little bits together that everything made sense.

The "intelligence community" had laid an egg.

They had blown it.

A year later, I was named one of the members of the bipartisan 9/11 Commission. We were tasked with learning what went wrong and figuring out how to prevent such a dastardly attack from ever happening again. I became privy to some of the intelligence available to the president and other leaders prior to the attacks, and so had a firsthand view of where things went awry and who deserved blame. There was plenty of that to go around, with President Bush deserving a fair share himself. Ultimately, I resigned from the commission over the way the administration stonewalled us, refusing to provide full access to critical intelligence documents. The man who did the stonewalling on behalf of the White House was Alberto Gonzales, then Bush's chief counsel. He practiced the same type of deception with the commission that later led to his disgrace and resignation as attorney general.

By the evening of 9/11, another dramatic moment happened in Washington. I was still watching television in my apartment at dusk when a lot of my colleagues from the House and Senate, both Democrats and Republicans, gathered on the Capitol steps. They held hands and sang "God Bless America." That kind of courage coursed through Washington after the attacks. The next day and the days following, all of my staff members came to work. It was their way of thumbing their noses at the terrorists. In those days, it seemed as if all of Capitol Hill was living out the old Winston Churchill quote from World War II: "You do your worst—and we will do our best."

Washington did its best in a massively bipartisan way to heal from the 9/11 attacks. There was a unanimous intent and desire to bring the attackers to justice. Immediately, in a bipartisan show of force, the Congress passed a blank check to go after the Al Qaeda terrorists in Afghanistan—the people the FBI said caused the attacks.

But before our troops got their marching orders, the Senate itself came under attack. It isn't unusual for a high-profile personality in Washington, D.C., to get death threats. When I was sworn in as head of the VA, I got death threats almost as soon as I showed up for work. Such threats come in to every Senate or congressional office, usually proffered by a harmless nut job looking for attention. The offices alert the FBI each time such threats come in, but they are considered a normal part of life in Congress. It is, however, highly unusual to receive an envelope full of poison capable of killing you and your entire staff in the morning mail.

That was what happened to Senator Tom Daschle, one of my closest friends. The poison was anthrax, and it arrived at his office in the daily mail on October 15. Several other contaminated letters had been discovered around the nation beginning on September 18, just one week after 9/11, and someone had already died by the time the letter arrived at Daschle's office, which was just down the hall from mine.

A note in the envelope read:

09-11-01

YOU CAN NOT STOP US.

WE HAVE THIS ANTHRAX.

YOU DIE NOW.

ARE YOU AFRAID?

DEATH TO AMERICA.

DEATH TO ISRAEL.

ALLAH IS GREAT.

Anthrax believed to have come from the Daschle letter is blamed for the deaths of two postal workers sorting mail in downtown Washington. Once it was known the Senate itself was targeted, Senate office buildings were shut down for several days.

The day of the anthrax attack, the Capitol physicians began to administer Cipro—an antibiotic strong enough to fight anthrax—to those who had tested positive for the poison in their nostrils. I never took it, but most of my office staff did. I ended up working on the Capitol lawn for a few days while they had us locked out of our offices. It was just me and my cell phone conducting the nation's business in the company of the squirrels and the chipmunks.

Soon the country and all of us in the Senate faced a bigger challenge to our political courage—but this one was drummed up by a president dead-set on waging war. I think the most telling story about the origin of Bush's obsession with Iraq is contained in Richard Clarke's book *Against All Enemies.* Clarke was the terrorism adviser to four presidents, three of whom were Republicans. He was the man put in charge of the White House Situation Room the day of the 9/11 attack. In the book, he tells the story of the president coming up to him in the Situation Room the day after and suggesting he try to connect the hijackers to Iraq. Clarke told the president that Al Qaeda, not Iraq, was clearly responsible, and that the FBI and CIA were in agreement on that point.

Just a few days prior to the attack, it was all Richard Clarke could do to get a meeting with Condi Rice about a possible terrorist attack from Al Qaeda. He had tried all year long to get a meeting with her about the subject, but nobody in the administration was interested. In fact, when the Republicans took over from Clinton, Dick Cheney demanded a briefing on Iraq. Only Colin Powell wanted a briefing on terrorism.

Why didn't George Bush take the goodwill of the world—not just the goodwill of the Congress, but the whole world—and go after the attackers? That will always be the question that haunts the legacy of his presidency for as long as there is American history. The answer is that the administration—Bush, Cheney, Wolfowitz, Rumsfeld— wanted to go after Iraq from the start. Never mind that U.S. troops had Bin Laden trapped in the Tora Bora mountains in Afghanistan precisely where Richard Clarke and his terrorism staff anticipated that they would go. Never mind that Bush had the might of the American military at his command with some of the best soldiers in the world on the ground within miles of Bin Laden's hideout. George Bush simply gave lip service to going after Bin Laden for a few months, then switched targets. It will always be a mystery to me why Bush set forth, arm in arm with his neocon comrades, and started a war with the wrong country. It already ranks as one of the great presidential mistakes in American history.

For me, the inauguration of George W. Bush as president ushered in a period I can only describe as unshirted hell. In those early years of his presidency and his war, I was to suffer the darkest days of my life and come to know the true depths of my own personal sense of loss and grief about what war had cost me.

★ 18 ★

"We're Going to War"

THE PENTAGON HAS given me chills all my life. When President Roosevelt, at the beginning of World War II, was asked where he wanted to build the new Department of War, he looked out the window, pointed at Arlington Cemetery across the Potomac, and quipped, "Put it over there." At the time, the Pentagon was a marvel of construction, completed in just a year and a half. It replaced the old War Department, which used to be located in the Old Executive Office Building, across from the West Wing of the White House on Pennsylvania Avenue. After World War II, President Harry Truman signed the Defense Reorganization Bill of 1947, which recast the War Department as the Department of Defense, something he thought sounded less aggressive after too many years of war. Truman also changed the Great Seal so that the eagle's head on the seal faced the set of talons holding the olive branches, not the talons with the arrows.

Despite the changes, the Pentagon has always reeked of war.

This day, September 11, 2002, was no different. I had been summoned to the Pentagon at the invitation of Secretary of Defense Donald Rumsfeld. Just entering the building made me antsy. I was

179

there, ostensibly, for a briefing on weapons of mass destruction. I felt a foreboding about what was to come.

For one thing, it was the first anniversary of the 9/11 attack. Why, I thought, would anyone set this briefing for today?

As a member of the Senate Armed Services Committee, it was not unusual for me to receive Pentagon briefings on various national security issues. Usually, the briefings took place in the Senate Armed Services Committee Room. If the briefing was classified, it took place in a secure facility within the Capitol. To be invited to the Pentagon for a briefing on weapons of mass destruction exactly one year after the 9/11 attack felt like a setup.

Something was going on, and I was afraid it was war. Though Al Qaeda had attacked us a year earlier from its base in Afghanistan, the president and his administration continued to make noises about attacking Iraq. A month earlier, in August, Vice President Dick Cheney had announced that there were indeed nuclear weapons in Iraq. No substantiation for this fantastic statement was offered. Then, on CNN one Sunday evening, National Security Affairs Adviser Condi Rice said she feared a "mushroom cloud" coming from Iraq.

For weeks, my Senate colleagues had been discussing the increased fearmongering coming out of the White House. I had a feeling the Pentagon meeting was part of that effort. I was ushered into a small reception room. To my surprise, about a dozen other members of the Senate were there. They were all powerful figures known for being strong on defense. Among the assembled were Senator Carl Levin, chairman of the Senate Armed Services Committee, along with Dianne Feinstein and John Kerry. Senator Dick Lugar, ranking Republican on the Senate Foreign Relations Committee, was also present.

After coffee and Danish, we went into a dimly lit conference room to see Rumsfeld. Just as he was about to begin, George Tenet, director of the CIA, walked in. Clearly, this was no ordinary briefing. Rumsfeld began. As he spoke, an aide scrolled through a PowerPoint display that listed all the nations that were members of the president's "Axis of Evil." These were places that Bush had outlined in one of his State of the Union speeches as threats to America. The states were ranked according to their weapons of mass destruction capability.

The door to the briefing room opened again. Vice President Dick Cheney strolled in, trailed by his ever-present shadow, "Scooter" Libby. All the president's war-making men had arrived. I sat up a little straighter, thinking that I might be witnessing an important bit of history.

As Rumsfeld proceeded with the briefing, it was painfully obvious that the real state in the "Axis of Evil" that had both nuclear weapons and the means to deliver them was North Korea. The other states listed—Syria, Iran, and Iraq—had little or no viable capability at that point, even according to the Pentagon's own chart. In the ranking, it seemed that Iran was second, Iraq third, and Syria last in terms of nuclear threat to the United States and our allies in the region.

When it came time for questions, just for spite, I spoke up and said to Rumsfeld and his administration cohorts, "It looks like, from your own chart, we should be invading North Korea." There was a stunned silence. I said that just to make a sarcastic point. After they'd spent two months beating the drums on Iraq, we all knew they wanted to take out Saddam Hussein. The odd thing was that they had gone through the dog and pony show of ranking the other states for our benefit. I certainly was not in favor of invading North Korea. I'd been in the DMZ separating North and South Korea. I had seen the combat troops standing trigger-ready on both sides of the border. I knew that an invasion of North Korea would cause an absolute bloodbath on both sides. Mainly, I just wanted to see if any member of the administration would admit that the data in their PowerPoint presentation very much pointed to North Korea, not Iraq, as the number one threat.

Dianne Feinstein said that she had traveled to Vienna and talked to the UN inspectors who monitored nuclear facilities. The inspectors there did not believe that Iraq possessed nuclear capabilities. Rumsfeld challenged her on the point. Then she said she had even talked to some of Rumsfeld's staff, and they agreed that Iraq did not have nuclear capability at this time. The secretary of defense sputtered for a moment, then shifted gears. He said that the United States wouldn't be able to get at some of the chemical and biological sites in some countries unless we used bunker-buster type nuclear weapons on them.

I was flabbergasted. In these tense times, and on the exact anniversary of the most deadly attack on American soil, the nation's top defense officer was talking about using nuclear weapons.

It seemed like crazy talk.

John Kerry asked a penetrating question about the plume from such a nuclear explosion. What would happen, he asked, if we attacked chemical and biological sites in Iraq with nuclear weapons while our troops were on the ground? What about the collateral damage that might be done in such an attack, to civilians and to neighboring countries exposed to such a plume? Rumsfeld put him off. He simply responded that you couldn't destroy the material completely unless you dropped tactical nukes on each site. As Kerry prepared to ask another question, the vice president, who had been quiet up to this point, chimed in.

Cheney said America was the only power in the world that could deal with Saddam Hussein. When he said that, I got a lump in my throat. He spoke as if no outcome other than all-out war with Saddam was possible. The implication was that since we were strong enough to do it, we should. The president's team obviously wanted to go after Saddam Hussein, not Bin Laden. How ironic, I thought. On the anniversary of the day Bin Laden and his Al Qaeda terrorist cadre attacked the United States, the vice president and the nation's top defense brass were all sequestered in the Pentagon talking about an "Axis of Evil" that for some reason didn't include Bin Laden.

*   *   *

I had begun to suspect that the administration had its own plans and was determined to carry them out. Listening to National Security Affairs Adviser Condi Rice and Cheney parrot their warmongering mantra on the Sunday talk shows, it was clear that what Colin Powell's deputy at the State Department later called a "cabal" between Cheney and Rumsfeld was, indeed, in control of American foreign policy. They were certainly in control of the war-making apparatus. None of them had ever heard a shot fired in anger. Yet here they were plotting a war the country *didn't* need to fight while virtually ignoring an ongoing war America *did* need to fight with Bin Laden.

It was a stunning moment. The president's men seemed so didactic and dismissive in their overt intent to start a war. I realized we weren't there for a briefing. We were there as a test audience for their plan to unleash the American war machine on Iraq. That explained why folks like Dick Lugar and Carl Levin were there. These were the nation's most respected voices when it came to international relations and national defense, and they were the voices most likely to rise in protest over such a half-baked scheme. By spilling the beans this way, in a formal, classified briefing, the assembled were essentially muzzled. None of us would be allowed to speak about what we had heard, lest we violate national security laws.

Senator Levin spoke up after Cheney. He said he had met with President Bush the day before and pressed the question of further UN inspections in Iraq. Bush had dismissed the idea out of hand, according to Levin. On that note, Rumsfeld called an end to the meeting and we were all ushered out to attend a Pentagon memorial service for those who had died in the 9/11 attack. I was struck by how weird it was for Cheney and Rumsfeld to use this national day of mourning to sell their war.

Other voices had been rising against war, even before that meeting. A few days prior, Senator Byrd had spoken at our Tuesday Democratic caucus luncheon meeting. He was absolutely enraged. He waved a copy of the U.S. Constitution, which he always carried in his pocket, and declared, "Only the Congress can raise armies and navies." He was so angry, yet so eloquent, as he castigated the president for dispatching all his administration war hawks to the Sunday TV shows the weekend of the first 9/11 anniversary. "And all they were talking about," said Byrd, was "attack, attack, attack!"

The memorial ceremony was held in the parking lot on the side of the Pentagon that had been penetrated and blown up by the attack plane on 9/11. I was amazed at the impact the loss of 186 Americans had on the Pentagon. One year later, in that same area of the parking lot, rows and rows of relatives and friends gathered to pay their respects.

On the way back to Capitol Hill, my car followed some charter buses carrying senators and congressmen from the ceremony. Going across Memorial Bridge, I saw my first antiwar protesters. They were wearing black and carrying black signs. Two or three were dressed in ghoulish costumes. They were already protesting the potential war in Iraq. As I rode back to my Senate office, I realized I had just heard the extent of the administration's sales pitch for the war.

My friend and fellow Vietnam veteran, General Hugh Shelton, former chairman of the Joint Chiefs of Staff under President Clinton, told me that if Saddam Hussein was taken out of power, "the Kurds, the Shiites, and the Sunnis will be at each other's throats like banshee chickens." He was not alone among the nation's military experts in warning Bush about the potential aftermath of the war in those early days. I have been told by sources that when the administration presented its evidence to the Joint Chiefs of Staff, attempting to make the case for a war against Saddam, two of the nation's top generals remarked, "Is that all you've got?"

But no matter! The Big Sale was on, already mapped out by Karl Rove, Andrew Card, Condi Rice, Dick Cheney, and the rest. This group had met from time to time in the Situation Room in the White House since 9/11. They weren't planning to make war on those who had attacked us on that day. They were planning to make war on those of us who questioned anything they did. I entered my office after the Pentagon briefing and memorial service and sat down at my desk, pondering the moment. I called my secretary, Elaine, in and said, "We're going to war."

And, I thought, there's nothing I can do to stop it.

★ 19 ★

The Last Race

THE POLITICS OF election year 2002 was dominated by the events of 9/11. George Bush and his political team made sure of it. With a nation afraid, the Bush team found themselves uniquely positioned to control the tenor of the election thanks to Osama Bin Laden, a name Americans were learning to fear. They used this new bogeyman, along with the catchall threat of "terrorism," as a club anytime anyone argued against their agenda. For the Republicans, "terrorism" became their new "communism." It was an evil, they told the country, that only Republicans were qualified to fight.

The Republicans had it all going for them, and that was bad news for a first-term senator like me. They had the Supreme Court, the House of Representatives, and the White House. They needed just one more puzzle piece to complete their sweep of the government—the United States Senate. They were still sore about losing control of the Senate in May 2001 after Jim Jeffords defected from the Republican Party and shifted the balance of power to the Democrats.

That event was the single most politically courageous thing I witnessed in my years in the Senate. Jeffords said at the time that he was leaving the Republican Party because his fellow senators had refused to provide full funding for the Individuals with Disabilities Education Act, which provided extra services to children with learning disabilities. But, in reality, Jeffords's maneuver had much farther-reaching consequences, weakening Bush's hand dramatically. It meant that the Senate was the only real obstacle Bush faced in pushing his Iraq agenda through Congress.

For me, the Jeffords switch and the Democratic takeover of the Senate meant I became chairman of the Armed Services Subcommittee on Personnel. That was the chairmanship I most coveted, as it put me in a position to look out for the troops. I could now, once again, care for those who had borne the battle. I felt like I had found my home in the Senate.

The bad news was that the Senate's balance of power teetered day to day. For anything to pass, it required the support of members of both parties. That meant there was no hiding from votes on controversial issues. With the Senate split down the middle, every issue was a potential minefield. I felt particularly on the spot as I was up for reelection in a state Bush had carried easily just two years before. Even though he remained plenty popular with the hometown crowd after 9/11, I still felt confident of reelection. In the wake of the new emphasis on national defense, I had an inside track. I had served my country in uniform. I had been wounded doing so. The people of Georgia and many people in America knew that. The Republicans could not take that away from me, or so I thought. Plus, I had voted for the president's tax cuts, taking away another possible avenue of political attack.

"Homeland Security will be our issue," bragged Republican senator Bill Frist of Tennessee publicly a month or so before the election. I figured I had that base covered as well, as I had been one of the cosponsors of the bill that created the Department of Homeland Security over the initial objections of the White House.

With that bill, Joe Lieberman and I had jumped ahead of the Republicans. Earlier in 2002, we, along with some others in the Senate, had introduced legislation to create a full-blown department at a time when the administration was officially saying that Tom Ridge's small White House operation was adequate to the task. The Bush team dismissed our efforts to create an entire agency devoted to security, but as our bill began to gain steam in the Senate, the White House abruptly shifted its position. In the White House version of the bill, however, all rights normally accorded federal workers, particularly union membership, were denied to employees of the new agency. It was preposterous. I agreed with Senator Byrd, who asked, "How can you make America more secure by making the workers in the Department of Homeland Security more insecure?"

With Democrats in charge and in the majority on the Governmental Affairs Committee, upon which I sat, I was able to help shepherd the bill to the Senate floor.

We faced challenge after challenge, partly because Joe Lieberman's name was attached to it. Joe, of course, had been the vice presidential candidate on Al Gore's ticket in 2000, and the last thing the Republican machine wanted to do was give him any credit for a major security initiative. They sought to undermine the bill and began providing amendment after amendment in committee. The ranking Republican on the Governmental Affairs Committee, Ted Stevens from Alaska, led the administration fight to weaken the bill through amendments. I voted against all of them. Our bill passed intact, and with the full complement of worker protections in place for anyone who worked in the newly created Department of Homeland Security.

Around that same time, I also cosponsored the bill that created the 9/11 Commission, designed to investigate the factors that led up to the attack and find out what the country should do to prevent one in the future. The Bush administration fought like hell against that bill as well, but we prevailed in the end, further strengthening my hand for reelection.

That meant the primary thing I had to wrestle with in the weeks before the election was the upcoming vote on the Iraq War.

Bush and his inner circle—Rumsfeld, Rove, Cheney, and Wolfo-witz—had decided to make the Iraq War the number one wedge issue for the election of 2002. If they could get the party faithful and the 9/11 fearful to back the war, Congress would have to go along. And anyone who didn't would be ripe for attack come Election Day. The Republicans even went so far as to set the vote for the resolution authorizing military force against Iraq for October, less than a month before the election. Unlike his father, the younger Bush proposed a resolution for war just before the midterms. The elder Bush, on the other hand, waited until a new Congress had been seated after those elections before asking permission to start the first Gulf War. The big difference was that the father made a conscious effort to avoid turn-ing the question of sending U.S. troops to war into a political issue, while the son did his damnedest to make going to war the ultimate one in the Republican quest to take back the Senate.

I had already had a lesson in Bush-style arm-twisting when the presi-dent was trolling through the Senate searching for Democrats willing to go along with his tax cuts. He invited me to the Oval Office to talk about the tax issue just a few days before the Senate was to vote in May 2001. I was there, in part, because Georgia was so Bush-friendly and polling in the state had shown the tax cuts were popular back home. When the White House called with the invitation, I was told the meeting would just be between me and the president, and that I should not bring any of my staff with me. That was not how things played out. Bush had his chief of staff, Andrew Card, sit in, while I was on my own. The president turned on the charm. He was jovial, made attempts at being witty, and referred to himself several times as "a rea-sonable guy." I tried to bring the conversation around to the tax issue, but that wasn't what the president really wanted to talk about. He wanted to make me feel good about him personally. I felt like I was in a fraternity rush and Bush was the rush chairman trying to get me to join. It was classic Bush bullshit. There was no substance involved, just a lot of backslapping. I didn't promise him my vote during our meeting. I felt like I had been taken in a game of three-card monte just for going. In the end, I did vote for the tax cuts, but only after they had been modified more to my liking in the Senate.

When it came to the war vote, rush chairman Bush was nowhere to be seen. In his place was attack dog Bush. Bush needed an evil to fight, and Karl Rove always made sure he had one. It made him look strong. And strength in a national leader in the wake of 9/11 was what people were looking for. The president and his salespeople were able to define Saddam Hussein as "evil" and people like me—Democrats in the Senate—as risks to national security. My neck was on the chopping block as I considered my vote on the Iraq War Resolution.

I had a meeting with my campaign team one afternoon in the fall of 2002, just before the war resolution vote. Geoff Garin, my pollster, said that there was a groundswell of concern about national security in the polls. He rightly observed that the question of war was a big issue in election year 2002 and said I needed to vote with the president.

I was in deep conflict on the Iraq War Resolution. The whole reason I had gotten into national politics was that I wanted to help keep our young people out of "stupid wars" like the one that had gotten me blown up. I told my political team that. They said I could *think* that all I wanted, but I could never say it publicly in this election. At the time, Bush had a 68 percent public approval rating in Georgia. Still, I didn't like the idea of voting for war—any war—when war had cost me so much. I argued that my military record was sufficient, that my being on the Armed Services Committee was sufficient, that having cosponsored the Department of Homeland Security legislation was sufficient to address the question of whether or not I was indeed protecting the national security of the United States. No one on my staff agreed. My campaign manager, Tommy Thompson, told me that if I voted against the war resolution, "you will quickly become the ex-senator from Georgia."

Still, I had major doubts about the war resolution. It smelled like war for political reasons, not national security reasons, just like Vietnam had been. I asked my friend and fellow Vietnam veteran John Kerry about it. John said that he thought military success in Iraq was achievable. He had flown in a helicopter over the battlefield a couple of weeks after the first Gulf War and described the American assault on the Iraqi ground forces as a "turkey shoot." Kerry told me he intended to vote for the resolution.

Bill Johnstone, my top policy adviser, put it more bluntly.

"Max, if you vote against the resolution out of principle, it won't make any difference. It will still pass, and you will be hung out to dry. You could lose your Senate seat over this."

I was not willing to risk losing my seat. I also knew that my constituents wanted me to give the president the benefit of the doubt and my support. And I rationalized that if I won reelection, I could live to fight another day. I would have six more years to care for those who bore the battle. After the election, I would be free to speak up for them forcefully.

The vote authorizing the war in Iraq came in the form of a resolution. The president already had a resolution approved by Congress to go after those who attacked us. Now he wanted a resolution specifically to go after Saddam Hussein. The resolution was rewritten again and again until it was cloaked in language soft enough to garner the support of moderates like me. The resolution required that Bush go through the UN first, but in the end, it gave him what he wanted. Dubya was given the authority to use our military "as he determines to be necessary and appropriate" in order to defend the nation. It was the Gulf of Tonkin Resolution, Part II. Its passage facilitated the creation of the Iraq War—the Vietnam War, Part II.

Given my leadership on two of their pet issues, and my vote for their war, I figured the only way the Republicans could beat me on the question of national defense would be to lie about me. Naturally, that's what they did.

By the time the Iraq War vote came down, I was in the final weeks of my campaign for reelection. I had an opponent handpicked by Karl Rove. Saxby Chambliss was a Republican congressman from the southern part of the state who had gotten out of Vietnam with a trick knee. That didn't stop him and the Republican Party from launching an ad against me that set what many, myself included, regarded as a new low in national politics.

It showed Osama Bin Laden's photo, Saddam Hussein's photo, and my photo alongside, as if I were a terrorist as well. A voice-over stated that I had voted against President Bush's Homeland Security proposal a number of times. The ad was an absolute distortion of reality. I had sponsored the Homeland Security Bill over the president's objections, and defended it when Republicans tried to gut it. To insinuate that I had anything to do with Saddam Hussein or Osama Bin Laden was absolutely preposterous. I had fought terrorists and paid a great price, while Bush, Cheney, and Saxby Chambliss had all ducked out of the war of our generation. Further, I had actually supported the president in the Iraq War Resolution. Still, the ad caused a tremendous stir.

Senators Chuck Hagel and John McCain, both wounded Vietnam veterans, were the first to come to my aid. "I've never seen anything like that ad," said McCain in a *Washington Post* article. "Putting pictures of Saddam Hussein and Osama Bin Laden next to a picture of a man who left three limbs on the battlefield—it's worse than disgraceful, it's reprehensible."

Chuck came over to me one day as we were walking through the tunnel between the Dirksen building and the Senate. Looking straight at me, he said, "There are some things more important than politics."

He offered to do a TV spot for me rebutting the ad, even though it was being aired by his own party.

Saxby Chambliss got wind of what Hagel had proposed. He called Chuck seven times in one day begging him not to side with me. Hagel asked him to take the ad down. Instead, Chambliss modified the ad somewhat, but still ran it. The ad still alleged that I had voted against the creation of Bush's Homeland Security Department 11 times. Then the ad stamped the word "misleading" over my face. The only true part of that ad was that I had voted against all the proposed Republican amendments that were designed to kill the bill.

In fact, it was Chambliss who was doing the misleading. In a debate against me just before the election, he dodged the question of Vietnam service by saying, "I had a bum knee. I had an old football knee that unfortunately they wouldn't take me." In reality, Chambliss was classed "I-A," meaning fit for service, twice during his college years. He sought and received five student deferments to get out of service, according to U.S. government records.

But the political season was already hot and heavy in Georgia that year, even without the dirty tricks and the war issue looming on the horizon. The Democratic governor of Georgia, Roy Barnes, had led a successful effort in the spring of 2002 to remove the Confederate battle emblem from the Georgia state flag. It made all the African Americans and progressive-minded people in the state happy, but it angered the state's rural white community something fierce. A white backlash resulted, especially among young white males.

Ralph Reed—onetime head of the Christian Coalition—had become a big mover and shaker in Georgia politics and was chairman of the Georgia Republican Party in 2002. His polling data showed that the flag issue was off the charts with white males. Reed saw an opening. He passed this information to the White House. Money poured in to Reed to register white males angry about the flag. When my friend Senator Paul Wellstone died a week before the election in a plane crash, Senator Bill Frist, head of the Republican Senatorial Campaign Committee, moved $700,000 in Republican money that had been earmarked for taking out Wellstone to Georgia so Ralph Reed could help take me out.

The weekend before the election, Reed assembled 10,000 Republican volunteers in Savannah, Georgia. They fanned out in 300 buses and went door to door all over Georgia to boost white male turnout. The thinking was that if they could drop the percentage of black voter turnout in Georgia to under 20 percent of the total by increasing white voter turnout, especially among males agitated over the flag, the Republicans could win. To help in that effort, Bush came to Georgia five times, including the weekend before the election, while Reed and his shock troops were banging on doors across the state.

It rained on Election Day in Georgia. It was a downpour. I knew that meant bad news for Democrats. Additionally, I had a sinking feeling that things weren't going to turn out well. The Bush-led, Karl Rove–inspired Republican politics had its moment in Georgia that day. They had trashed John McCain in 2000. They trashed me in 2002. And later, they would "swift-boat" John Kerry. As Kerry told me in 2004, "They took away my service." That was how I felt.

It fills me with sadness that it is considered an acceptable political tactic to question the patriotism or military record of any serviceman or servicewoman who served an honest tour of duty in a war zone. The attacks on McCain, Kerry, and me, all decorated wounded combat veterans, are a shameful legacy of the Bush administration, and among the most shameful political stunts in the nation's history.

By early election night, it was clear I was not going to win. I called Saxby Chambliss and congratulated him. I lost by 140,000 votes, roughly the same number of white male voters who were motivated to turn out in an off-year election to show their displeasure over the flag issue. For the first time in years, the percentage of blacks that turned up at the polls came in at below 20 percent.

Democrats around the state lost. I lost, the governor lost, the speaker of the Georgia house lost, and many Democratic members of the state senate and house who had voted to change the flag lost. Forty counties flipped from Democrat to Republican in south Georgia alone.

The Republicans had scored their biggest win in Georgia since the end of Reconstruction in 1876. And, with my defeat and the defeat of Jean Carnahan in Missouri, the Republicans took back the U.S. Senate.

Bush and the Republicans now had all three branches of the federal government. They had the Supreme Court, the U.S. Senate and House, the presidency, and all the agencies of the federal establishment. I can so well remember after I lost, shopping in a food store and seeing a picture on a magazine cover of Bush and Karl Rove hugging each other and smiling broadly in the wake of their dramatic win. It burned my soul to the core. With the Republicans in charge of all the levers of power, George Bush had what he wanted—an open path to war. And I had helped him get there. Twenty-one Democrats, one Republican (Chafee), and one Independent (Jeffords) voted against the resolution.

They were right.

I was wrong.

I have to live with that mistake for the rest of my life. But I also have to reckon with having been outwitted politically and tactically, and I strongly suspect a lot of below-the-radar chicanery went into ensuring my defeat.

The Diebold machine company is based in Ohio. Among other things, it manufactures voting machines.

The state of Georgia saw the debacle with the state of Florida and the "hanging chads" in 2000 and decided that Georgia would not be subject to such embarrassment. Governor Roy Barnes and Secretary of State Cathy Cox, the chief election officer of the state, decided to purchase and install new, high-tech "black box" voting machines in every precinct in Georgia for the election of 2002. Georgia became one of the first states in the nation to be all computerized. The situation was ripe for fraud.

The state gave the contract to Diebold for the installation of the machines. The election officials who normally run elections in Georgia were not up to speed on the technology of the new computerized machines and so had to rely on technicians from Diebold to set everything up, from programming them to inserting the names of candidates. As is the law in Georgia, the machines were tested for fraud before the election. Apparently, the run-through went well. But, less than 24 hours before Election Day, according to a Diebold whistle-blower who told his story in 2007, the head of Diebold sent a team to install a computer "patch" in each of the 5,000 machines to be used in Fulton and DeKalb counties.

Fulton and DeKalb counties provide the only Democratic stronghold in Georgia. DeKalb is majority black, and Fulton has hundreds of thousands of black citizens as well. Both counties have been reliably Democratic for years. Ostensibly, the patch was installed to correct a problem with the clocks in the machines. The job was done in the dark of night in a warehouse in the Atlanta area. According to various news accounts, including a 2006 *Rolling Stone* article by Robert F. Kennedy Jr., the whistle-blower said he and others were told not to talk to election officials about the patch or the supposed repair job. The orders came from the head of Diebold's voting machine operation, Bob Urosevich, who personally delivered the patch from company headquarters in Texas.

The clocks never worked.

The machines were clearly adjusted by people who were not election officials. I don't know if the adjustment flipped Democrat votes to Republican, as has been alleged. The Diebold machines do not provide a verifiable paper trail in the form of ballots, or even a receipt showing how a vote was recorded. There is nothing for election officials to review in the event of a recount.

I do know that I was ahead of Republican Saxby Chambliss by six points in public polling leading up to the election. Democratic governor Roy Barnes was 11 points ahead of Republican Sonny Perdue.

We both lost.

Later, in 2004, the president of Diebold sent out a letter stating that he was "committed to helping Ohio deliver its electoral votes to the president." That state also uses a good deal of Diebold voting equipment. Bush won in Ohio over John Kerry, claiming the presidency amid numerous accounts of people in Democratic strongholds pushing "Kerry" on the screen and seeing "Bush" highlighted as their choice.

America cannot allow our elections to be so vulnerable to corruption. In this age of high-tech computer hacking, the need for a verifiable paper trail associated with our elections could not be greater. We get receipts with every bank machine transaction we conduct. Election officials should be able to get one when we vote.

Immediately after the election, I took my girlfriend, Liz, and lit out for St. Thomas in the Virgin Islands. I planned to do something there I had never done in my life. I was going to propose marriage to a woman.

The circumstances were not going to be quite like I had imagined, particularly the part about being newly reelected right before I popped the question, but I decided to go through with it anyway. I had always equated having a wife with having a "real" life like everyone else. I bought an engagement ring and had an old Robert Browning quotation inscribed on top of the jewelry box: "Grow old along with me! / The best is yet to be / The last of life, for which the first was made." Liz accepted, but the best was not yet to be for us.

Instead, the worst was about to happen.

Losing my race for reelection was having a profound effect on me. Another grenade had blown up in my face—this time on the political battlefield rather than the military battlefield. But it felt the same way. When I lost my senate seat, I lost my way of coping with life after Vietnam.

Back in Washington after the trip to the Caribbean, I sat powerless and watched as my staff packed up my life. As they took the plaques and photographs off the walls, especially the big picture of me with Senator Russell, I felt like crying. Liz and I went back to Atlanta for Thanksgiving, but for some reason I couldn't celebrate. I couldn't enjoy anything. I felt miserable inside. The afternoon of Thanksgiving 2002, I started crying, and I was to keep crying off and on for the next two and a half years as the worst depression of my life swallowed me whole.

✶ 20 ✶

An Infamous Commission

ONE OF THE first things I did back in Washington after I lost the election was corner Tom Daschle on the Senate floor and ask him to appoint me to the 9/11 Commission. I had been one of the original cosponsors of the legislation that created the investigatory body over the objections of the White House, and I was about to be out of a job come January. It seemed like a good fit. Daschle graciously agreed.

Serving on the commission made sense to me in many ways, and I knew it would be a high-profile effort. I believed it would provide some purpose and direction for my life. It wouldn't be the Senate, but I thought it would be something that I could sink my teeth into.

Before I left the Senate, Daschle invited me to meet with some of the family members who had lost loved ones in the attacks. Listening to those families, their eyes filled with grief and suffering, I wondered, What good could come of this? How can we help these people heal? I decided that I would pull no punches and get to the bottom of the issues. I had a new mission in life.

I thought the 9/11 Commission would be the most powerful and responsible government commission since the commission investigating the attack at Pearl Harbor. I thought the goal was to figure out what happened so we could make sure that such an event would never happen again.

I was wrong.

The White House, especially Dick Cheney, fought the creation of the 9/11 Commission all the way. Ultimately, it was the families of the victims who forced the president and Congress to agree to its establishment. Time and again over the next year, those families would call press conferences and demand presidential action in the face of Bush's inaction. It was their involvement that ultimately forced Bush and Condi Rice to agree to testify before the commission, although without swearing to tell the truth.

Bush, Cheney, and others in the administration would do their best to hamstring the commission until the end. I have come to believe that their goal was simply to protect themselves from blame and keep their plans for war in Iraq on track.

Appointed in early January 2003, more than a year after the attacks, one of the first things I did as a member of the commission was to read up on Al Qaeda and its history. I also looked at how our government, particularly President Roosevelt, responded to the attack on Pearl Harbor.

Within the first week after that tragedy, Roosevelt had set up a commission to investigate it and all its ramifications. Just 10 days after the attack, he relieved both the naval commander at Pearl Harbor, Admiral Husband E. Kimmel, and the army commander, General Walter Short, of their jobs based on the commission findings. Every aspect of the government's inner workings, from diplomacy to military readiness and intelligence, was laid bare for the commission to examine. And in the end, Roosevelt got his man: Within three years, he had personally given the order to shoot down the plane carrying Admiral Yamamoto, the Harvard-educated enemy warrior who planned the attack.

During that length of time, there were at least four commissions that looked at the December 7, 1941, fiasco, and their findings led to government reforms. The conclusions of those commissions resulted in the National Security Act of 1947. That act created the Department of Defense (rather than the Department of War), the U.S. Air Force (rather than the old U.S. Army Air Corps), and the Central Intelligence Agency (rather than the Special Operation Units of World War II).

At its inception the CIA was asked to make sense of all the intelligence information coming in to the United States government from various bureaus and agencies. The commissions studying the Pearl Harbor attack concluded, among other things, that intelligence in the U.S. government was "stovepiped"—not readily shared with other agencies, especially other intelligence agencies. Consequently, there was no unified voice presenting the latest intelligence to the president and the Congress to help them "evaluate the threat to the United States."

The creation of the CIA was supposed to change that. For decades now, the president of the United States has gotten President's Daily Briefs from the CIA, highlighting our nation's most valuable intelligence. Those briefings are presented to the president routinely every morning wherever he is around the world.

Eventually, however, the CIA mission began to change. The agency got more involved in espionage during the cold war and moved further away from its original role as a sort of information clearinghouse. In the 1950s, the CIA began its dark work of assassinating foreign leaders and setting off government coups in other nations. Eisenhower liked the CIA and its covert nature and began employing the agency's spies more and more, subtly shifting the nature of the agency itself. He authorized a number of secret missions, including a plan to topple Castro in Cuba. When President Kennedy came to office, the plan to remove Castro was still very much alive. Kennedy bought it, which led to the Bay of Pigs disaster. After that, Kennedy didn't think much of the CIA's field capabilities. He vowed to return the CIA to its original purpose of gathering information from the existing intelligence units of the federal government and presenting it to the president in a centralized way. But Kennedy was assassinated before he could follow through with his plan.

Come Vietnam, Lyndon Johnson again embraced the cloak-and-dagger side of the CIA. He encouraged the agency's spies to work side by side with the American military in Vietnam, especially with Special Forces units. I saw some of that stilted relationship during my time in the army.

As a young signal officer in 1967, I was summoned to a CIA safe house in Qui Nhon, a city on the South China Sea. I was in charge of a radio outpost in Qui Nhon that supported my unit, the First Air Cavalry Division. Since a great deal of the division's supplies came in at the Qui Nhon port, my radio team worked around the clock communicating division resupply operations. Unbeknownst to me, our radio post was located near the CIA safe house. One day I got a message from one of my guys that a CIA officer wanted to talk to me in person. The CIA guy had been bugging my guys about using our radio to talk to his superiors in Saigon. That was a definite breach of our orders, so I jumped in a jeep with "Top" Marcus, my company first sergeant, and drove the 30 miles to Qui Nhon.

Top Marcus was a lot older than me. He had been with Merrill's Marauders in Burma in World War II and had served as a young radio officer at the Big Three conference in Yalta at the end of that war. He had seen a lot of war.

On the trip down to Qui Nhon, as we drove along the snaking roads of the Central Highlands and then down the hills that sloped into the port city, Top pointed at the Vietnamese peasants working in the rice fields, just as their ancestors had done for centuries. We had just come from the sprawling American base camp at An Khe, a place with electricity, refrigeration, and a thousand other conveniences unknown to the farmers knee-deep in the rice paddies. Top looked at me and said, "We'd probably be much better off if we tore down our base and used the money to give each one of these Vietnamese a chance to improve their lives." I've come to think he was right, and not just about Vietnam. It clutches my heart when I think of the hundreds of thousands of people who would still be alive, the millions of families that wouldn't have been torn asunder, and the generation of children who wouldn't have known war. So it is when an army of liberation becomes an army of occupation. The killing just goes on and on. Sometimes, as Top said, it's just better to give the money to the locals and leave.

In Qui Nhon, Top and I made our way to an old house built in the nineteenth century during the French colonization of Indochina. We entered and found three Americans in civilian clothes sitting on sofas in a large living room. Three of my radio guys from our outpost in town were already there, summoned by the CIA. One civilian, obviously the lead CIA officer, approached me and said, "Why can't I use your radio to send some messages to Saigon? You've got secure radio Teletype here."

That was true, but nonmilitary personnel could not use it.

"This rig belongs to the First Cav and the U.S. Army. I can't let you use it," I told him. "You've got to go above me to get the OK."

He looked at me a minute.

"Do you know about the buildup north of here by the North Vietnamese?" he asked, mad enough to blow smoke.

"No, sir. I don't know about it."

He squinted his eyes and squared his jaw before he spoke. "You should know about it. The North Vietnamese are building up like crazy up north. They didn't tell you that?"

"No, sir," I replied. "I didn't know that."

"I need to get word to Saigon. I need to do it now."

"Yes, sir. I know. But I'm not authorized to let anybody use this system other than army folks. You'll have to go higher than me to get approval."

The conversation ended. My men, all five of us in uniform, got up to leave. I remember thinking that the CIA's little outpost didn't seem too worried about being secretive, with American soldiers coming and going in broad daylight and a bunch of CIA guys inside dressed like they were fixing to go bowling. As Top and I drove away, he said, "Did you see what happened? They taped the whole thing."

"They did? Who the hell do they think we're working for, the other guys?"

"Nope," Top said. "That's just the way they do things. They're spooks."

I had never met the CIA agent before, but I could tell the guy didn't like me. It was also obvious he had a beef with normal military intelligence. There were other radios he could have used right there in town. We figured he was trying to avoid talking to somebody in the military intelligence unit, maybe just because he didn't like them, or maybe because he didn't want to share his information with them. Why else would he be trying to get a combat unit like ours to let him use radio gear?

I returned to my platoon at the 1st Cav base in An Khe. I called the guys together and relayed what the CIA spook said about forces massing in the north, and that it might mean there was a big attack brewing. I told them to practice rolling out of their bunks, hitting the floor, and grabbing their weapons. And then I passed what I had been told on up the line to my commanding officer. This was in October 1967. Three months later, February 1, 1968, the North Vietnamese launched the Tet offensive, the most massive attack of the war. Tet is the Vietnamese New Year, and the 1968 holiday inaugurated the Year of the Monkey. The attack put a monkey on the back of every American serviceman in Vietnam.

The north's sneak attack was successful in that it caught our military planners by surprise. I could not understand how that happened.

It made no sense. Clearly the CIA knew something was up months before it happened if its operatives were blabbing about it to regular army soldiers like me and the four guys from my unit. We were just radio guys. We weren't in any kind of command position. Was it possible that nobody in the CIA had told their counterparts in the army about the enemy troop buildup for three months?

In 1982, more than a decade later, the entire fiasco between the CIA and military intelligence went public. CBS aired a big story about the rift between the different intelligence arms of the two entities and the bad blood between them. There was much finger-pointing. No resolution ever came of it. The CBS story suggested that General Westmoreland—commander of U.S. forces in Vietnam from 1964 to 1968—had hidden evidence of the pending Tet offensive from the president and others because showing the true strength of the North Vietnamese forces would have caused political troubles back in the States, especially in terms of maintaining support for the war itself.

Westmoreland sued CBS for libel in 1982, seeking $120 million. The two parties quietly settled out of court in 1985. Westmoreland got nothing. The Tet offensive was simply labeled an "intelligence disaster" and the country moved on. But for me, what happened with Tet remains instructive. I believe it illustrates how easy it is for those in power to ignore, squash, or manipulate any intelligence they don't like. Like 9/11, Tet showed that the creation of the CIA did nothing to prevent the nation's intelligence communities from stovepiping information as they had done with Pearl Harbor.

After 9/11, the entire nation wanted to know who attacked us and why. The president selected Henry Kissinger as chairman of the commission charged with answering that question. I thought it was a great choice. I had come to know Kissinger during my six years on the Senate Armed Services Committee and once had him over to my Senate office for tea. We enjoyed each other's company immensely and talked about a lot of things, including, to my delight, the fact that he believed I was carrying on the bipartisan spirit of my predecessors, Dick Russell and Sam Nunn. That afternoon he told me that Vietnam had taught him, "You can't solve political problems with the military."

I agreed.

I called him to congratulate him on his 9/11 appointment. I told him I was looking forward to working with him. But Kissinger didn't take the job. All of us on the commission had to disclose any interest in or connection with a foreign government. Kissinger apparently couldn't do that. I called him on the phone again to express my regret that he wouldn't be leading our effort. He chuckled and said in that distinctive accent, "I'm eighty years old and I've got to make a living."

I think that was where the commission began to go awry. Ultimately, when the commission had to wrestle with the big dogs in Washington, especially the big dogs at the White House, we lost virtually every battle. Minus the gravitas of a Kissinger-like figure in our camp, the administration just steamrolled right over us.

In Kissinger's stead, Bush installed a mild-mannered, retired Republican governor from the state of New Jersey, Tom Kean, as chairman. Kean was likable enough, but at 67 and president of a small liberal arts college in New Jersey, he wasn't exactly the tiger we needed to tame Washington and tackle the White House about the most serious attack on the nation since Pearl Harbor.

Although the commission was supposed to be "independent" and answer to no one, the White House cast a long shadow over our operations. In order to get anything out of the staff assigned to the commission for research and other help, we had to go through the Bush-appointed commission staff director, Dr. Phil Zelikow, a Condi Rice protégé. And staff members were required to go through him to talk to us. The administration was obviously putting a close hold on information flowing back and forth between commission members and staff personnel.

A few weeks into the investigation, we began to cut to the chase. We agreed that the main issue was this: What did our government know and when did it know it? That was the famous question asked by Senator Howard Baker from Tennessee when he served on the Watergate Committee investigating the Watergate break-in and the subsequent cover-up by the Nixon White House.

It was the ultimate question too for President Bush.

As commander in chief, what did the president know and when did he know it? Did he know enough before the attack happened that something could have been done to prevent it? The commission never got a straight answer.

Straight answers were hard to come by from any government agency during the year I spent on the commission. We were treated like representatives from a foreign country: Virtually every request was ignored. Over the course of the year 2003, the commission was forced to subpoena the Federal Aviation Administration, the North American Aerospace Defense Command, the Air Defense Command, and the Department of Defense. All of those agencies ultimately answer to the White House, and all of them refused to provide access to any information without a subpoena.

The fact that we were having to subpoena the FAA to find out what was going on in our airspace prior to and during the 9/11 attacks told me that the administration was deliberately and calculatingly slow-walking the commission in order to run out the clock and have the commission expire without having done its job. But the agencies couldn't hide for long. We were able to compel them to turn over what we wanted to see.

Once we obtained the audiotapes and other records we sought from the FAA, NORAD, and the Department of Defense, it became clear those agencies had been misleading the public, the Congress, and now the 9/11 Commission regarding their various responses to the attacks. For instance, NORAD and the FAA reported to the commission and in press interviews that they were tracking the hijacked aircraft during the attack and had military jets ready to shoot down United 93, the flight that crashed in Pennsylvania. But the subpoenaed records suggest that neither agency was aware of the hijacking of that flight until after it had crashed. The commission debated pushing for obstruction of justice charges against each of those government entities, but ultimately simply referred the matter to the inspector general within each agency.

A much tougher nut to crack was the White House itself.

Long before a man named Alberto Gonzales became famous for misleading Congress as attorney general, he was President Bush's lawyer. In that capacity, he represented Bush's interests before the commission. Gonzales later gained further notoriety for his role in covering up the illegal destruction of secret CIA videos of torture sessions with Al Qaeda prisoners. The *New York Times* reported in December 2007 that Gonzales was privy to their destruction in 2005 even as a federal judge ordered the tapes to be preserved. What's more, he and other White House officials had been discussing the destruction of those tapes with the CIA since 2003. Those tapes had been requested time and again by the commission for the purpose of determining what, if any, information the CIA had obtained from captured Al Qaeda operatives. Requests for them were made to CIA director George Tenet, Gonzales, and numerous Bush administration officials. It was after their illegal destruction became known to the world through that *New York Times* article that Tom Kean and Lee Hamilton, the Democratic vice chair of the commission, wrote their extraordinary op-ed piece in the January 2, 2008, *New York Times*. In that piece, they wrote, "As a legal matter, it is not up to us to examine the CIA's failure to disclose the existence of these tapes. That is for others. What we do know is that government officials decided not to inform a lawfully constituted body, created by Congress and the president, to investigate one of the greatest tragedies to confront this country. We call that obstruction."

That's what we were up against in the White House.

More and more as our investigation progressed, evidence pointed to the fact that only the President's Daily Briefs from the CIA would paint a true picture about what the president and the nation's intelligence agencies knew about any potential Al Qaeda threat.

We knew that getting them would be difficult, especially because Gonzales flatly refused to give the commission access to them. The White House had already been down this road of halfhearted cooperation with an earlier congressional investigation of 9/11, the Joint Intelligence Committee headed up by Senator Bob Graham of Florida. That group never got to see any of the presidential briefs, and even then it had to delete 20 pages of its final report to the public and Congress because of "sensitive" materials regarding a foreign country—Saudi Arabia.

I don't know exactly what was in those 20 pages. But I know Bin Laden is a Saudi. And I know that over 100 members of the Bin Laden family were flown out of the United States immediately after the 9/11 attack. The White House cleared the flight out of the country within days of the attack. Did any of them have any connection to the hijackers?

The commission was not to get a chance to publicly ask such questions of Bush or Cheney, both of whom refused to testify under oath. In the meantime, we interviewed more than 1,000 people and reviewed millions of pages of documents, many of them classified. But the White House continued to stonewall on the daily briefings.

Time after time, Tom Kean and Lee Hamilton went to the White House to press the commission's case for seeing them. Time after time, they were rejected. Tim Roemer, a former congressman from Indiana, and I were sick of it.

It was time for a showdown.

Late one night in 2003, safely ensconced in a CIA safe office in Washington, we had it out with our fellow commissioners. For me, it came down to this: If the commission couldn't see the daily briefings, the commission couldn't do its job.

When Senator John McCain originally pushed for the creation of the commission, he insisted that it require a majority vote in order to issue a subpoena. We had easy majorities when it came to voting to subpoena the FAA and the Department of Defense. But that was not the case when it came to issuing a subpoena to a sitting president a year before the next election. The commission was equally divided between Republicans and Democrats. When it came down to issuing a subpoena for Bush's briefings, we split along party lines.

That night, as Tim and I made our case, we almost got our sixth vote. One of the Republicans wavered, but ultimately retreated back into the fold.

We failed in the subpoena bid, but we came darn close and that put a scare into the White House. Tom Kean and Lee Hamilton went back to Gonzales with the threat of an imminent subpoena. The White House played "Let's Make a Deal." Gonzales offered Kean and Hamilton a weird choice. A few of the commissioners could come to the White House and see the handful of daily briefings that the president considered relevant, and then take notes. Those notes would be reviewed by White House personnel before they could be shared with the other commissioners. Roemer and I thought that this was ridiculous. Our position was that if you trusted one commissioner, you trusted all of the commissioners.

Kean and Hamilton wanted to accept the deal. I did not.

I resigned. My statement at the time went public. I said, "If this decision stands, I as a member of the commission cannot look any American in the eye, especially family members of the victims, and say the commission had full access. This investigation is now compromised. This is *The Gong Show.* This isn't protection of national security."

Tim Roemer went public too. He said, "To paraphrase Churchill, never have so few commissioners reviewed so few important documents with so many restrictions. The ten commissioners should either have access to them or not."

Eventually, after receiving a handful of the daily briefings, the commission learned that a President's Daily Brief from August 6, 2001, was entitled, "Bin Laden Determined to Strike in U.S." It contained information about Al Qaeda seeking to hijack passenger jets and casing buildings in New York. Ultimately, we learned that Osama Bin Laden and Al Qaeda had been mentioned in 70 different presidential briefs provided to Bush between January 2001 and the attacks themselves. There were mentions of Al Qaeda cells working in the United States in those briefs. Clearly, they were important, but we were never to see many of them.

In the end, the commission learned through testimony before the commission and a book by Richard Clarke that Clarke and George Tenet had been warning the White House that an Al Qaeda attack was coming for months before September 11. But in the months before the attack, Clarke has said he was unable to get the White House's attention despite repeated requests for a meeting. Tenet said he warned the White House specifically in July 2001 that "the system was blinking red."

In 2007, Gonzales resigned as attorney general after being caught misleading Congress about his role in the firing of federal prosecutors. Additionally, he was fingered as one of the four White House staff people, including Dick Cheney and Harriet Miers, who participated in discussions about whether or not to destroy the CIA tapes made while torturing suspected Al Qaeda operatives.

The most important conclusion of the 9/11 Commission was that the nation needed an "intelligence czar" to be the ultimate focal point at the top of the pyramid to make sense of all the information gathered by the intelligence community. It was the best recommendation of the 9/11 Commission, and amounted to essentially the same recommendation made by Roosevelt's Pearl Harbor Commission, which had created the CIA for exactly that purpose.

Part of the problem with the nation's intelligence community is that the Defense Department has historically controlled 80 percent of the funds, while the CIA has had just 20 percent. To rely completely on the CIA to detect threats from terrorists all by itself is unrealistic in terms of budgetary priorities because the Defense Department is the agency with the money. Ultimately, as we know now, the Bush administration actually used the DOD to manufacture false intelligence about Iraq. Having an intelligence czar might have thwarted the infamous Rumsfeld-led neocon outfit that created the false intelligence used to justify going into Iraq.

Ultimately, the 9/11 Commission disproved that Iraq had anything to do with the attack. It was all Al Qaeda, as the FBI rightly announced to the nation the day of the attacks. Of course, it was too late. The president was already one year into his Iraqi adventure by the time the commission's findings were released.

In the end, I believe the administration decided to thwart the commission's work in order to protect the president from blame and continue the war in Iraq. The 9/11 Commission will go down in the history books like the Warren Commission, which investigated the assassination of President Kennedy. Both will be remembered as commissions that did not firmly resolve the questions they were asked to answer.

As Supreme Court justice John Paul Stevens told a *New York Times* reporter after reading the 9/11 Commission report, "I wanted to see a second opinion."

I did too.

★ 21 ★

"We Are Drowning in War"

ALL THROUGH MY days on the 9/11 Commission, a battle raged inside of me. Part of me was fully engaged with the terror investigation, and part of me was disappearing into a personal abyss.

The commission met much less often than I would have liked, and I found myself at loose ends. Home with my new fiancée, I'd fall to pieces and weep. After a few months, our relationship became strained. My emotional state was turning out to be more than Liz could handle.

Until then, my life as a public servant had made it possible for me to be not just a leader but also an inspiration to people from all walks of life. I had even been featured in a motivational video shown to people coping with traumatic injuries. I felt my life counted for something, and that had been a crucial part of my healing.

After my defeat in 2002, I lost all of that. I lost my confidence and my sense of purpose. I lost a sense of meaning in my life. I also lost my income. Suddenly I found myself broke with two nice apartments, one in Atlanta and a brand-new two-bedroom for Liz and me in D.C., where she had just gotten a great new job and expected to stay. I wanted to move back to Atlanta and retreat to the place where I had

215

been most happy. Liz wouldn't hear of it. So I let go of my apartment in Atlanta. It was a big mistake. It was another amputation. I loved that little apartment. I'd had it for almost 20 years. It was on the 12th floor with a balcony that looked over forests toward the city skyline. I used to sit on the balcony in the mornings and let the sun hit my face. I had all my personal treasures there, and my parents were just a half hour away. It was the one place in the world where I always felt safe and secure. I think that place provided me with a sense of home, a feeling of being grounded. I used the excuse of closing down the apartment to donate or throw away a lifetime's worth of awards and memorabilia. Truckloads of plaques and awards that I had been given since I was a state senator in the 1970s were just tossed out. I didn't want them anymore. I felt like all the tokens of my political life were just reminders of what I had lost. I donated my Senate papers to the Richard B. Russell Library at the University of Georgia, and my most precious personal memorabilia—war medals and such—to Stetson University, my alma mater.

Losing my senate staff meant losing my driver and the assistants who had helped me get around and get by in the world at large. Every job I had held since 1976, when Jimmy Carter appointed me head of the VA, had come with a full staff at my disposal. The day-to-day help and friendship my various staffs had provided at the VA, as Georgia secretary of state, and as a senator had nurtured me and deeply improved my quality of life.

Once they were gone, my handicaps and limitations were put into stark relief, both to me and, more importantly, to Liz. There was no hiding the fact that I was a 60-year-old man with the basic mobility of a 90-year-old. The more I depended on her, the more I felt like a burden. My anxieties began to take over. I found myself dwelling on them and finding no release: What am I going to do now? How am I going to get around? How am I going to get stuff done?

I was reduced to setting up a phone in the community party room of our apartment complex so I could have some semblance of an office.

I used the big table in there as my desk. I ended up going into debt to pay for a guy to come over for about four hours a day to help me get around town and collect my dry cleaning and such. I hadn't felt so low since my first days after Walter Reed, back in my parents' home.

Depression began to sweep over me. I grieved for the time I had once been whole, and I grieved for the time I had been a U.S. senator. I was inconsolable, and Liz and I fought more and more. It wasn't her fault. I was simply coming apart at the seams. More and more, I couldn't relate to her, and she became increasingly frustrated with my inability to cope with day-to-day life. This was not the life she had bargained for.

John Kerry's first wife, Julia Thorne, struggled with depression. She wrote a book, *You Are Not Alone: Words of Experience and Hope for the Journey Through Depression,* in which various people share their stories of how depression felt to them. I ran across a comment that stuck with me. One gentleman quoted in the book said, "Sadness is a cold. Depression is cancer." That was what I had, a cancer of the soul. It was deep and dark and real.

Good friends encouraged me to hang in there. Bill Clinton sent me a wonderful book by William Styron entitled *Darkness Visible,* the story of Styron's own personal struggle with depression. Bill told me that he too had suffered through a major depression, and there was light at the end of the tunnel. Hillary called and told me that she and Bill had been kicked to the curb and run over many times in their lives. They had bounced back, just as I would.

But that wasn't happening. I wasn't recovering. What really sent me over the edge was the invasion of Iraq in April 2003. I couldn't believe I was seeing another generation of young Americans sent into a muddled situation with no serious plan to win and no exit strategy.

To me, it was Vietnam all over again. I couldn't bear to watch the shock and awe of war broadcast right into my living room. I couldn't read the newspapers or listen to the radio. It was just war, war, war, everywhere I turned. All of that war news triggered deep emotions about war in general for me, particularly anger at the people who start wars. Here, once again, was a war being waged by a bunch of old men who had never been in battle and didn't understand the terrible human toll involved.

One day after coming in the front door and finding me listless once again, Liz looked at me and screamed, "Tell me you're on medication!"

I wasn't. I hated the idea of medication. I hated the thought that my brain was out of control, that it wasn't working right and I needed medication to fix it. I thought the cure for depression was to read another inspirational book. Boy, was I wrong: I have a shelf of them to prove it. Without drugs, I couldn't concentrate. I couldn't sleep. My brain just wouldn't work. When I did drift off at night, I had horrifying dreams. I remember one I had after my good friend Mary Landrieu won a runoff for her Senate seat in 2002, shortly after I'd lost my seat. In the dream, two cars raced down the New Jersey Turnpike at 90 miles an hour. They were neck and neck, jockeying back and forth. Then one of them crashed into a brick wall and exploded into flames while the other one kept going.

That was me. I had crashed and burned in life. The election was just like the grenade—over and done in an instant, with no appeal. No, we can't put your life back together again. No, you can't have your limbs back. No, you can't have your Senate seat back. That life is over now.

At Liz's prodding, I began taking my first antidepressant. It was Paxil, and I hated it. It blunted my blues from deepest black to dark purple, but it sure as hell didn't cure me. All it did was stabilize me at a slightly more tolerable level of misery than the one I had been at. Of course, different drugs work for different people. With Liz urging me to do so, I sought psychiatric help for the first time.

Thanks to those sessions, I was soon to learn that I hadn't left my war years behind me like I thought. I had just buried them under layer upon layer of scar tissue. The Senate defeat and the war in Iraq quickly ripped all of that away, leaving the great trauma of my life as bare and raw as it had been in 1968. It all conspired to transport me right back to the days of being blown up in Vietnam and lying on the ground dying. For the first time, I began feeling the total hopelessness and fear of the battlefield, reliving again those first desperate moments after I was blown up. My body and brain reacted accordingly. On high alert, my adrenaline ran wild. My brain chemicals became depleted.

The day I sat down across from the top psychiatrist at Bethesda Naval Hospital for the first time, I cried bitterly. He studied me for a while, then said, "I want to invite you to a meeting at my house."

I agreed. It turned out to be another Twelve Step program, this one for Washington types whose lives had crashed and burned for one reason or another. The night of my first meeting was cold and snowy. The house was in Georgetown, one of Washington's oldest and toni-est neighborhoods. A group of men I didn't know hauled me through the ice and snow at the curb and carried me and my wheelchair up a flight of steps to get me inside. The psychiatrist looked at me and said, "Welcome to the last house on the block." He called it that because people who came to the meeting had tried everything else and noth-ing had worked for them in their recovery. For them, and for me, it was, indeed, "the last house on the block," the last chance for success-ful living.

Everybody in that room had lived lives of total achievement, total success. Most of them were patients of the top psychiatrist in the navy. They were atomic scientists, famed top gun jet pilots, psychiatrists, senators, congressmen, ex-senators, ex-congressmen, and top military officials. Everybody in there had tried everything else before they ended up at "the last house on the block." High public office, power, money, fame, fortune, sex, drugs, liquor, women—none of those things had saved anybody in the room from crashing and burning. All of them had thought about suicide, and some had actually tried it. One man had held a gun to his head not long before the meeting. For the first time, I felt surrounded by people who understood my craziness, my sense of having lost it all. By the end of the night, I felt like I had found a place of total love, total acceptance, and total understanding.

The meeting was good for me, and so was my weekly counseling session, but after a couple of months, I could tell it wasn't enough, that it wasn't going to do the trick. I was just treading water. My anxieties were all still there. I had cycled through various drugs after Paxil, but they all did me in. They hurt me and confused me. They left me feeling like a zombie. They didn't make me feel better, just terrible in a different way. I quit taking them.

I had a friend in Miami named Howard who was going through an intense depression himself. I called him, and he said he was seeing a counselor there named Michelle and that she was saving his life. I knew I needed to find somebody like that. I asked for Michelle's phone number, and Howard gave it to me. I talked to her and told her the condition I was in and that I needed to get my life back. I asked her to recommend someone in the D.C. area. She said she would check it out.

Meanwhile, I started talking to my friend Charlie Wolden again. Charlie was one of the three men who had come to my aid on the battlefield when the grenade went off. He had helped save my life in 1968.

Now I needed Charlie to help save my life again.

Charlie and I had kept up with each other since we had reconnected after my appearance on the TV program about combat medics. We had talked on the phone a number of times, but more and more, I sought advice from him. Charlie had actually become a professional counselor to war veterans. After getting out of the marines in Vietnam, he had turned around and joined the Air Force as a B-52 bomber pilot. He was a successful Air Force major, but then started having trouble getting his life together. He finally walked into a VA Vet Center—the program that I had created when I was head of the VA—and sought help.

He told me the Vet Center saved his life.

Now I was turning to Charlie to save mine all over again. He told me that I needed someone who knew how to counsel combat veterans, not just people with depression. "Veterans are like cookie cutters. They're a lot the same, although each one is different too." Coincidentally, Howard's therapist in Miami called me back with the name of a lady at Walter Reed who was a specialist in post-traumatic stress disorder. I knew what PTSD was in a general way, but I didn't really understand how it manifested itself, as I had spent the last 40 years refusing to believe I had it. I asked Charlie about it.

"How are you feeling?" he asked.

"Well, I'm tense, I'm filled with anxiety, and I feel like hell. I feel like something horrible is about to happen at any moment and there is nothing I can do to escape it."

"That's PTSD, Max. It's an anxiety disorder. It can be full of fear and tension. It was for me."

For the first time in my life, I connected my own anxiety with PTSD. I thought I had avoided it. But I had it in spades. Even down to little things I just thought were my own personal quirks, like triple-checking all the stove burners and door locks at night and before I left home. I had been doing that and a hundred other things for decades, all in an effort to stay safe in a dangerous world.

It was also Charlie's insight that what I had experienced on the battlefield of politics was an exact replica of what I had experienced on the battlefield in Vietnam. I never made the connection until Charlie said it out loud. Clearly, my life had been blown up all over again and it had triggered every survival nerve in me. And the rapid escalation of violence in Iraq in late 2003 and early 2004 only sent me spiraling deeper into misery.

Soon I reported to the trauma counselor at Walter Reed, whom I'll call Val. Meeting her was a turning point. She had lost a husband in Vietnam, and could understand my pain. On my first visit with her I wept uncontrollably.

The irony did not escape me. I had come to Walter Reed in that same hopeless, helpless condition in late April of 1968. The doctors and nurses at Walter Reed had put me back together so well that I had lived a full life in the years after I left there. They had helped me become, in Hemingway's great phrase, "strong at the broken places." Yet here I was, almost 40 years later, helpless and hopeless at Walter Reed once again. What the hell was going on? Instinctively, I knew I was in the right place. I knew that the staff at Walter Reed understood war.

In my first visits with Val at Walter Reed, I saw some young wounded soldiers. That was tough for me, but not nearly as tough as it was about to become. My return to Walter Reed coincided almost perfectly with a massive increase in the number of Americans killed and wounded in Iraq. Most of the casualties from Iraq and Afghanistan are U.S. Army casualties. Walter Reed is the first place they are sent when they return to the States.

Once the war ramped up, like clockwork, three times a week, a large U.S. Air Force hospital plane loaded with patients would land at Andrews Air Force Base in Maryland. Coming from Landstuhl, Germany, the casualties were straight off the battlefields of Iraq and Afghanistan. I knew what being wounded in a war halfway around the world was like. I instinctively knew what these patients were going through before I'd even met them. I had made that trek myself before any of them had been born. Shortly after I began meeting with Val, Walter Reed was full to the gills with a new generation of wounded.

Every time I would go to Walter Reed and look down the corridors full of young soldiers in wheelchairs or hobbling on crutches, some with their arms missing, some with legs missing, some with portions of their faces gone, I felt like I was in a time warp. It was as if I was right back in Walter Reed as a patient myself, watching everyone hobble or roll up and down the halls. Nothing had changed, and to be back in that situation almost 40 years later was overwhelming.

I remember the day I saw my first female amputee. Sometimes after my therapy, I would go to the orthopedic ward. One afternoon, there was a young army sergeant in there—three stripes, a buck sergeant—lying in bed. Her right leg was intact, but her left leg was sawed off just like you would slice off a slab of beef at a butcher shop. She was a pretty girl.

I asked what had happened.

"Well, the LT said we had to go out on night patrol. I told him it was dangerous because we weren't fully up-armored and you can't see anything at night, but he said we had to go anyway. I thought about refusing, but I couldn't disobey a direct order. He put me in the lead vehicle, which I knew was the worst place to be. As soon as we left the base, I knew that we were going to get hit because the white flares in the sky changed to green flares. That was the signal when they knew we were coming, those green flares. Sure enough, we got hit. The bomb was right under me. It blew my leg off."

All I could think was, Oh, my God, we're sending women to get blown to hell! I was left wondering about who would send these young soldiers out on a night patrol in the desert where there is no place to hide. What the hell are they going to do in the dark? That sergeant lying there with her leg open and raw like a piece of steak, that got to me. I had seen amputees for 40 years. I had been an amputee for 40 years. But I had never seen a woman amputee, not from war.

Slowly I faced up to the most horrible part of it all, the thing that was making my recovery so hard.

I had voted to give George Bush the power to start his war. Almost 40 years to the day after I got blown up in Vietnam, I had raised my hand and voted for the Iraq War Resolution. I was nothing but a part of another Congress that gave another weak president too much power. I had tried telling myself that it wasn't my fault, that the resolution would have passed anyway, but sitting there in Walter Reed again, confronted by the human horror of what my vote had enabled, there was no escaping the truth. Deep in my soul, I felt like I blew it. When my turn came to protect another generation of young people from fighting and dying and getting maimed in another unwinnable, unnecessary war, I had blown it.

Every time I went back to Walter Reed, I saw the brokenness of the Iraq War. And more and more, I felt for these kids. I could see they were coming back not just with physical wounds, but with massive postwar stress. Doctors came up with a new word for what the soldiers from Iraq were suffering from: polytrauma. Polytrauma meant you were screwed up in multiple ways. Sending all facets of the American military—active duty, reserve duty, and the National Guard—on tour after tour meant that the soldiers never had time to calm down. They were always on alert, sent into combat over and over again, for years at a time. Psychologically, it was called hypervigilance, a classic symptom of PTSD. I knew what that was because I had it too. I was always on alert, always looking for danger. It had become impossible to settle down or relax. I could see the same edge in the eyes of the kids at Walter Reed.

The casualties making it back to the United States were the worst that had ever survived war. Most of the casualties in previous wars were due to gunshot wounds. The casualties coming back from Iraq were different. In the case of this war, most of the casualties were due to explosive devices, but not the Vietnam version. In the Iraq War, the explosive devices were so powerful that even if you didn't get hit with shrapnel, you could get caught up in the concussive impact of the explosion, strong enough to rearrange the internal parts of the body and the mind. Thus the term "traumatic brain injury"—the signature wound of the Iraq War. A study conducted by the staff at Walter Reed in 2006 found that 62 percent of the wounded from Iraq had some degree of brain injury. With new injuries came new challenges for the staff at Walter Reed.

Ultimately, a special three-week PTSD treatment course was created to deal with the worst of these cases. My counselor, Val, ran the course. It was her job to teach soldiers who had been through hell how to calm down and soothe themselves, how to leave the battle behind. Val began asking me to meet with the groups as they came through in batches every three weeks. For me, it was a nightmare, like a bad dream I couldn't wake up from.

The irony of the thing was that back when I was feeling hale and hearty with a concrete spike up my rear end as a U.S. senator, I was interviewed for a little film about people who had been through traumatic experiences and put their lives back together. I actually gave them the title they ended up using for the film. They called it *Strong at the Broken Places,* after the Hemingway quote that I often use. In the video, I gave my whole motivational spiel. I said the question is not whether or not you have been hurt, wounded, or blown up. The question is, Do you recover? In the video, I said that in my case, by the grace of God and the help of friends, I had gotten "strong at the broken places."

So what does my trauma counselor use to inspire these poor kids from Iraq and Afghanistan? The video I'm in! They see me there on-screen, a disabled veteran, my handicaps very visible, and it looks like I have my act together. Unbeknownst to them, I'm in therapy with the same counselor they are, broken into more pieces than some of them. I wasn't strong at the broken places anymore. I was shattered, sitting in the office for therapy every week, wiped out, done. No fiancée, no hope, no future, no job, no income. I felt that my life was over, and I couldn't stop crying. Then, literally on the other side of the wall from Val's office, there I was on-screen giving this uplifting message, saying, "You can get strong at the broken places. You can do this. I did it. Turn your hurts into halos, your scars into stars."

The first time my counselor sent me in there, everybody recognized me from the video. I was like a show-and-tell exhibit. I just started talking to them, asking what had happened to them. One guy said he just hadn't been able to come home because of all he'd seen and done. He said, "The only thing that's holding this whole thing together for me is the ink mark on this Iraqi woman's finger after she voted. That's the only thing I saw over there that was worthwhile in any way. That's the only thing with any meaning for me."

I knew how he felt.

Another guy, a young black guy who had already been to Iraq once and been hurt in an explosion, was being sent back just as soon as they could get his mind right. He had this recurring nightmare. "Me and my squad are out in the desert. A helicopter dropped us off, but they don't come back for days and days. They keep saying they are coming back, but they don't show. Then we get a message over the radio that says, 'We aren't coming back. Put a grenade in your mouth and blow yourself up.'"

That's where he was, that sense of total aloneness, total isolation, just him and his troops, desperate and without hope of rescue. I knew where he was coming from. There was no meaning for him. Just kill yourself. That was his Iraq. That was my Vietnam. I knew that sense of loss of support back home. That's what it felt like when Johnson announced he was dropping out and suing for peace moments before I took off for Khe Sanh. George Bush abandoned 200,000 troops on the battlefield when he left the presidency, just like Johnson did. They both retreated to their Texas ranches and left the soldiers who had followed them into battle "twisting slowly, slowly in the wind," to borrow a phrase from Watergate.

I kept going to Walter Reed for three years, until 2007. The war raged on, the casualties kept on coming, faster and more of them as time went by. One day during my counseling session, Val looked at me with sad eyes and whispered, "We are drowning in war."

It was getting to her as well. The whole hospital was overwhelmed. They had run out of space. By 2007, 30,000 people had been wounded in Iraq alone. About 4 percent of those wounded had at least one limb amputated.

In less than a year from the time Val said the hospital was drowning in war, the *Washington Post* ran an exposé on the situation at Walter Reed. They found 1,000 soldiers stuck in barracks that made living conditions in Baghdad look good. It was a national outrage. Heads rolled. The secretary of the army was fired. The commander at Walter Reed was fired. Another Washington commission was formed. Bob Dole and Donna Shalala headed up the commission and made recommendations. There was much stirring about, but little was done.

One day, I was early for our session, so I went to the cafeteria to get some lunch. Walter Reed is now in a new location, but going into the cafeteria was like going back in time. There were tables set up without chairs for those who didn't have legs and needed room for wheelchairs, just like there had been in 1968. I remember the first time they took me to the cafeteria from my ward to sit at those tables. I was totally freaked out: All the regular army folks were just milling around and getting their lunch, like having tables full of amputees was just a normal, regular part of everyday life.

Sitting at those same types of tables 40 years later, I saw a lady sitting in a wheelchair eating with a woman who was obviously her mother. I went over to eat by them. When I got to the table, I saw the woman in the wheelchair had no legs, just like me. And her right arm was mangled, just like mine. My first thought was, Oh, Lord, she has no idea what's in store for her. Poor thing.

We got to talking and I learned that she was a helicopter pilot with the Illinois National Guard. She had been flying a chopper in the battle of Fallujah in Iraq when she took a rocket-propelled grenade right in her lap. It blew the helicopter out of the sky. Her copilot managed to crash-land and pulled her, barely breathing, from the burning wreckage. Her life hung in the balance for 10 days after surgery, just as mine had.

We became fast friends. One day over the phone she confided to me that she wanted to make her life count for something. Hearing her say that, I saw myself in her. She went through all kinds of fittings and hell learning to walk on artificial limbs, as I had. Then one day, a year or so later, she called me up and asked me to come to a fund-raiser for her. She was running for Congress. I showed up at her event in Illinois and made my way to the stage area. She came walking toward me on her artificial legs. You see a woman in a skirt and the legs poking out from the bottom are brushed aluminum and shiny titanium from the knee down, that's a stark sight. But it was marvelous as well. And what an inspiration. Her name was Tammy Duckworth and I campaigned for her. She lost, but not before she had learned to run without legs. That afternoon, she told me that I had been her inspiration. I was blown away. Then she said she was a female Max Cleland. When it was my turn to introduce her at the mike, I told the crowd that I was a male Tammy Duckworth minus the sex appeal.

Tammy soon got appointed head of the Illinois Department of Veterans' Affairs and was one of three names bandied about by the Obama administration as a candidate to run the VA. She has since been named an assistant secretary.

The amazing thing is that Tammy is still in the National Guard as an army major serving as a flight safety officer. She told me that more than anything, she wants to fly again. That kind of spirit is just unbelievable. Seeing it in her reminded me that I had been like that once. In fact, I had been like that for 40 years. Tammy became my hero. I'm fairly certain she is the only person to have been profiled by both *Vanity Fair* and *Soldier of Fortune* magazines.

I met a lot of the Iraq kids at Walter Reed through a man named Jim Mayer. He lost both legs in Vietnam just like me, but he was able to walk on artificial legs because he still had knees. He had served as my executive assistant when I ran the VA. Once the Iraq War cranked up, Jim became known as the "Milk Shake Man" around Walter Reed for his habit of bringing McDonald's milk shakes to the new arrivals on the amputee ward. McDonald's named him their Customer of the Year because he bought so many milk shakes. He'd sit and talk with the kids, try to draw them out of their shells. When they got discouraged over their lost limbs, Jim would reach down and slide his pant legs up to show them that he had no legs. Most of them couldn't believe it. They were stunned that this guy who seemed perfectly normal and capable of getting around in the world had no legs. Jim was great therapy. Eventually he got a local restaurant to agree to provide a free steak dinner and plenty of booze to all the new arrivals on the amputee ward every Friday night. That has gone on for years. When he found a particularly tough case, he'd sic me on them.

Through Jim, I met one young soldier from an island in Micronesia. He was another triple amputee with no legs. I sat down to get to know him, and all he talked about was hunting, fishing, and running up and down the beaches back home. Sun, sea, sand, coconuts, and shrimp—that's all he knew from life on a tiny island in the Pacific. But he told me there were no jobs there. When the U.S. Army came offering lots of money if he'd sign up, he joined. They took him, an islander from nowhere, gave him a bunch of money, and shipped him off to a desert war thousands of miles away where he got blown up. I remember talking to him, trying to connect, and all I could think was, What is this kid going to do? Go back to live in a hut on his island? Run, jump, and play in the sand? I don't think so. The young man will need an electric wheelchair and all kinds of special accommodations for the rest of his life. The kid wasn't even a U.S. citizen, but we took him and sent him to our war. I was left wondering what we as a nation had become. We're hiring people who don't even get to live in America to go fight our wars?

We have a draft today, but it is a draft by hunger. We have an army made up of people who, in many cases, joined because it represented the only economic avenue out of the places they came from. Fifty percent of the casualties from Iraq are from towns of 2,000 people or less, according to Congressman Ike Skelton, House Armed Services Committee chairman. These aren't kids who are going to Harvard. They don't have those kinds of opportunities. They don't even have job opportunities anymore. And now these soldiers— some two million Iraq veterans by the end of it—are coming back from war to a country with a severely depressed economy. The percentage of homeless Iraq vets is on the rise, and so are incidents of domestic violence on U.S. bases. But soldiers fear being drummed out of the service if they report psychological problems while on active duty in a combat zone. These veterans need treatment instead of being kicked out of the army and denied any VA benefits. And they need jobs.

I had been meeting with Val for months. I was still weeping. She said, "You're about a quart and a half low in terms of your brain chemicals. You're caught in a depressive cycle. You need some chemical help." I had refused to take anything after bad experiences with several drugs, but Val thought it was time to try again. A hometown doctor I called for advice put it to me succinctly when he said, "Circumstances create depression. Chemicals perpetuate it."

I knew that as much as I hated medication, something had to give. I wasn't getting better. I wasn't getting my life back. And I was still living on the edge of nothingness. Maybe I did need some chemical help. Val thought it was the only thing that would tip the balance, but she didn't know what to try.

We had both heard horrible stories about people going from medication to medication over a long period of time and getting nowhere, as I had done. It was at this point that the good Lord intervened. At least I see it as an intervention now.

I had a speaking engagement at Brown University in Providence, Rhode Island. The trip turned out to be providential in every sense of the word. While there, I met the dean of the medical school at dinner. His name was Dr. Eli Adashi. He took one look at me and could tell something was wrong. He asked if I felt all right. I told him I was struggling with depression. Then he asked about medication. I told him my history and he said, "You're trying to walk without crutches. You're going to need some help." He handed me his card, and on the back he wrote "Cymbalta." I had never heard of it. Dr. Adashi said it was brand-new and that I should try it as soon as possible.

Val took me to a psychiatrist at Walter Reed, who wrote a prescription for me. The more I found out about it, the more I thought it might be helpful. It affects two of the three main brain chemicals that keep us sane—serotonin and norepinephrine. I started taking it and I began to feel better. It didn't leave me in a stupor of confusion. My self-doubt and depression began to ease. Within weeks, I was beginning to make a turnaround. I went whole days without crying, then whole weeks. Within a year, I believed I was actually getting "strong at the broken places" mentally and emotionally. Walter Reed had done it again.

President Bush decided to close Walter Reed and fold it into the Bethesda Naval Hospital in Maryland in 2011. It is a terrible shame for our military veterans and for the country at large. Now, at Walter Reed, the young doctors must look elsewhere for a career in medicine. They're leaving what Val calls "the mother ship" of army medicine.

I can't imagine my own recovery without Walter Reed. I see the closing of the 99-year-old institution as another Bush administration disaster. Meanwhile, our troops are still dying in Iraq. And, Walter Reed—my Walter Wonderful—is still drowning in war even as they try to close the doors forever.

★ 22 ★

Band of Brothers

JOHN KERRY CALLED me on my cell phone one day in 2003 while I was driving to my parents' house in Lithonia. I switched him to the speakerphone so I could drive and talk to him at the same time—when you've only got one arm, holding a cell phone while you drive presents obvious problems. We shared our latest news. My news was that I was starting to come out of my depression and was trying to find the way back into my life.

John's news was bigger.

"You've got to get back in the game, Max. I'm running for president and I need you to be there with me."

"OK," I said. "I'll be there."

John Kerry's full name is actually John Forbes Kerry—JFK. For me, getting back in the game with this second JFK was, as FDR termed it, "a rendezvous with destiny."

I had been struggling along in a couple of jobs before John's call. An old family friend, Danny Amos, appointed me a member of the board at Aflac, the insurance giant, just a week after I lost my Senate seat. It wasn't my life's calling by any means, and the board only met four times a year, but it helped pay the bills. My other job wasn't

233

much more fulfilling; I had been nominated by Tom Daschle, then Democratic leader in the Senate, for a position in the Export-Import Bank of the United States. The bank's main role is to provide loans for American companies looking to export goods overseas. The board members are appointed in pairs by the president, usually a Republican and Democrat each time. In my case, it was President Bush who appointed me. This was only a year after he had helped defeat me. I was nominated along with a woman who had been the president's girlfriend at Harvard while he was in business school there. She and I became friends. Through her, I learned that Bush had appointed me over the objections of his senior staff. Perhaps he felt guilty. Later I asked her to tell the president that I had forgiven him and Karl Rove for trashing me and ending my political career. She told me he was touched. I was grateful to have the job, but in the end, I felt like I was just spinning my wheels at the bank, headed nowhere.

So, when John called, I knew I had to help the new JFK win the presidency. It meant an opportunity to restore the old Kennedy legacy and wrest the fate of the nation out of Bush's bumbling hands. JFK was John's hero, just as he was mine. His example led both of us into politics. Kerry actually got into a fistfight defending Kennedy's campaign at a Kennedy for President rally in 1960—my kind of guy. In his own quest for the presidency, John Kerry would not let his staff use the initials JFK to abbreviate his name on schedules and such, insisting instead that they use JK.

In reality, both JFK and JK were so much alike it was spooky. Born to fine families in Massachusetts, Kennedy and Kerry both came out of Ivy League schools in the Northeast. Kerry joined the navy just like JFK, and volunteered for swift boat duty, the PT boat equivalent in the Vietnam War. Both men fought in the wars of their generations and both were decorated for saving the lives of their fellow soldiers. Kennedy had his *PT-109* crew campaign with him, while all but one member of Kerry's two swift boat crews stood with him as he announced his campaign in Charleston Harbor in South Carolina. I didn't get to help the first JFK win. I wasn't going to pass up this opportunity to help the second JFK.

I got back in the game.

When I signed on with Kerry in 2003, there were just five of us veterans who traveled to New Hampshire for a Veterans Day parade in November 2003. It was that way for weeks. At the time, Kerry was looking like a longer and longer shot for the presidency. He was 30 points behind Howard Dean in December 2003, just a month before the New Hampshire primary. The Kerry team calculated that he might be able to survive a loss in Iowa. But if he didn't win New Hampshire, which was literally in his own backyard, his backers would leave him. The rub was that if he didn't win Iowa, he would very likely be unable to stop the Dean juggernaut from rolling over the Granite State. Dean was riding high on a populist wave of antiwar sentiment, and Kerry couldn't touch him for a time because Kerry had voted for the Iraq War Resolution.

I was invited to a meeting with the campaign's top fund-raisers at Kerry's home. They were his closest friends, and they were worried about winning, especially with Kerry running so far behind Dean. Kerry urged them to hang in there. Then he asked me to say a few words. Off the cuff, I came up with the theme I would carry as I introduced him for the rest of the campaign. I said John had gone through war and had been wounded and changed by it. Understanding war, a President Kerry could get us out of the mess in Iraq and return the country to the economic prosperity of the Clinton years. I finished with, "John Kerry may not be a member of the greatest generation, but he's the greatest of our generation to be president of the United States."

I had first heard that line about Vietnam veterans being "the greatest of our generation" from General Hal Moore of the First Air Cavalry, coauthor of *We Were Soldiers Once . . . and Young*. I always liked the idea. The crowd applauded vigorously. Then John's wife, Teresa, came over and hugged me. She turned to the group and said, "I was a Republican before they attacked Max Cleland for being unpatriotic. I love Max Cleland and I'm glad he's here." Teresa and I hugged again and became fast friends.

Shortly after that, in early December 2003, I made my first visit for Kerry to Iowa, along with about a dozen veterans, most from Vietnam. The band of brothers had grown somewhat. A member of our group, Del Sandusky, had been the pilot on one of the swift boats Kerry commanded. Sandusky knew Kerry better than any man alive. They shared a special bond that had been forged in combat. He was the classic "old salt" and showed it. He helped me resurrect myself. Campaigning too quickly proved great therapy, something it had been since Vietnam. It was my way to fight back against Bush, Karl Rove–style politics, and the Iraq War.

Just before our group went back to Iowa for Kerry in January 2004 for the final push of the primary campaign, I developed a miserable cold. I was coughing my head off every night and living off antibiotics and cough syrup. Lying in bed a few days before I was supposed to get on a plane to Iowa for Kerry, I started coughing so hard that the reflex action of my heaving body actually threw me off the end of the bed and into the dark. I instinctively put out my left hand to brace myself. I hit the floor and wound up breaking the third bone in my hand. It swelled up so badly I could hardly even touch my chair, much less push it. A doctor wrapped it with some gauze and an Ace bandage and said that was about all that could be done. It would have to set itself. My hand being out of commission was a major problem. Without it, I had little mobility and independence. Simple tasks like opening a door became nearly impossible. The day before I was to leave for Iowa, John Kerry called and said, "I hear you hurt your hand. Stay home."

"No, John. I'm not staying home. I'm coming to campaign with you. I've lived through worse than this." John laughed and said OK. He knew I wouldn't have missed helping him for anything in the world. Broken hand and all, I hit the Iowa countryside like there was no tomorrow. At that point, there really wasn't a tomorrow for John Kerry. It was do-or-die time.

The state of Iowa shuts down in the wintertime. There is not a green blade of grass to be seen. The cornfields that dot the state in the springtime are just dirty snow and bare stubble, as forlorn a landscape as the Russian tundra.

On my first stop in northern Iowa, I got out of the car and an aide started pushing me through the snow. The right wheel spontaneously fell off my chair. Unbelievable. A broken left hand, and now, for the first time in 40 years, a wheel falls off my wheelchair. During the day, I made do with another wheelchair, but I needed a left-hand-drive model that I could control myself. I would just spin in circles in a standard wheelchair, because I couldn't steer the right-hand side. Frantic calls went out, and we located a left-hand-drive chair across the state line in Nebraska at the Omaha VA hospital.

I called the Omaha staff right away.

"This is former senator Max Cleland and I need a left-hand-drive wheelchair."

A beautiful female voice whispered to me over the phone, "You're not in the system."

I was thunderstruck. How could I, a triple amputee who had lived and been treated in government hospitals for 40 years of my life, not be in the system? I just laughed and said, "Sweetheart, I *am* the system."

We went across the river to the state of Nebraska and, after much huffing and puffing, got my wheelchair from the hospital. I think they considered the broken wheelchair that I took to them what they used to call in Vietnam "a combat loss."

I usually led off my stump speech for John with the line "If you see wheelchair tracks in the snow and they stop, start digging." That line always got a laugh. Then I launched into my pitch. My argument for Kerry was simple. He was a veteran. He had seen war. And as John said over and over on the campaign trail, directly referring to the Iraq War, "We should never go to war because we want to, but only because we have to."

I was up in northern Iowa just before the caucuses when a truly significant event happened. Back in Vietnam, Kerry's swift boat had come under attack just after picking up a Special Forces officer at a secret rendezvous point in the Mekong Delta. The guy who was being picked up had been leading a band of Chinese mercenaries into Cambodia. As Kerry's swift boat and the others in his group were heading back downriver, guns began blazing at them from the jungle riverbanks. The Special Forces officer fell overboard. Kerry turned his boat around and went back into the battle zone. Standing on the bow of his ship, he leaned over into the water and grabbed the Special Forces officer and pulled him back on board. He saved the guy's life. A few days before the campaign in Iowa ended, that Special Forces officer, Jim Rassmann—a registered Republican—called the Kerry campaign from his home in the Pacific Northwest. Rassmann had seen a news article about Kerry and the writer mentioned the incident. Rassmann cried as he read the story. He couldn't believe that the guy who saved his life out of the drink during a firefight in the rivers of South Vietnam was running for president. He asked if he could campaign for Kerry.

The staff was excited.

There was a very emotional reunion in Des Moines when Jim Rassmann mounted the stage and saw John Kerry for the first time since Vietnam. They embraced powerfully; tears were shed. The moment seemed to solidify everything we were trying to say about Kerry in Iowa. That he was a combat veteran, that he risked his life for his fellow soldiers, and that he was the real deal, not like the phonies who started the Iraq War and occupied the White House.

On the night of the caucus, I was posted at the state veterans' home, where we had worked hard to win over the residents. Watching an Iowa caucus meeting unfold was the darnedest political event I've seen in my life. It was like an election for seventh-grade president. The partition between the two halves of the recreational hall at the home was pulled together, dividing the room in two. Somebody announced that one side of the partition was Precinct A and the other side was Precinct B. "All you for candidate A over there, and all you for candidate B over there in that corner, all you for candidate C stay in the back," someone yelled. It was unbelievable to me that this was the first test for anyone looking to occupy the most powerful office in the world.

As a candidate, the critical thing was to remain viable. That meant in 2004 that you had to have the support of at least 20 percent of the caucus voters present in the room. If candidates didn't meet the 20 percent threshold, they were no longer "viable" and no one could vote for them. Once you found yourself backing a candidate who wasn't viable, you had to cast your vote for one of the folks who was still viable or just leave the caucus and go home.

As time went on, both precincts of the state veterans' home went heavily for Kerry. It was a predictor of things to come. Kerry carried Iowa and upset Dean in the process. Later that night in a Des Moines hotel, I stood on a stage with John and Teresa and the head of the National Firefighters Union and other hard-core Kerry supporters. I heard John Kerry give one of the best speeches of the entire campaign. What I didn't know was that he had just been diagnosed with pneumonia. The campaign did not want that to get out, because Kerry was coming off a bout with prostate cancer just months before.

But we were ecstatic with the win. Our fondest hopes had come true. Kerry had achieved an upset victory in Iowa and was now the

lead dog in the presidential sweepstakes. Teresa leaned over and whispered in my ear, "We really got 'em this time, didn't we?" I had to
agree. It was an awesome victory. The next day, we headed to New
Hampshire.

John Kerry rode in there with fire coming out of his nostrils. He
could sense victory. He could sense winning in New Hampshire and
going all the way to the White House. Ted Kennedy showed up. The
firefighters came on board. The policemen came on board. Kerry
would go on to win New Hampshire and the Democratic nomination. I knew he would make things right in Iraq, which I thought
would help make things right for me as well.

Just prior to the Democratic National Convention in Boston, Kerry's campaign manager called me and asked if I would introduce John
to the convention. I told her I'd be thrilled.

I had been called upon to introduce John Kerry on the day he
announced for the presidency, and since then, I had introduced him
dozens of times in situations and states all over the country. But this
was going to be at the Democratic National Convention. What we
used to call "the pucker factor" back in the army was going to be
much greater for me. There would be thousands of people hooting
and hollering and carrying signs and dancing in the aisles and I was
going to be in the middle of it. Not only was I going to be in the
middle of it, I was going to introduce the Democratic nominee for
president of the United States in front of millions of people watching
on television. After I hung up, I thought about what a long road I had
traveled since waving my little lipstick-and-cardboard Adlai Stevenson
sign on Main Street in Lithonia, Georgia.

Bob Shrum helped write the initial introduction, but I worked to
perfect it all week long, and rehearsed in the convention hall, where I
got used to reading off the giant teleprompters. The line I wanted to
end with was "Now, ladies and gentlemen, reporting for duty again,
the next president of the United States, John Kerry." The day before

the speech I was told that Kerry wanted to use my last line for his opening line. OK by me. This convention was about him, not me.

On the big night, I was able to relax and be as comfortable as humanly possible up there onstage with 60 million people watching on television. I had rehearsed my lines and done my speech so many times I was starting to really feel it. I got out there in front of the world and told them that John Kerry had been an inspiration to me since he stood up against the Vietnam War right after earning medals for heroism. And I told them how I had come back from Vietnam questioning things myself, just as John had. I said that the man was one of my heroes even before I had met him. Then, after I served alongside him in the Senate, I realized he was really my brother.

As I got toward the end of the speech, I started to get excited and the crowd began to really get going, not so much from my talk but with the anticipation of John coming out on the stage. By the time I got to, "Ladies and gentlemen, the next president of the United States, John Kerry," the crowd was roaring so loudly nobody could hear a word. It was the same kind of pandemonium I had seen on TV in 1952.

They had told me John would be coming up from the audience, instead of offstage, but I didn't know which side he would emerge from. It was something he had learned from a Howard Dean speech in Iowa, where Dean came out of the crowd to great effect.

I was swiveling my neck around onstage looking all over for him while everybody went crazy. John came up from my right, gave me a big hug, and then went around and hugged all his swift boat crew members, who were arrayed along the back of the stage. Del Sandusky told me that John hit him so hard on the back of the head that his false teeth nearly flew out of his mouth. When the nominee stepped forward and said, "I'm John Kerry and I'm reporting for duty," the crowd went through the roof.

After Kerry's speech, all of us who campaigned for him and all the Democratic candidates who had campaigned against him joined together on the stage. The balloons came down and John Edwards's little kids practically swam around the stage in them.

John Kerry had just become the Democratic nominee for the presidential election of 2004. He was about to run into the biggest ambush of his life.

★ 23 ★

Swift-Boated

THE "SWIFT-BOATING" OF John Kerry stands as one of the most sordid moments in American history. The attack on his record as a young navy officer in Vietnam was like a dead mackerel in the moonlight—it both shined and stunk at the same time. It shined because it garnered so much publicity and was so shocking. It stank because it was all lies.

Never in the history of presidential politics has a distinguished war veteran running for the presidency been so maligned, trashed, smeared, and lied about in terms of his military service as John Kerry in 2004. Americans had always respected military service as an asset in a commander in chief. Americans had actually elected five generals to the presidency: Washington, Jackson, Harrison, Grant, and Eisenhower. None of them, Democrat or Republican, ever had their military records shredded like John Kerry. Candidates for the presidency had been attacked politically before. Andrew Jackson, the "hero of the battle of New Orleans," who successfully fought the British in the War of 1812, was once called a jackass by one of his opponents. Jackson promptly adopted the donkey as the symbol of the Democratic Party. But nobody denied that he was a hero.

Kerry had his courage, heroism, and patriotism challenged by veterans of the U.S. Navy's swift boat force in South Vietnam. Save for one example, these weren't men who served with him. For the most part, the only thing they had in common with him was they served on the same kind of boats in the same war.

Snippets of critical comments by these veterans about Kerry's leadership as a swift boat commander were melded into a TV spot that was initially funded by a Texas millionaire with strong ties to the Republican Party, George Bush, and Karl Rove. He was a Houston developer named Bob Perry, whose home-building company was worth hundreds of millions of dollars. At that time, Bob Perry was the largest contributor to the Republican Party in Texas and gave a total of $8 million to conservative causes during the 2004 election cycle. Perry gave more than $4 million of that money to the Swift Boat Veterans for Truth organization, after helping get it started. Ultimately, Swift Boat Veterans for Truth spent $22 million in TV ads against John Kerry, and continued its attack right up until Election Day.

It was all lies, yet, thanks to news outlets like Fox News and Rush Limbaugh's radio program, the allegations began to gain credence. In addition, two men, John O'Neill and Jerome Corsi, wrote a book on Kerry's service in Vietnam entitled *Unfit for Command: Swift Boat Veterans Speak Out Against John Kerry.* O'Neill had been recruited by the Nixon White House in the early 1970s to attack Kerry after John testified before the Senate Foreign Relations Committee against the Vietnam War. O'Neill—whose law partner had served as Bush's lawyer when he was governor—was from Texas and had served on the swift boats, but never with John Kerry. The two men had, in fact, squared off on *The Dick Cavett Show* in the early '70s, arguing about the Vietnam War, but that was the only time they had met. The dirty tricks of the Nixon years surfaced again in early '04, when O'Neill volunteered as the leader of the swift boaters who went after Kerry.

The fact that the term "swift-boat" has come to have a pejorative connotation in America is truly tragic. Those officers and men who served on those vessels in the southern portion of Vietnam patrolling the rivers and streams in the Mekong Delta south of Saigon sustained some of the highest casualty rates of the Vietnam War. If you were a swift boater, the odds were very good that you were going to get either killed or wounded. As a matter of fact, Kerry witnessed, up close and personal, the death of another young officer when the man's boat was blown asunder by an enemy mine as they ran along a river. John himself was wounded three times. He earned three Purple Hearts. Facing an enemy ambush one day, he beached his boat and charged into the jungle after a rocket launcher–toting Vietcong attacker. The man had aimed his weapon at Kerry's boat. John killed him and saved his crew, for which he was awarded the Silver Star, the nation's third-highest decoration for heroism. Kerry knew how to respond to an ambush on the battlefield. You charge it, you attack it. You wipe them out before they wipe you out. That was the kind of man I wanted in the White House.

After his third Purple Heart, the U.S. Navy sent John Kerry home to the States. He had performed his duty. He had gotten a few holes in his T-shirt.

So why did the Republican smear machine, George Bush and Karl Rove, with their point man, John O'Neill, go after Kerry's military record and try to destroy him with it when U.S. Navy records confirmed and documented his heroism?

The answer is that they wanted to do to him what they did to John McCain and me—take legitimate military service in combat, turn it around, and make it suspect. The goal was to show George Bush—a man who clearly ducked out of his military obligation to the nation—as strong and his opponent weak. Rove and company went after Kerry even though they had to lie to do it. They had no shame.

Kerry has been unfairly blamed for his campaign's slow response to the swift boat ambush. John wanted to respond quickly and immediately. I know he did. He was on the phone with his campaign headquarters from his car daily urging them to put together a response ad. The campaign manager and the people who were in charge of communications, Bob Shrum and Stephanie Cutter, resisted. They didn't believe that a response was necessary until it was too late. It was a critical miscalculation. Kerry certainly had better political instincts than his team. In any case, it was two weeks later before he addressed the question directly by saying the swift-boaters had lied. But much of the damage had already been accomplished.

As the Kerry campaign geared up to fight back, I got a call—the campaign wanted me to confront George Bush personally while he was on vacation in Crawford, Texas. I jumped at the chance. I was so furious about the way this president had gone after McCain, after me, and now after Kerry that I was ready to spit nails. I would have done anything to fight back.

After landing in Texas, my driver, Adil Durrani, and my press aide, Tara McGuinness, drove down to Crawford, in Central Texas. The swift boat attacks were ringing in my ears. But by then, John McCain had come to Kerry's defense just as he and Chuck Hagel had come to mine when I was under attack. McCain called the swift boat attack on Kerry "dishonest and dishonorable" and asked the president to pull the ads. That's what I wanted to ask Bush to do as well. I had been given a letter signed by six members of the Senate, all of whom had served in the military. One of them was Democratic senator Dan Inouye, who had received the Medal of Honor, the nation's highest award. The letter asked the president to stop the attack on Kerry's war record.

There's a small two-lane road that goes to the Bush ranch, just outside Crawford. It's the only way in or out. As you pass down the road, there is a schoolhouse on the left. The schoolhouse is about three miles from the Bush compound. That was where the press holed up during the hot days of August 2004. I didn't stop at the schoolhouse, but as I went by it, the press gaggle jumped in their cars en masse and started their cameras rolling. They chased me all the way to the ranch. Looking in the rearview mirror, I saw a stream of cameras and cars that stretched into the distance. I felt like I was in a Burt Reynolds *Smokey and the Bandit* car chase. I finally rolled up to the main entrance of the Bush compound. By the time I got out of the car and hopped into my wheelchair, there was a strange mixture of Secret Service and media surrounding me. One man stood in the group with a VFW cap on his head. My job was to get the letter into the hands of a Secret Service agent and tell him to deliver it to the president.

I started rolling toward the closest Secret Service agent, press people moving out of my way as I did. The Secret Service agent started running. I tried to push my wheelchair toward him, waving my letter and saying, "This is a letter asking the president to stop the terrible attacks against John Kerry." The Secret Service agent just kept running. Then the man with the VFW cap started running after me, saying, "I'll take it. I'll take it." Clearly the president's plan was to prevent me from giving the letter to federal employees like the Secret Service guys, and instead hand it to a private citizen—the VFW guy—who had no access to the president himself.

I tried to find another Secret Service agent. I saw one, and moved toward him. He started running too. It was a strange feeling to see the Secret Service running away from me, a former U.S. senator. Frustrated, I got back in the car. Ultimately, nobody got the letter. I certainly wasn't going to give it to the VFW guy, because I knew he was just a plant to defuse the situation.

I asked my driver to turn around, and we went back down the three miles to the schoolhouse. There was a gaggle of press like I had never seen. I got out in the dirt parking lot and gave the president hell.

I was madder than a hornet. I knew that the mackerel shining and stinking in the moonlight had rotted from the head down.

One day, before the swift boat attack on John Kerry, the two of us were riding the little subway car that runs under the Capitol from the Senate chambers to the Dirksen Senate Office Building. We were alone. I asked him a question that had been on my mind for years. I knew he had received the Silver Star. I had too. But I told Kerry that I felt guilty about my Silver Star, that I felt like I got credit for something my men did. Kerry said, "Someone other than you made the judgment that you deserved it. It wasn't you. You didn't ask for it. Just accept it." Believe it or not, that made me feel better.

I didn't write the evaluations of my performance as a young officer when I was in the military. Someone else did. Neither did John Kerry. The American people should accept that verdict too. John Kerry earned his three Purple Hearts, his Bronze Star, and his Silver Star. Yet right-wing radio still revives from time to time the old lies about his service. As late as November 2007, three years after Kerry's defeat for the presidency, Rush Limbaugh claimed that the Swift Boat Veterans for Truth "were right on the money and nobody has disproven anything they claimed in any of their ads, statements, written commentaries, or anything of the sort."

In 2008, T. Boone Pickens offered a million dollars to anyone who could disprove the claims made in the ads. When the Kerry office sent him a letter signed by the swift boat crew members who served with Kerry, proving his war record, Pickens dismissed the letter as irrelevant because, according to him, it didn't refer to the ads.

It was all bull feathers. The U.S. Navy proved John Kerry was a hero 40 years ago when it gave him those medals.

★ 24 ★

A Time to Heal

ON ELECTION DAY 2004, John Kerry got just 43 percent of the veterans' vote in America. Swift-boating had worked. Amid allegations of voter fraud and a calculated suppression of the Democratic voter base on a dreary and rainy day in Ohio, Kerry lost that state and thus the presidency. My Vietnam veteran brother, John McCain, had lost to Bush's political assassination machine in 2000. I had lost to the same crowd in 2002. Now another Vietnam brother, my own contemporary JFK, had lost to them as well.

It was time to let go of all the pain those losses and all the others in my life had cost me.

It was time to heal.

I had made great strides in my recovery after discovering that Cymbalta worked for me. And the time on the campaign trail had been therapeutic as well, giving me purpose once again. But I still wasn't all back. I still wasn't reconciled with all I had lost, and there remained vast reservoirs of grief inside me. My counseling with Val at Walter Reed continued.

All through my therapy, Val had talked about my need to own my past and take control of it, rather than letting it dictate my future. I felt

249

like I was a long way from that. I didn't really even like my past. One day, just as I was starting to get really worked up about all the crap that had befallen me in life and asking when it would all end, Val stopped me abruptly by holding up both hands like a traffic cop. She looked directly into my eyes and shouted, "Whoa, whoa, whoa . . . Where's your faith?"

"The hell with faith. I'm hurting. I'm struggling. I'm suffering like I've never suffered before. What's faith got to do with any of that?"

But Val persisted, as she always did.

A theme had emerged over the years as my counseling sessions went on, with Val returning again and again to my need to become reconciled with my life as it was. She said that until and unless I did that, I would be unable to find happiness, because I would forever be searching for a life I could never have again. She also talked about "reintegrating" my sense of self back into my personality, since everything that defined me had been blown all to hell twice in my adult life. Val said she had had such a reconciliation moment when she went to her 45th high school reunion. There, in a few short days, she had rediscovered the beautiful little girl she had been before life happened to her, before she grew up, before her husband was shot down in Vietnam and killed. Seeing herself as everyone else remembered her had helped her reclaim that part of her personality, a happier part that she had lost along the way. Val said I needed to make the same journey back in time to remember who I really was, who I had been before life and its various explosions had happened to me. She said I needed the same healing.

Over the years, we talked about putting the shattered pieces of my life back together. We talked about the need for me to find a sense of wholeness, even a new sense of self. In our counseling sessions, I began to realize that so much of my life had been defined by war. Even before I was blown up, I was an ROTC cadet in college. Then I was a soldier. Then I was a wounded patient. After all of that,

I headed the VA. Ultimately, I went to the Senate and cast a vote for war. All along the way, I had been tied to war. I was either training for it, serving in it, recovering from it, or voting for it. I knew I had to find a new self-image outside of military service. Even politics was a kind of war for me, and the cost of defeat on that terrain had been nearly as great as the cost of almost losing my life on a battlefield. I had to move on and find out what it was to just be alive. I needed to find joy in the fact that I was still alive rather than spending my days cursing the life I was forced to live. I needed time to heal from the trauma of war and the trauma of politics, and find myself—my real self—again.

As God would have it, in the early spring of 2008, my cell phone rang. It was a fellow named Toby Warren, a volunteer aide and driver to retired lieutenant general Hal Moore. I had met General Moore when I ran for reelection to the Senate in 2002. He had come over to Atlanta from his home in Auburn, Alabama, to campaign for me, though at that point we didn't really know each other well. We had breakfast together, then held a press conference at the state capitol with a group of veterans behind us.

General Moore had been my hero since he led his unit as a lieutenant colonel with the First Air Cavalry Division in the first major battle of the Vietnam War in 1965. I had been on active duty just a few months as a young second lieutenant at the Army Signal School in Fort Gordon, Georgia, when I first read about the dramatic battle between elements of the First Air Cavalry Division and the North Vietnamese army. It set the tone for the rest of the war because so many were lost and nothing whatsoever was gained.

On the phone, Toby relayed an invitation from Moore to a "leadership retreat" in Vail, Colorado, hosted by a wealthy financier named Dick Strong. General Moore would be there, along with a small group of other leaders. Toby told me that Moore had personally requested my attendance. There was no way I could say no to him.

I headed off to the snowy mountains of Colorado with another Vietnam veteran, Bill Chapman. Bill was my hometown buddy and had earned the Distinguished Flying Cross while serving two tours in Vietnam as a helicopter pilot. When we got to the retreat, held at a house nestled in the beautiful snow-covered mountains of Vail, I was stunned to find another hero of mine attending the conference, Scott Carpenter, one of the original Mercury 7 astronauts in the U.S. space program back in the early 1960s. Going to school at Stetson University in Deland, Florida, I had gotten up early one morning and driven to Cape Canaveral to watch a rocket carrying Scott Carpenter blast into the sky. In those early days of the space program, just lifting off and landing safely in the ocean without blowing up was a success. He and the other astronauts, like John Glenn, inspired my generation. They were the best of the best. It was an idealistic and meaningful time for me and for America, and it was a thrill to meet him.

During the conference, Toby handed me a book he had written about General Moore's personal effort to come to terms with Vietnam and the grief of losing his wife, Julie. Toby had entitled the book *A General's Spiritual Journey*. The title caught me off guard. I knew General Moore to be one of the best military leaders and best generals of our era. The last thing I expected was that such a warrior would ever have had a "spiritual journey." Certainly, I didn't have any notion that his spiritual journey could be like mine.

But it turned out to be so.

General Moore and his sidekick, Joe Galloway, had written an earlier book, *We Were Soldiers Once . . . and Young,* that captured my spirit and the spirit of the nation. The book told the story of Moore's battalion, the First/Seventh Cavalry, in the battle of the Ia Drang Valley, later known as the Valley of Death. In November 1965, Moore's unit of 450 men had unwittingly been dropped into a clearing surrounded by 2,000 North Vietnamese soldiers ready to massacre them. They quickly realized they were completely hemmed in, with no possible avenue of retreat. At the time, it seemed like Moore would meet the fate of an earlier, more famous general who once commanded the Seventh Cavalry: George Armstrong Custer.

Outnumbered five to one, but determined to survive and be victorious, Moore and his little band fought night and day for three days. By the time the enemy withdrew, Moore had lost 79 soldiers, while his men had killed over 1,000 North Vietnamese.

Unlike many battlefield generals, Moore was very close to his soldiers and knew them by name. He had spent 18 months training them at Fort Benning, Georgia, before President Johnson ordered the unit to Vietnam. The men he had lost had haunted him ever since the war. He wrote *We Were Soldiers Once . . . and Young* as a tribute to them.

Early in the 1990s, Moore and Galloway went back to the Valley of Death and met General Moore's counterpart, Lieutenant General Nguyen Huu An, the North Vietnamese commander of the troops who had tried to wipe him out and who was also now retired. Moore told me later that in his study of the battle of Dien Bien Phu, the defeat that caused the French to pull out of Vietnam, he had learned that the North Vietnamese were infatuated with head-on frontal assaults. At Dien Bien Phu, the Vietminh never attacked the French rear. With that in mind, Moore put all his soldiers up front in the battle of the Ia Drang Valley. He didn't have a choice, because he was so badly outnumbered. But it left the rear open. In discussion with General An, Moore said, "Why didn't you attack my rear? It was open." General An's mouth dropped open with a gasp.

It seemed both men hungered for the same sense of closure. At the end of their meeting, the North Vietnamese general grabbed Moore by the shoulders, then hugged him and kissed him on both cheeks. In response, Moore gave the general his wristwatch as a seal of their friendship. Before parting company, the two men, who had tried their damnedest to kill each other, had dinner in Pleiku, in the Central Highlands of Vietnam, in what Moore called a "two-rat-per-room hotel."

Later, on the occasion of General An's death, Moore returned to Vietnam and visited the general's home. There, set in a hallowed place in the den, Moore found the wristwatch he had given General An.

In *A General's Spiritual Journey,* Moore relates that he had arranged to visit his old battlefield before the encounter with his former enemy. One night, just before a monsoon drenched his party, the general "walked the perimeter" once again by himself. He thought of the names of all those who had been lost. He heard the sounds of battle once again and stared into the darkness that now enveloped the place where he had spent the most harrowing hours of his life.

Later that night, the rain ceased. The stars came out over General Moore as he stood upon the battlefield where his men had died. Suddenly a meteor shower of extraordinary proportions appeared, and the falling stars filled the sky. It was as if Moore's troops were saying good-bye to him and helping him deal with his grief. It was as if God were saying to this man of honor that his troops were all right and that he too would be OK. Moore found some peace that night.

Something came over me as I read that part of the general's spiritual tale. I wept—and then I quit. I was OK. Somehow, in finding that one of my lifelong heroes was struggling along the same road I was on, was searching for the same sense of meaning, I found what I had been seeking as well. I found some peace in the fact that I was still alive after all.

Later, when Mel Gibson played the role of Hal Moore in the movie *We Were Soldiers,* Moore attended the premiere at Fort Benning. After the movie, Moore ducked out a side door of the movie theater. He was observed praying quietly. He was praying for his lost soldiers.

Mel Gibson and General Moore share a favorite prayer, the Universal Prayer of Pope Clement XI. One of the lines of the prayer General Moore quoted to me directly:

"Discover to me, O my God, the nothingness of this world, the greatness of heaven, the shortness of time, and the length of eternity."

* * *

To me, this insight into life is the essence of a great warrior and a spiritual man. I came to see Moore's determination to come to terms with his war, his grief, and his life as an ultimate testimony of faith.

What is faith? One of the best definitions leads off Moore's book about his spiritual journey. The quote is credited to Patrick Overton, a minister and college professor. It speaks to my heart in a deep and very encouraging way:

"When we walk to the edge of all the light we have and take that step into the darkness of the unknown, we must believe that one of two things will happen. . . . There will be something solid to stand on, or we will be taught to fly."

General Hal Moore continues to step forward beyond all the light he has and take that step into the darkness of the unknown. His example has encouraged me to do likewise. Before he left Fort Benning for Vietnam, Moore told his troops, "I can't promise that I will bring you all home alive. But this I swear before you and before Almighty God: That when we go into battle, I will be the first to set foot on the field, and I will be the last to step off, and I will leave *no one* behind. Dead or alive, we will all come home together."

In the battle of the Ia Drang Valley, Hal Moore was the first one on the ground and the last one off. And he brought all his soldiers home.

So what does faith have to do with it?

I have come to the end of all the light that I have many times. I've had to step out into the darkness of the unknown. Always, even though I didn't know it, and even though most of the time I didn't believe it, one of two things happened: There was something to stand on, or I was taught to fly.

I wasn't supposed to have this life I've had. I wasn't supposed to live after getting blown up by a grenade. I never should have made it back. But I did. And once I got back, I just kept making it a little further. No one thought I'd learn to walk again. Or swim. Or drive. Or get elected to the United States Senate. In the end, I just kept going and pushing because I couldn't stand the alternative. I have achieved great things, and been left so far down that even surviving another day seemed impossible. The only way over the obstacles for me has been to keep pressing ahead. I realize now that I've been taught to fly so many times in my life that there is nothing left for me but faith. And not just in God, but in myself. After climbing back from this latest valley, I've come to realize that I will always find a way back up the mountain simply because I keep trying every single day, inch by inch.

On January 6, 2009, six years to the day after I left the Senate, and 12 years after I had initially been sworn in to that body, I went back onto the Senate floor again. The occasion was the swearing-in of new members of the Senate and of older members who had been reelected.

There I encountered two of my other heroes, Senators Bob Byrd and Ted Kennedy. Much had changed for them.

Byrd was in a wheelchair, his left eye partially closed by palsy. His face was swollen somewhat, but when he saw me, he greeted me with the same gallant charm he has always possessed.

"Max Cleland, how good to see you. You're my hero," he muttered softly, taking my hand in his.

"You're mine, Mr. President Pro Tem," I replied with as much ardor and affection as I could muster.

Ted was standing up by his desk, a cane in his hand.

I went up and gave Ted a big hug. We had become fast friends during my six years in the Senate, and he was as delighted to see me as I was to see him. Pointing at me, he said, "This guy Cleland is a real sailor." We laughed about a day years earlier when he had taken me sailing off the shores of Cape Cod. The crew had lashed my wheelchair to the boat to keep me from rolling overboard. Ted had his favorite dog with him that day, and seemed in total command of the craft and of life when he was at the wheel. I have a picture I treasure of us together on the boat. He's wearing sunglasses, his hair wind-blown. Even as an old man, he looks the very picture of the Kennedy mystique that seduced me into a life of politics those many years ago.

Before we parted company, he suggested we hold "another meeting of the Senate Water Resources Committee." That was what Ted always called our trips to the Senate steam room, where he and I would often hit the Jacuzzi together. He waved at me as I left him. "Come back down to the shore sometime," he called, his voice trailing off.

It seemed so sad that these last lions of the Senate should be going out this way. Byrd was more and more feeble, and Ted had been stricken with brain cancer. But as I left the Senate floor that day, I felt a sense of completeness and peace in place of bitterness. I had a sense that I had done my time in Washington, and didn't need to go back. It was a feeling that had eluded me since I lost my seat.

And then came the inauguration of Barack Obama. America had self-corrected. It was a transformational moment for me for the most unexpected of reasons. I watched the inaugural address with my father in his house in Lithonia.

Midway through, there came a point that lifted me up and changed my world. Obama was speaking of those "who have carried us up the long, rugged path towards prosperity and freedom."

When he spoke the words "For us, they fought and died, in places like Concord and Gettysburg; Normandy and Khe Sanh," my heart skipped.

I couldn't believe he said Khe Sanh. It was an amazing moment for me, to finally get recognition, almost 41 years later to the month, for the battle that had changed the course of my life. I had never heard anyone mention my battle among those other battles, each so famous for its part in preserving American freedom in the world. To hear it equated with them was life-changing for me. It made me feel like my sacrifice mattered after all. The war that had taken so much from me was part of America's story.

Obama was five years old when the siege of Khe Sanh was raging. Whether it was a young staffer or an old warrior or the new president himself who made sure that it was in the speech, I didn't care. He had said it, and I stored it in my heart.

More than my specific battle, though, Obama recognized all those who had borne the battle to keep America alive. Even more important, he had singled us out as those to whom the nation should look for examples of selfless sacrifice for our country. He asked others to sacrifice as we had. As he spoke, I felt the parallels between Obama's words and an earlier president's call to sacrifice for our nation. Standing on a tombstone in Arlington Cemetery as I watched them bury my president so long ago, I had dedicated myself to answering that call. Obama's words were an affirmation that I had, indeed, done what I could do for my country. The acknowledgment helped slay some of the bitterness inside me. That a new president with a new agenda and a new politics still remembered those of us who had fought old, misguided battles told me that my sacrifice was still something worthy of honor—never mind how meaningless I felt my war had been.

As January 20 drew to a close, I began to feel a certain kind of release from the rancor, anger, and frustration that had stung me for so long. I began to mellow a little. As the evening closed around me, I could feel myself letting go of the hurt.

Over the next few months, I gained everything I needed—a new perspective on life, a reconciliation with my past, a sense of wonder about God's creation in nature, the warmth and love of true friends, and an appreciation that somehow, through it all, God provides. I shall take that as the watchword for my new life. As the marvelous former chaplain of the U.S. Senate, Dr. Lloyd Ogilvie, liked to say, "What God desires, he inspires . . . What he guides, he provides."

As I rebuild my life, I remember an anonymous poem I received during my days as head of the VA. I came across this item recently while going through my possessions, separating the things I wanted to throw out from the things I wanted to keep. I have adopted the sentiments expressed as my own:

I have dreamed many dreams that have never come true,
I've watched them vanish at dawn.
But I've realized enough of my dreams, thank God,
To make me want to dream on.

I have prayed many prayers when no answer came,
Though I waited patiently and long.
But answers have come to enough of my prayers,
To make me keep praying on.

I have trusted many a friend who failed me,
And left me to weep alone.
But I found enough of my friends true blue,
To make me keep trusting on.

I've sown many seeds that fell by the way,
For birds to feed upon.
But I've had enough golden grains in my hand,
To make me keep sowing on.

I've drained the cup of disappointment and pain,
And gone many days without song.
But I've sipped enough nectar from the roses of life,
To make me want to live on.

☆ ACKNOWLEDGMENTS ☆

WITHOUT BEN RAINES, this book would not have been written. He has been my collaborator, friend, coworker, counselor, therapist, and chaplain. My thanks to him is profound. Additionally, I thank Professor Doug Brinkley, the eminent American historian, for getting us together. Also, Bob Barnett, my agent, was on the case early and stayed on it until the job was done. My thanks to him and his legal assistant, Jacqueline Davies. Thanks to Bill Johnstone and Lynn Kimmerly, my great friends, and thanks also to the numerous members of the staffs I've had over the years. You have helped me immensely. My editor at Simon & Schuster, Priscilla Painton, deserves a great deal of credit for believing up front in me and Ben, and the story we would put together. We both offer thanks to our parents. We would not have been here to show the world what we could do if they hadn't raised us right and believed in us completely. And we both thank Shannon and Jasper, Ben's wife and son, for tolerating the pair of us during this endeavor.